Managing People

Second edition

Jane Weightman

Jane Weightman BA, MSc, PhD is a psychologist and was associated with the
Manchester School of Management at UMIST from 1980 to 1997, since then she has
written and implemented training within organisations. She has carried out research
into a wide range of management-related topics. Previously, she worked in the field
of mental handicap as a researcher, teacher, lecturer and county adviser. She has
written widely in a range of journals, and her books include *Competencies in Action*
(1994), also published by the CIPD.

The Chartered Institute of Personnel and Development is the leading publisher of books and reports for personnel and training professionals, students, and all those concerned with the effective management and development of people at work. For details of all our titles, please contact the publishing department:
Tel: 020-8263 3387
Fax: 020-8263 3850
E-mail: publish@cipd.co.uk
The catalogue of all CIPD titles can be viewed on the CIPD website:
www.cipd.co.uk/bookstore

Managing People

Second edition

Jane Weightman

The Chartered Institute of Personnel and Development

Published by the Chartered Institute of Personnel and Development,
CIPD House, Camp Road, London, SW19 4UX

This edition published 2004
First published 1999
First edition reprinted 1999, 2001, 2002, 2003 (twice)

Designed and typeset by Fakenham Photosetting Limited, Fakenham, Norfolk
Printed in Great Britain by The Cromwell Press, Trowbridge, Wiltshire

British Library Cataloguing in Publication Data
A catalogue record of this book is available from the British Library

ISBN 0 85292 9943

Chartered Institute of Personnel and Development, CIPD House,
Camp Road, London, SW19 4UX
Tel: 020 8971 9000   Fax: 020 8263 3333
Email: cipd@cipd.co.uk   Website: www.cipd.co.uk
Incorporated by Royal Charter   Registered Charity No. 1079797

CONTENTS

List of Figures

List of Tables

Preface

This book is written to the CIPD Core Management Standards for managing people. Part 1 looks at ways of understanding individual people. Part 2 examines the environmental factors that affect the work of individuals. Part 3 contains practical material on how to manage people more effectively. Each of the chapters starts with a small case study based on a true situation to emphasise the issues dealt with in the chapter. At the end of each chapter I ask you to consider how you would react to the case study in the light of what you have read, and give my views. Each chapter also contains questions and activities for you to ask and do yourself. These aim to give you the opportunity to reflect on what you are reading and to apply it to your own situation. I hope you will use some of them. It is only by trying to apply the material to real situations that you will learn to manage people more effectively.

The Fundamental
Characterisics of People

PART

1

Introduction to Managing People

This chapter deals with the following key ideas. There is a description and discussion of **Psychology, Sociology, Unitarism, Pluralism, Contingency theory** *and* **Ethics**. *These are academic ideas that inform our understanding of how to manage people. The chapter also includes descriptions and discussion of the practical application of these in terms of* **Human Resources, Management** *and* **Leadership**. *There are specific examples from McDonalds and the NHS. There is also a section on how to use this book at the end of the chapter which might help you use the book for your own purposes.*

OBJECTIVES

When you have finished reading this chapter you should be able to:

■ **understand the different systems of thought involved in social science which could be useful for analysing how to manage people**

■ **describe the main approaches of personnel management and human resource (HR) professionals**

■ **discuss some of the central debates in management such as unitarist versus pluralist, management versus leadership, and the ethics of leadership.**

INTRODUCTION

Managing people is an extremely important part of making organisations work well. Managing people means acknowledging that the people in the organisation are an important part of getting things done. There are several different ways of approaching this assumption. The human resources (HR) approach assumes that no amount of clever work with figures, or of expenditure on the latest technical equipment, will deliver anything unless people agree to work in co-ordination with each other. This applies to everyone in the organisation. An alternative view is that of industrial relations writers, who assume there is basic conflict in the employment relationship. This makes mutual accommodation necessary because the conflicting interests can never be reconciled. Whichever perspective you hold, studying the management of people will be useful to you at work. By understanding other people and how they interact, you will be able to get things done more easily. This applies to you whether you are a team leader, manager, or have no particular formal responsibility for managing other people. Managing people means understanding both formal and informal relations between people at work.

M West (2002) reports a study that compares the mortality rates of 61 NHS hospitals. These rates were linked amongst other things to the human resources practices of the hospitals. The hospitals with the lowest mortality rates, everything else being equal, were those with appraisal schemes, quality training and training in teamwork. This demonstrates how very important managing people effectively can be.

WHAT ARE THE DIFFERENT STRANDS OF THOUGHT THAT INFORM THIS AREA?

Ideas and evidence from several traditions of study are used by people to try to analyse and understand the issues associated with managing people. First, there is material that originates in the social sciences: this includes psychology, sociology, political theory and philosophy. These subject areas have developed individual specialisms in organisation analysis and practical management applications. For example, there are organisational psychologists who look at organisational behaviour. Much of the industrial relations material uses models from sociology and politics to analyse some of the conflicts at work.

Second, there is material from what Americans call 'management specialists': ideas, research and practice that are devoid of any academic pedigree but look particularly at work organisations from the management perspective. This group includes work by various sorts of experts. It may be that of successful managers who have written autobiographies – for example Sir John Harvey-Jones (1994), one-time chairman of ICI, or Bill Gates (1996), founder of Microsoft. It can also be that of systematic researchers of management such as the study of core competencies in organisations by Prahalad and Hamel (1990). Or it can be management textbooks where assumptions are made about the nature of the management task, for example Handy (1985). Subsections of this body of material contain contributions from people working with a personnel, training and development perspective, nowadays called 'human resource management'. Each of these specialisms has a contribution to make to understanding managing people.

Gareth Morgan's highly influential academic book *Images of Organization* (1997) argues that there are seven quite distinct ways of looking at organisations (see Table 1.1). Each is a different sort of probe into a complex area, and each is appropriate for giving us an insight into some aspect of an organisation's working. An organisation is all of these things at the same time. For practitioners it is only by having a variety of strategies for investigating or 'reading' the situation that one can be effective. At the very least, if everything we know has failed, this list might help us generate something else to try.

The present book tries to use material from a wide range of different disciplines. Part 1 concentrates on the individual and contains material from a psychological perspective – with its language of behaviours, motivation and feedback. Part 2 mostly uses the language of social science to look at the variety of work situations and emphasises such things as context, cultures, norms and roles. Part 3 looks at the organisation as a whole and uses language from a variety of disciplines. From engineering comes the language of systems, structures and control. From politics comes the language of power, influence and authority. From management comes that of overall responsibility. From theology comes the language of vision, leadership and commitment.

As you may begin to understand, the study of managing people involves the range of human language and analysis. It is also the case that there are several different ways of looking at the same behaviour or issue. Sometimes these differing views are compatible – but not always. Learning to deal with this diversity of views is at the heart of managing people.

Table 1.1 *Ways of looking at organisations*

1 Organisations as machines with:
  orderly relationships
  clearly defined parts
  determined order

2 Organisations as organisms with:
  adaptation to the environment
  life cycles
  survival techniques

3 Organisations as cultures with:
  patterns of belief
  daily rituals
  own language

4 Organisations as political systems with:
  authority
  power
  the right to manage or defend individual rights

5 Organisations as brains with:
  think-tanks
  strategy formulation
  corporate planning teams

6 Organisations as psychic prisons with:
  the trap of one-way thinking

7 Organisations as instruments of domination with:
  some having influence over others
  work hazards

Adapted from Morgan (1986)

Throughout this book you will find boxes like this one with specific examples of the points being made in the text. These may be examples from individuals, organisations or research materials. They are all 'real' examples. Some of the activities at the end of each chapter are also there for you to generate your own examples. The idea is that by applying your theoretical reading it makes more sense and is more memorable. By generating your own examples you will see whether the argument of the text makes any sense to you. You are also more likely to learn things you use.

What are the social sciences?

The two disciplines in social science that are most relevant to managing people are psychology and sociology. Other disciplines normally included among the social sciences are economics, geography and political theory. They are not included in detail in this book, although the idea of people as economically and politically active is important for understanding organisational life and is included throughout the book in discussions about the analysis of how things are done.

When I tell people that I am a psychologist they usually say something like 'Oh, I'd better be careful then, as you can read my mind.' Fortunately for us all, this is not true. I cannot read people's minds. Another confusion is that psychology is the same as psychiatry. It is not. Psychiatry is concerned with particular accounts and treatments of people with mental illness. So what is psychology?

Psychology is normally defined as the study of behaviour. It may be animal or human behaviour. Such a study can include detailed descriptions of particular behaviours – for example how we learn; it may also include some analysis to try to account for why these behaviours happen in the particular way they do. By looking at the underlying structures and hypothesising about the effects of previous experience and the environment in which it takes place we try to understand questions such as:

- Why do people choose to do different things?
- Why does one person reject this course of action when the previous person did not?
- Why do decisions change?

Psychology usually tries to account for the behaviour of individuals, but it includes what happens to them when they are in groups large and small.

A particular branch of psychology relevant to our needs is organisational psychology. People working in this area apply the findings and models of general psychology to work organisations. They also carry out research into organisations to try to improve our understanding of them and generate new models. As with all psychology, there is particular emphasis on the effect on individuals and their effect on others. This includes questions such as: What do managers do? How do groups influence each other? How can changes in people's behaviour be dealt with most effectively? I use several examples from this discipline in this book.

Sociology is concerned with the social, group and institutional aspects of human society. There is some overlap with all the other social sciences. What distinguishes sociology is a desire to understand the influences and agreed norms of the institutions of society that affect the behaviour of its members. Sociologists look for generic (general across groups) concepts and patterns that can help to explain social activities. They examine such questions as: What are the roles we play? Which institutions are most dominant in society? Does the nature of the community affect the individual's choice of career? How do bureaucracies work? What distinguishes professionally qualified workers from other groups? Are there different sorts of conflict? What are the effects of different cultures?

These enquiries can then be used to analyse specific examples such as the role of a senior manager, the profession of accounting or the culture of the National Health Service. Of all the social scientists, sociologists are the most interdisciplinary – sharing insights and ideas with economists, geographers, psychologists and political scientists as well as with philosophical and religious writers. This interdisciplinary tradition is useful for analysing and understanding work organisations. This is particularly so when we try to understand a specific organisation as compared with another, or the position of a particular group within the organisation.

Other disciplines from social science that are also involved in studying organisations and the people in them are economics when considering performance management – see Chapters 13 and 14; and political science when considering power – see Chapter 7. Some other disciplines are also influential: for example, history and cultural studies will tell us about the context of organisational behaviour, while engineering provides some of the control and systems language that certain management writers use.

What methods do social scientists use?

Social scientists use many different methods to study behaviour. Some psychologists use biological methods to study the biological basis of behaviour. This type of study seeks to determine what the limits of behaviour are and what the inherited components of behaviour are. For example, how is memory stored in the brain (see Greenfield, 1997)? Other psychologists use a scientific framework but study behaviour. They set up carefully controlled experiments in the laboratory where everything is kept the same except one thing; any differences in behaviour are then accounted for by the variation in the one factor. As an example of this type, one study tells us that *any* sort of additional attention to people at work improves their productivity on routine tasks – the so-called 'Hawthorne effect' which was found by psychologists in some early work in factories (Mayo, 1939).

Yet other psychologists and sociologists study behaviour in its natural setting, trying to use systematic description and analysis to account for the behaviour. This might involve questionnaires, interviews or observation. Examples would be studies of stress in teachers, or of how new recruits behave on an induction programme. Sociologists use interviews and observation to collect their data. Sometimes they use outsider, non-participant, observation; on other occasions the study is conducted by a member as participant observation. Unlike psychologists, they rarely use controlled experiments, preferring to study real situations.

You will notice that throughout this book I refer you to some quite old writings. The development of any discipline is never even; sometimes there is a rapid increase in knowledge and theory while at other times progress is slower. The past decade or two has seen a marked change in confidence in psychology and sociology, with an increase in the variety of views. In psychology there are two areas in which there has been marked consensus about genuine development: physiological psychology, where studies of the brain's mechanisms are increasing our understanding; and developmental psychology, with its analysis of how children develop. In other areas of the social sciences there is rather less sign of new fundamentally agreed theories.

Most of the basic description and analysis of behaviour has been done. Some writers have indulged in introspection and self-analysis about where next for social science (see, for example, Kline 1989). Many psychologists and sociologists are now looking at higher-order models and integrations. Many are looking to applied areas such as the study of the mentally ill or of work organisations to help develop these higher-order models using the basic research of older references as their starting points.

What is personnel management and human resource (HR) management?

Personnel and HR work is directed at employees – finding them, training them, arranging for them to be paid, explaining management's expectations of them and justifying management's actions to them. The HR, or personnel, function of management is carried out by all managers. In all but the smallest organisation it is also partly carried out by specialists. This is to ensure consistency of treatment and to operate systems such as performance appraisal and job evaluation, which have value only on an organisation-wide basis. HR specialists are concerned with satisfying employees' work needs and with modifying management policy and actions that might otherwise provoke an unwelcome reaction. Human resource management

(HRM), the more recent term for the work of personnel specialists, implies a more strategic view of the part people play in the success of an organisation. It might be said that HRM is when the chief executive uses personnel.

Personnel management is defined by Tyson (1987) as managing the employment relationship. Tyson suggests that this has led to three types of personnel department. First is the clerk of works type, where the department gives administrative support but has no involvement in business planning; the principal activities for personnel staff are recruitment, record keeping and welfare. The second type is like the contracts manager, concerned to meet each event with a system as part of the policy network; personnel staff are involved with informal agreements and understandings and so become part of the political life of the organisation. The third type is that of the architects, who seek to build up the organisation as a whole and would call themselves HR; in this type of personnel, staff devise explicit policies which affect the corporate plan and have a system of controls integrated between line management and personnel. Not surprisingly, professional personnel managers prefer to see themselves as architects. For example, HRM experts claim expertise in managing change – a crucial area for most organisations.

As a line manager, your relationship with the HR or personnel function will depend upon its role in the organisation. If it is 'clerk of works' it will be a source of information and support for quite specific things. If it is 'contracts manager' or 'architect' you are more likely to be discussing, debating and deciding with its members how to proceed in particular areas.

Personnel management professionals are currently inclined to call themselves human resource managers, which emphasises the strategic business orientation, although the British professional body is called The Chartered Institute of Personnel and Development (CIPD). Useful books in this area are by Marchington and Wilkinson (2002) and Foot and Hook (2002).

CENTRAL DEBATES ABOUT MANAGING PEOPLE

There are as many views on how to manage people as there are individuals. These views reflect our political, social and ethical views of organisations. I give some of these variations below.

Unitarist or pluralist?

Many people would like to think that the history of thought on organisations is developing in an evolutionary manner. This has the attraction of integrating everything currently known, implying that the latest is the best. This is certainly the position of many management consultants who peddle their versions of the latest thinking to various organisations. However, there seem to be some fundamental differences in the basic assumptions of some schools of thought that have not been reconciled or integrated.

This has been well described in a technical book by Burrell and Morgan (1979), who argue that some contrasting assumptions could never be reconciled. For instance, some people believe that organisations can be one happy family, believing in the same ideals as a strong leader; technically this is called the 'unitarist view'. An example might be the Body Shop and Anita Roddick. Other people believe that organisations are made up of people with a variety of views and beliefs that should all be heard; technically this is the 'pluralist view'. Most universities are examples. The choice between unitarist and pluralist views seems to be a matter of personal preference amongst individuals, but the effect on an organisation of the leader's style can lead to a whole organisation being unitarist or pluralist – see, for example, the choices of leadership model discussed in Chapter 10.

For those of us concerned with the practical business of managing people in organisations as part of our working life, it is perhaps best to be pragmatic – to try to find the analysis that seems to make most sense of the particular problem presented at any one time rather than hold to one view through thick and thin. This approach of 'it depends on the situation' is called 'contingency' theory.

Managing or leading people?

Whether we hold a unitarist or pluralist view when it comes to managing people, there are both 'hard' and 'soft' approaches. The hard mechanistic approaches of control management can be compared to the soft concerns of the human relations models of leadership. These are no longer seen as stark alternatives but rather as options that most effective operators will combine in practice. Let us look at some of the practical implications of this in the ways managers behave towards others.

Hard management

The hard approach includes the view that by carefully analysing the work to be done managers can specify exactly how things should be done and so become more efficient. This mechanistic approach has always had the appeal that if we only spend just a little more time and effort analysing things we shall have a perfect system. Modern examples of this approach are to be found in some exponents of the quality movement and competencies approach:

- The quality movement is enshrined in standards – the most commonly used one is the international standard, ISO 9001. For example, very detailed quality standards specify the exact nature of the memos that should be sent if there is a complaint.
- The competency movement is an approach to recruiting, developing and rewarding staff that looks in detail at what they should do to meet the required performance. Competency lists have been seen to include such minute detail as 'smile at the client when they first come to the reception desk'.

An example of the hard approach can be found in the catering industry. Here there is the desire to break down the whole job of catering into its component parts and get less skilled, and less well paid, people to do the more menial tasks. This approach expects people to comply with the carefully laid down analysis of what is required. A well developed example of this is the McDonald handbook of tasks involved in the burger business.

These hard approaches, where tasks are carefully specified, are useful where a high degree of conformity is required, where there are many temporary or unskilled staff, or where there are major crises to be dealt with. Their disadvantage is that the more prescriptive an approach is, the more people will work to rule and show no initiative, as it is 'more than my job's worth'.

Soft management

In contrast, the soft approach to management tends to put the emphasis on getting the right things for people to do. It includes an appreciation of individual styles and motivations. Here there is a great deal of discussion of empowering people to control their own work and of allowing people to express their views on how things could be done better. The softer approach emphasises the fulfilment of individual talents. It is about developing people over a period of time and allowing them to make different contributions at different times in their careers. Some of these softer approaches emphasise individualism, and others the building of teams; but all encourage individuals to feel that what they are doing is worthwhile and worth making a commitment to. Some of this is expressed in very caring terms, which makes those from the hard approach suspicious. An example is how some restaurants allow individual employees to express their personal service to the customers in a variety of different ways.

> Several organisations are giving staff a choice about their work. This is so they maintain a leading edge and retain good staff. Some choices available are:
>
> Job seeking – BP allows individuals to put their CVs on the intranet to receive internal matches.
>
> Projects – Otican encourages employees to create projects
>
> Learning – Unisys gives everyone access to all their training provision
>
> Mentor – McKinsey allows their staff to choose their own coach or mentor
>
> Rewards – AstraZeneca has a range to choose from
>
> Location – BT allows people to work from home
>
> Time of work – BT has a portfolio of work times to choose from

These softer approaches emphasise autonomy and collegiality and are most appropriate where the full commitment of the people in the team is necessary – for instance, when a situation is new and everyone needs to deliver a service. An example is when health visitors in clinics were faced with a new recommendation on the best way to put babies in their beds to prevent cot deaths, but no one knew quite which was the most effective way of communicating this to parents. Each health visitor was encouraged to use his or her own personal skills and judgement on how to get the message over to parents.

There does seem to be some need for bringing both hard and soft approaches together. One possible way of doing this might be to systematise some of these softer approaches so they can be evaluated alongside traditional harder methods. One such way was some work I did with my colleague Royston Flude at Kellogg plc where we were asked to look at management competencies throughout the organisation. As our starting point we used a list of competencies issued by the Management Charter Initiative (MCI), now called Management Standards Centre, the National Vocational Qualification (NVQ) body for management competency standards. We (Weightman and Flude, 1996, unpublished) felt that the different competencies could fall into four distinct groups:

- managing activities that were about getting things done and the actions required by the business

- managing the analysis of information and resources to solve problems and reach decisions that involved thinking
- managing people and dealing with one's own and other people's feelings
- managing the vision, values and assumptions that underpin the organisation. This involves understanding one's own values and expressing them in strategic ways.

The first two groups of competencies might be described as the hard approaches to getting the right things done and the latter two groups as the softer approaches. We found that teams needed all four groups of competencies. We also found that the more senior managers were, the more of the second two groups of competencies they needed and the less they could do of the first, although they often still had to supervise competencies from the first two groups. The exercise highlighted the need for different competencies within a team and the fact that both hard and soft competencies are required for sustainable, excellent performance. This work was based upon the Motivational Driver Model (or FIN) developed by Royston Flude.

The importance of trying to develop both hard and soft competencies can be seen within almost any organisation. There are times when we need the analytical, hard competencies of making the most of the resources available to us. At other times we have to deal with other people and our own feelings, using the softer competencies. It may be that we personally take more easily to one group of competencies than the other. If we are to become useful members of a work organisation, we do need to try to acquire at least a modicum of competence across the whole range.

Currently there is a fashion for associating the word 'management' with the hard approaches, and the softer approaches are associated with the word 'leadership'. This is at the heart of much discussion in HR/personnel and management circles. See for example the change of vocabulary in the standards for CIPD Core Management from earlier sets; now there is great emphasis on the soft skills of leadership and developing commitment. This is reflected in the changes in the content of this book compared with its predecessor (Weightman, 1993). The emphasis has moved from looking at the mechanics of co-ordinating the organisation, management, to encouraging individuals, leadership.

SOMETHING TO DEBATE

Throughout the book there will appear boxes like this one headed 'Debate' which take a central debate of the topic being discussed. Some of these will be particular to the subject. Some will refer back to the central debates mentioned here. They are intended to allow you to decide for yourself what your view is. You might want to use them as a starting point for a seminar discussion to see what other people think. They could certainly be the basis of further investigation to look at other people's writing.

The ethics of leadership

If we are going to manage other people, what are the ethical issues of doing so? Ethics has become a popular topic in many business schools. This sounds great but, as Rowe (1997) points out, ethics can be taught in two very different ways. It can be taught using the models of absolute values, or as theologians and philosophers call them 'first principles' – that is, the absolute right and wrong ways of doing things. But it can also be taught in terms of how we all have our own way of seeing things. According to this view, values are relative to individuals and the situations in which they find themselves – the right way depends on the context. The first is very much like the unitarist view of organisation and the latter like the pluralist or contingent view.

The first model is always popular with those in senior positions and can be paraphrased as the principle of the leader always having the right way. In this model there is an élite of people who can claim a special connection to absolute values. The special claim might be based on ownership, ability, personal charm, success or other factors. The second model is more democratic: it argues that we all start from our own unique perspective and we have to prove by argument that our perspective is a better approximation of reality than anyone else's. Users of the first model can claim infallibility whilst those of the second persuasion always have an element of doubt. The first demand compliance, the second rely on credibility to get things done. Chapters 7, 10 and 11 all have further discussion of this.

The ethics of leadership can be seen from either of these perspectives. Is the leader claiming some superior position or does he or she take the democratic approach in order to encourage each person to offer their best? Where you stand on this dichotomy will tell you what sort of leader you are and will also tell you how vulnerable you are to a fall. The absolute version is always less flexible than the contingent model. Chapter 10 deals specifically with leadership, but several times throughout the book there will be suggestions on how to influence those who work for you. When you use these suggestions, try asking yourself whether some claim for absolute values is appropriate or whether a more democratic approach might be effective. The style of your leadership has implications for you as well as for those you try to lead. I believe that if you try to achieve an unobtainable absolute you are more likely to be frustrated than if you adopt the more pragmatic, contingent view of leadership – but then I was ever the pluralist and relativist. Make your own view, but try to know yourself; whichever ethical position you hold, knowing yourself will help you to lead and manage people more effectively.

Chapter 13 has further discussion on the ethics of management, this time on the ethics of managing performance.

HOW TO USE THIS BOOK

This book is an introduction to managing people. It is intended to be used, as well as read. Each chapter can be read separately and in any order as I refer back and forward to related chapters. The order of the chapters follows the sequence of the indicative content list of the CIPD's Professional Standard, Managing People. You may prefer to use the chapters in a different order. For example, following the employment cycle: recruitment, training, appraisal, motivation and stress. Or you might want to look at chapters dealing with the individual first, then the group and finally the whole organisation. I have included a route map at the beginning of each chapter to enable you to find the section you need.

I have included various devices in each chapter to try to help you develop your understanding and be able to apply the theory to real situations. These include:

Route map At the beginning of each chapter there is a section, in *italics*, where the key ideas from the chapter are indicated in **bold** and cross-referenced to other chapters. This lists the theories and abstract academic analysis that are most relevant to the chapter. These are the backbone of studying management. Then I list the related practical methods and techniques for managing people. They are the application of the theories. The aim is to reinforce your understanding that systematic theories, models and concepts inform the development of applications and ways of managing people. These in turn are expected to assist the achievement of organisational and individual goals. If you like, it is a tagging of the component parts of the study and practice of managing people. I have also listed the specific examples given in the text that are trying to illustrate this connection.

Objectives At the beginning of each chapter there is a series of bullet points with the main learning points of the text.

Case study At the beginning of each chapter is a small pen portrait of someone and a dilemma facing them at work. Each of them is based on a real person whom I know well. For obvious reasons I have changed names and some small details so that they cannot be identified; many of them are still working in the same organisations. I have included a few questions for you to consider as you read the chapter.

Activities At the end of each chapter is a list of activities. Some are questions for you to answer individually, some are to be answered as a group, for example a seminar group. The idea is to make you apply your reading. This should aid your understanding and your learning about the material. By gathering your own examples of the material given you gain experience of the ideas and so will learn more than just reading. See the Kolb cycle, described in Chapter 3, for further discussion of why this approach to learning is used in this textbook. Answers to some of these activities are given at the end of the book.

Have I met the objectives? At the end of the chapter is a series of questions asking you to check whether you have learned the main points.

And finally At the end of the chapter I ask you to say what you would do in the case study in the light of what you have learned. I also give a brief summary of my view, not necessarily the only correct view.

Examples Throughout the chapters are boxed text with specific, real examples taken from my own work or from other written material. These are all real, recent cases where people have had to manage others to achieve something worthwhile. Look at them and ask questions such as: does the theory apply in this case? Of which point in the text is this a good example? In some of the more applied chapters there are also smaller examples within the main body of the text to illustrate the application. Again, these are real examples of real people faced with having to do something.

Debate Each chapter has a boxed text with some central debate described. They are intended to provoke you to start developing your own point of view. You will certainly have a view, but may not yet know quite what it is.

Theories, models and concepts I have tried to give brief descriptions of theories and models. These are important analytical tools for any discipline and are at the heart of academic study. There is very little difference between a theory and a model. A theory is usually more established and has been tested over time. Both models and theories involve concepts. These are the specific ideas that make up the model or theory. The more seriously one undertakes to study a discipline the more detailed an understanding and development of models and theories one needs. By using these theories we can develop a more systematic study of managing people. The more robust the theory or model, that is the wider range of people and places it applies to, the more important the theory or model is. These are the areas upon which you need to concentrate your learning. They distinguish the professional from the amateur.

References These are the books, articles and other sources I have used to find the information. The author's surname and date of publication are given in the text and a list is given in full at the end of the book.

Further reading I have recommended two or three specific books on each subject. Some are other textbooks or academic books but some are from more general reading such as novels or biographies.

Key words At the end of the book I have given a list of key concepts. This should allow you to have a quick reference to see if you have covered the salient points of the book. It Is also a quick revision aid before exams. I have not given definitions here – you will need to look them up in the index and read the text.

ACTIVITIES

1   Can I think of any behaviour at my work that a psychologist could usefully study, and how such a study could be beneficial?

2   What contribution to understanding my situation at work could a sociologist make?

3   Do we have an HR or personnel department? What type is it? When did I last use it?

4   Do I prefer the one-happy-family approach of the unitarist or the diversity approach of the pluralist?

5   Can I think of three hard approaches to management used in my organisation? Can I think of three soft approaches used in my organisation? What are the effects of these? Are they appropriate?

If you are in a seminar group, exchange details of your examples with colleagues to see if you agree about the classification hard/soft.

6   If you were going to do research on how universities manage their people you would start with some questions. You would then need to decide which discipline – psychology or sociology – would best answer these questions. Then decide what methodology you would use. Decide which discipline and what methodology you would use for the following questions about universities:

How should we train newly appointed lecturers?

What does the Dean do?

What will be the effect of amalgamating two departments?

How can we resolve the complaints from the local residents about the noise coming from the student halls of residence?

How can we motivate the porters to allow late evening use of the building?

HAVE I MET THE OBJECTIVES?

1   Can I list three different approaches to analysing how to manage people?

2   What is the difference between psychology and sociology?

3   What is the central debate of unitarists versus pluralists?

4   What is the difference between management and leadership?

5   What are the main issues about the ethics of leadership?

FURTHER READING

Foot and Hook (2002) and Marchington and Wilkinson (2002) are excellent textbooks in personnel/HRM. Marchington and Wilkinson is the more serious academic text of the two and is the course book for the later CIPD qualifications.

A very useful introduction to the whole business of management is an American publication by J Magretta and N Stone, *What Management Is: How it works and why it's everyone's business* (2002) Profile Business. It is clearly written and free of jargon but written with the authority of the Harvard Business Review, one of the main journals for management research.

Individual Differences

*This chapter deals with the following key ideas: theories of **personality, psychoanalysis, behaviourism, humanistic psychology, intelligence, personal constructs, social learning** and **perception**. These are all ways of trying to understand and explain individual differences. This chapter includes a description and discussion of **people's attitudes and the diversity of people at work**. These are the practical aspects of understanding individual differences at work. The theories discussed in this chapter are an important underlying basis for the concepts in other chapters. For example, they inform material in Chapter 5 on job design, Chapter 8 on selection, Chapter 9 on training and Chapters 13 and 14 on reward management. This chapter has a specific example from the military.*

OBJECTIVES

When you have finished reading this chapter you should be able to:

- understand the principal ways in which human beings differ

- explain the principal ways in which human beings differ

- describe some psychological models for analysing personalities

- describe some of the causes of the differences between people

- understand and explain some of the ways individual differences may help organisations

- understand and explain some of the ways individual differences may create problems for the organisation.

Nick's dilemma

Nick was head of a large business team. He was also a very keen sportsman. The team included 20 people based in the office and 20 sales people located throughout the country. The company was celebrating the 50th anniversary of its foundation. Nick was allocated £60 per person to hold some sort of jamboree for his team. The only rules were that there should be some event to which the entire team was invited. How was Nick to decide on what would suit everyone?

Should he capitalise on the cohesive, young group in the office and have some energetic day out such as go-karting? Should he ask for suggestions? Should he arrange a traditional dinner, so no one would be offended? Should he try to emphasise the team or do something more dramatic than the other teams? Would it matter if not everyone came, as long as they were invited?

There are two main reasons for understanding individual differences at work. First we need a range of people to work with so that a variety of talents and attitudes are available to develop our work. Second we need to be able to work with this range of people reasonably and smoothly so we can get things done. If we are going to work successfully with a range of people we have to come to terms with the fact that there is quite a wide variety of people doing the same job. If we were all the same it would be not only very boring, but also detrimental to the organisation, as there would not be a sufficient breadth of experience and opinion when we needed to solve problems. By understanding and tolerating these differences we are more likely to get a co-operative, productive effort from those we come into contact with. This does not mean we have to understand and tolerate all behaviour, indeed that would amount to indifference. If we are to work with other people we need to try to influence some people to behave differently as well as tolerate individual differences.

I have included here three concepts about individual differences to demonstrate how we can analyse the differences between people. This type of analysis can be used to select and develop people differently. We might want to use it to ensure we have a sufficient variety to balance our team. It can also be used when we want to change a person's behaviour at work. By understanding why an individual may behave differently we are more likely to be able to celebrate the difference, accept the difference, or to find a convincing way of helping him or her to change, rather than just saying 'I want you to be different'. The three concepts used are personality, perception and diversity.

WHY PEOPLE HAVE DIFFERENT PERSONALITIES

We all need to understand other people in everyday life so we can make friends, understand our families and influence each other. An important step in our understanding is the need to see things from the other's point of view, an extremely difficult thing to do. To do this we have to analyse something about his or her personality. One way of doing this is to have some models to help us analyse. In other words, one way of understanding more about the nature of individual differences is to look at the theory of personality.

In everyday use, the term 'personality' describes the impression a particular person makes upon others. The differences in our personalities are the sum of the differences between us. Inevitably there are lots of theories of how and why our personalities are formed and what they are derived from. There is no one best theory of personality. The theory or theories that seem to account best for our own and other's behaviour will vary from time to time and place to place. We are also likely to be attracted to theories of personality that fit our own personality. Our view of personality will also affect how we interact with people. It is well worth understanding what that view is so we can interpret the effect we may have on others and modify it where appropriate.

Some models for understanding individual differences of personality are given here, but there are many others. The three main contrasting schools of thought on personality are those of the psychoanalysts, the behaviourists and the humanistic psychologists. These three views are still the most influential. Let us look at each in turn and see what insights they can offer into behaviour in organisations.

Psychoanalysis – Freud

Psychoanalysis is dominated by the theories of Sigmund Freud (1962), developed from his work in Vienna at the beginning of the twentieth century. Freud concluded that personality consisted of three separate parts: the 'ego', the 'superego' and the 'id'. The 'ego' is made up of the individual drives we are born with that focus a person's nature. It will make people act differently from those around them and interpret the world differently. The 'superego' is learned from society. It represents the injunctions of parents, schoolteachers and other important members of society about what is acceptable behaviour and what is not. The superego can have a modifying effect on the ego, which suggests that basic drives are modified by society. The 'id' consists of the basic, animal instincts that make us aroused so we get going and become involved with our surroundings.

Freud argued that personality develops through a series of traumatic stages when these three aspects of personality are in conflict, and trying to get them into some sort of harmony is the business of maturing. The classic stages described by Freud include the following:

- first, the early period of breast feeding with its implicit intimacy between mother and child which leads to anguish when the child is required to give it up
- second, the anger felt by children over the external control implicit in toilet training
- third, the disapproval of childhood sexuality demonstrated by society
- fourth, the difficulties for all of us in learning to control anger and aggression in socially acceptable ways.

Freud argued that these traumas get pushed to the back of the mind but continue to affect our behaviour into adulthood. The most obvious example is what we call the Freudian slip, when we say something with a hidden meaning instead of what we intended. For example, if an individual uses a favourite brother's name when talking to the less preferred brother. Another example is that the early experience of toilet training may result in a need for order and tidiness in adult life.

So how does a Freudian approach apply to behaviour at work? As well as the general implications of analysing how we deal with anger and aggression, another way in which a Freudian approach can be useful at work is through the idea of 'defence mechanisms'. These are devices we subconsciously use to defend ourselves from being psychologically undermined. We use these when we feel under stress and they give us relief. The most common defence mechanisms are:

- Fixation: individuals become rigid and inflexible and stick to known procedures and behaviours.
- Rationalisaton: individuals cover up their behaviour and contributions with elaborate explanations.
- Regression: individuals behave in a less mature way than is usual or appropriate for their age or responsibility.
- Projection: individuals attribute their own motives and feelings to others where this is inappropriate.

All of these can be demonstrated at work.

Perhaps Freud's greatest contribution to our understanding of behaviour in organisations is the message that we must consider the whole person and everything that has happened to them to understand their personality. The main criticisms of his theories are that they are based on a very small sample of Viennese bourgeois life in the early part of the twentieth century, and that by placing so much emphasis on childhood they make it difficult to see what we can do to change ourselves once we grow up. By their nature, the theories are very difficult to test and collect data about objectively.

To show how psychoanalytical theory could be used in understanding organisations, let us look at Dickson's (1976) use of a Freudian analysis applied to the work of people in the army. He demonstrated how military life attracts those who like regimentation and orderliness, and suggested that this was due to the individuals' early childhood experiences. With so many people in the military falling into this category, there are not enough who can be flexible when the rules, regulations and procedures do not cover a particular circumstance. Dickson maintained that since those with potty training traumas tended to be drawn to military organisations there should be nothing surprising in the fact of military incompetence because of lack of flexibility.

Psychoanalysis – Eysenck

Hans Eysenck was a British psychologist who did much to popularise the subject of psychology through books such as *Know Your Own IQ* (Eysenck, 1962). He was also responsible for the widespread use of the terms 'introverted' and 'extroverted', originally proposed by the Swiss psychiatrist Carl Jung. Eysenck's main suggestion is that we differ in our basic state of arousal – that is, how much stimulation we require to get going both physically and mentally. Those with an introverted personality are naturally highly aroused so any extra stimulation sends them into a state of anxiety. By contrast, extroverted people are in a low state of arousal and consequently need a lot of stimulation to get them going. This distinction suggests that introverted people will seek out quiet whereas extroverts will thrive in large noisy gatherings. Eysenck (1976) has proposed that there is a continuum from the most introverted to the most extroverted. He has also suggested that people differ on a dimension he calls neuroticism as opposed to stability. Eysenck argues that a stable extrovert has quite a different personality from a neurotic introvert.

How does this apply to the world of work? The logical conclusion from this theory is that the two individuals' behaviour at work will be quite different; the stable extrovert could tolerate a more robust environment than the neurotic introvert, whilst an environment that suited the neurotic introvert would probably seem boring to the stable extrovert. Eysenck did a good deal of research to support his theory. He has been criticised for the nature of some of the research, particularly that associated with racial differences, and for his emphasis on the role of nature and genetics.

Much of our everyday understanding of personality has come from Freud, Eysenck and other psychoanalysts. The usefulness of psychoanalytic models for analysing people at work lies in their message that there may be deep-seated reasons for strange behaviour. The models are also useful in giving us some basic vocabulary to describe the differences between people. However, the drawback of using only a psychoanalytical view of personality is that there is such an emphasis on the early years, and this gives the impression that nothing can be done later about people's personality. It can lead to a feeling of hopelessness if someone does not fit in.

Behaviourism

Behaviourism is dominated by the work of the American psychologist BF Skinner. His main contention is that we learn through our experiences and that these experiences affect who and what we become. With others (1953), he explored in minute detail how behaviour is learned – see Chapter 3 for further details. Skinner emphasised the external control of behaviour: we behave in the way we do because of our history of reinforcement or rewards. According to behaviourists, a stimulus evokes a response from the individual, which in turn evokes a reaction that may or may not be reinforcing to the individual. Where the response leads to a reinforcing reaction the individual is more likely to respond in that way in the future. For example, if every time we offer to wash up we are given a grateful hug we are more likely to offer again in the future, assuming we like hugs from that person; if we are told we are washing up in the wrong way, at the wrong time, we are unlikely to offer again, unless of course we like being told off!

By studying observable behaviour and the effect of different rewards given at different times, the behaviourists have built up a detailed understanding of the technology for specific learning. It has proved highly successful in teaching new skills. Many computer programs for teaching are based on this 'programmed' learning. The idea is to make the instructions as clear as possible, and when the correct response is elicited a reward is given: it may well be 'Well done' or something more concrete. The behaviourists have suggested that if we can discover which reward, or reinforcement, each individual prefers, learning will take place more effectively. Reward is defined as that which the person will work for. The process of manipulating people's behaviour by adjusting the instructions, task and reward is called 'behaviour modification'.

Various models of personality are used in organisations for assessing the personalities of people wanting to join the organisation. Psychometric tests – that is, systematic tests – have an increasing popularity in the assessment of personality. In psychology circles there is much debate about this, as the reliability of the tests and the ethics of assessing something as personal and private as one's personality are not clear cut. On the other hand, the personality of a candidate is inevitably assessed at interview with a view to seeing whether the candidate will fit in with the work group. Might it not as well be done by a systematic test as by guesswork? A widely used test is the Occupational Personality Questionnaire (OPQ) developed by the British consultancy company Saville and Holdsworth. The various forms have 30 scales of personality attribute, covering such things as persuasive, active, modest and critical. An individual profile of these attributes can then be compared with the desired qualities of the person-specification for a particular job. These questionnaires have to be administered by specially licensed people. The results are often then used by others responsible for the decision.

There are clear implications here for managing people. If personality is learned and dependent on the history of reinforcement, then managers can institute a suitable system of rewards to elicit the behaviours that are required to run an organisation effectively. The only task is to analyse the desired behaviours and reinforcements in sufficient detail and with enough accuracy for individuals to be motivated to behave appropriately. Luthans and Kreitner (1975), amongst others, developed this idea. They gave reinforcement schedules, analysis of behaviour and the training necessary to enable managers to put it into effect. The application of their ideas does seem to improve productivity. It can be seen in such training schedules as that of the McDonald's fast food chain, where very detailed schedules about how to cook and serve a burger are laid down and have been used to train people throughout the world from an astonishing range of backgrounds. In a less meticulous way, the idea of rewarding appropriate behaviours is implicit in all performance-related pay schemes, which are discussed in more detail in Chapter 13.

The limitation on applying this approach comprehensively is the difficulty of including the idea of intrinsic rewards. These rewards are when we are motivated by our desire for fulfilment and development, reaching our potential as emphasised by Maslow, as I discuss in Chapter 12. However, much of the current approach of sophisticated organisations to tailor work to individuals through flexible working, variety of rewards and performance appraisal schemes fits in with a behaviourist model. Another limitation of the behaviourist approach is that it tends to assume that workers are entirely dependent on leaders and managers getting the analysis right, whereas many people work in environments in which some degree of self-control and personal responsibility is necessary. There are also ethical issues related to the degree of control and obedience we are prepared to accept at work. Very few of us have difficulty in accepting the use of behaviour modification techniques to teach mentally handicapped children to feed themselves. But most of us would object to having the same techniques applied systematically to us by a manager with complete control over us at work – assuming of course that someone was clever enough to analyse both the task and the rewards accurately enough to persuade us to comply.

Humanistic psychology

Humanistic psychology has been very influential among organisational psychologists and in the study of organisational behaviour. Unlike the other two schools of thought outlined above, it is not dominated by one outstanding figure for it is really about ideals. It is more a description of what 'could' and 'should' be than an analysis of what 'is'. The central belief is that we all have within ourselves the capacity to develop in a healthy and creative way. The emphasis is on becoming independent, mature adults who can take responsibility for our own actions. There may be distortions due to the vagaries of parents, schools or society, but we can overcome these difficulties if we are prepared to take responsibility for ourselves.

Maslow is usually seen as the founding father of this school, with his idea of the self-actualising personality (see Chapter 12). He outlined the concept of people who work for themselves to see how far their abilities will take them. By putting this concept at the top of his hierarchy of needs, Maslow was obviously advocating it as an ideal that we should aim for.

Some of these ideas have been further developed into the concept of various 'intelligences'. Intelligence was described by Piaget (an important child psychologist) as 'what you do when you do not know what to do'. It is thought that individuals have a range of intelligences covering various behaviours. For example, Lucas (2001) suggests we have multiple intelligences, such as:

Linguistic	Mathematical	Visual
Physical	Social	Practical
Musical	Environmental	
Emotional	Spiritual	

Individuals will vary in the extent to which they develop and rely on these aspects of behaviour. We each have a different profile of these 'intelligences' and may prefer to use one above another. There is a great deal of interest in these ideas within organisations. One reason is trying to develop tests that will describe the intelligence of individuals. This is used in the selection of staff. The most popular personality questionaire is the MBTI – Myers Briggs Type Indicator® and is increasingly used. However, not everyone agrees that it is a sufficiently bias-free way to select staff.

Carl Rogers (1967) has also been very influential amongst humanistic psychologists. He described a sequence of stages that an individual goes through in becoming a fully functional person.

- The first stage is the need to be open to experience and to move away from defensiveness.
- The second stage is a desire to live each moment more fully and immediately, rather than to relate everything to the past.
- The third is when individuals increasingly trust themselves physically, emotionally and mentally.
- The fourth stage, ideally, is when individuals take responsibility for themselves and their actions.

To help us to go through these stages, Rogers advocated using other people as a resource to interact with. He argues that only by sharing experiences and developing trust do we come to know and trust ourselves.

Consultants working in organisations will often be operating from the particular standpoint of humanistic psychology. The enthusiasm for participation in decision-making, ownership of ideas, autonomous work groups, and developing potential, all fit within humanistic psychology. One particular application is the concept of stress and the analysis of sources of stress. The cure is dependent on this diagnosis, but usually some increase in openness and trust is advocated with higher degrees of autonomy and self-management being associated with a healthier organisation.

The problem with using humanistic psychology as a model to understand personality is that not everyone shares these ideals. Given the unproven nature of some of the basic tenets, it can be difficult to persuade non-believers of the benefits of the proposed changes suggested by a humanistic analysis.

Other theories of personality

There are a huge number of models and theories of personality. They include models from the disciplines of theology, philosophy, psychology and literature. All of these disciplines have interesting insights into the nature of personality but the two included here have particularly influenced the thinking of people who study organisations.

Personal construct theory – One group of theories that has been widely used by people studying organisational behaviour rejects the idea of motivation and single stages in personality development and emphasises the individual's conceptualisation of his or her world. Kelly (1955) introduced the idea that we all construct our own worlds. We each see things differently and interpret things differently using our own dimensions and models; this means we each construe the world differently. One dimension he used was the process of 'attribution', by which we make sense of our world by making assumptions, or attributions, of what is causing things to happen. By having these attributions we hope to be able to predict and control social events. Each of us will have different attributions and so perceive the world differently. Because we enact many roles and engage in continuous change we have constantly to practise this process of construction. Kelly's theory is called 'personal construct theory'.

Kelly has also been influential methodologically. Various techniques based on Kelly's original device, the 'repertory grid', have been developed to discover what 'constructs' each of us is most likely to use. This is very widely used by social scientists in research into organisations.

Social learning theory – A related group of concepts are the social learning theories. These deal with the learning of behaviour, and particularly the learning of maladaptive behaviours – see, for example, Bandura (1977). These theories emphasise the role of dysfunctional – that is, unhelpful – expectancies or self-concepts. Expectancies can be dysfunctional in a variety of ways. If we wrongly expect a painful outcome we are likely to avoid a situation. If this is a wrong expectation we may miss out on the good times. For example, if you fear that closeness will bring pain you are likely to act in a hostile way that leads to rejection by others, which in turn confirms the expectation that closeness will bring pain. Dysfunctional self-evaluation can be exemplified in the person who has no standards of, or capacity for, self-reward and so is bored and dependent on external pleasures. It can also be seen in the person who has set overly severe standards for himself or herself. These standards can lead to self-punishment and depression. All these can be a problem at work. The recommended therapy from a social learning point of view is 'modelling', 'guided participation' and 'desensitisation'. These all involve taking things slowly, step by step, towards the full objective.

DEBATE – NATURE OR NURTURE

One of the continuing debates in philosophy from Plato onwards has been the relative contribution of our inherited characteristics, nature, and our upbringing, nurture. This is not just an academic issue as it has practical implications involving the extent to which we can modify our own or someone else's behaviour. If our ability to learn languages, acquire new skills and adopt new attitudes is all laid down by our inherited characteristics then how we grow up and whom we work with will not affect this ability. If, on the other hand, such abilities are influenced by the environment in which we develop it is important to look at what influences we are experiencing and what influence we are having on others.

Traditionally psychologists, sociologists and social anthropologists tend to focus on the effect of the environment on the child. This does not mean that they assume that the child is infinitely pliable, but they do assume that nurture plays an important part. More recently there has been greater interest in the nature part of the debate as new biological techniques have meant greater understanding of genetics and the brain's construction. If we consider some of the models of personality, we can see that their different assumptions about human nature have implications for analysing organisational behaviour. The Freudian model is a conflict model with an emphasis on how innate, antisocial impulses become restrained by society. Behaviourists take a view that behaviour is entirely shaped by the environment, claiming to be able to train any child towards any goal. Humanistic psychologists usually assume a gradual unfolding of nature through nurture that continues throughout life. A team leader would need to treat team members differently if they were seeking to elicit a change in behaviour, depending on which of the approaches was taken.

PERCEPTION

Another useful concept in trying to understand individual differences is what psychologists call perception. 'Perception' is the term used to describe the process of selecting, organising and interpreting incoming stimuli. We each do it differently, and so perceive a different real world.

The real world is so stable and familiar to us that it seems curious to discuss the differences of real worlds. But this familiarity and stability of the world has more to do with our own mental processes than the actual sensory input, which is constantly changing. Because we organise the incoming message into our stable view of the world we make it seem stable to us. But your stable world is a different one from mine.

There are several reasons why people may perceive the same situation differently:

- *Physical sensitivity*: human organs are sensitive only to a limited range of things. For example, none of us can see X-rays. Some people are more or less sensitive than others – for example, partial sight or hearing makes a difference to the stimulus received.

- *Selective attention*: we notice some things and not others. For example, at a party we can concentrate on one conversation and ignore others; we focus on what is important to us. If, however, someone mentions our name we usually hear it – even in a conversation we are not part of.

- *Categorisation*: we categorise the cues as they come in. The incoming stimuli are fitted into one of our existing categories – these categories include concepts, ideas and associations built up in our memory as a result of experience such as education. This process may well be influenced by language; we fit things into our existing pattern of understanding.

- *Limits on our capacity*: we can deal with only a limited amount at any one time. The limit is set not just by how much is coming in but also by the ease of categorising the stimuli. The time we feel most overwhelmed at work is when many difficult communications are coming to us. The office party, when there are probably just as many communications, is nothing like as daunting because the communications are easier to categorise and it is easier to decide what action to take.

- *The environment*: our expectations and the context will determine the kinds of categorisation we apply. If we are expecting to see our colleague at the airport, it is surprising how often we misidentify someone else before we meet the right person. Whereas if we meet the same person in the supermarket it may take us a little while to remember his or her name.

- *Individuality*: our attitudes and personalities will influence what we perceive. They generate expectations. A prejudiced person sees the behaviour of those whom they are prejudiced against in a negative way, whatever actually happens: a friendly act will be seen as false, a casual attitude as sloppy, a remote stance as difficult – and so on. This in turn will affect the behaviour of the perceiver, creating the beginnings of a vicious circle.

The act of perceiving is a constructive process in which we try to make sense of our environment by attempting to fit it to our experience. The real world is different for each of us, as we perceive it differently. As you work with people, you will undoubtedly be faced by people perceiving things differently from yourself. Sometimes this is because of a different job perspective and access to information, sometimes it is due to the amount of time and commitment we have given to the topic. It is usually possible to resolve the difference by means of a discussion that unravels the basis of the different perceptions. This exploring of different perceptions can clarify issues and lead to a new perception by both parties. Where it does not we may have a problem, and this is discussed in Chapter 14.

To overcome the difficulty of being reported for sexual harassment at work, many US companies are asking their staff when they are in any sort of relationship with another person at work to sign a 'love contract'. This will allow everyone to perceive the behaviour differently and still maintain dignity at work. Clearly sexual harassment is a matter of perception, as you need to know whether there is consent!

EQUAL OPPORTUNITIES AND DIVERSITY

So far, this chapter has dealt with the psychological models that can help us analyse individual differences. There is also a social component to why people are different. Individuals' cultural and economic backgrounds will influence the norms that are set for them, the socialisation they experience, and the choices available to them. Norms are the socially acceptable, 'normal' way of doing things. Socialisation is the process by which our behaviour is shaped by those around us so we fit in and become socially acceptable. The next chapter has more on social learning. Different ethnicity, gender and abilities will also account for individual differences, because individuals will have been treated differently as children and as adults in both overt and covert ways. To say that people are different does not mean that some are superior, merely that their experiences differ.

Fair treatment

One aspect of managing people that has attracted attention over the years is how to ensure fair treatment for different people and ensure that all people's talents are used. This is important for three reasons – ethical, business and legal. The ethics of treating people differently for some reason other than their ability to do the work required is not acceptable in modern, liberal democracies. The ability to do the work required always includes some understanding of acceptable behaviour. What is meant by acceptable behaviour, and where the line is drawn, is the subject of much debate and changes over time. For example, the position of smokers at work has moved from a common behaviour to total banning in many places of work in 30 years.

The business argument for fair treatment is that by having a diverse workforce there will be a variety of talents available to the organisation. The diverse workforce will also have experience and knowledge of a variety of customers, so the organisation will not become too detached from the general population. The legal aspect of managing for diversity is the legislation on equal opportunities and discrimination about gender and race. Table 2.1 gives a list of legislation that to some extent protects people from discrimination. Under European legislation there is increasing pressure not to discriminate on the basis of people's sexuality, age or disability. It is expected that UK legislation will implement this. This is known as equal opportunities legislation. The inequality of opportunity that is experienced in selection, training and promotion by women, ethnic minorities and those with disabilities has been hotly debated since the 1960s and is further discussed in Chapter 8.

Managing diversity

In many management books, and particularly those covering personnel or human resource management, there is increasing use of the term 'managing diversity'. This is used where in the past a phrase derived from 'equal opportunity' was used. There is a different emphasis as well as a change of vocabulary. The concern of the earlier equal opportunities movements and legislation was to help different groups cope with a dominant male, white, able-bodied

Table 2.1 *Equal opportunities legislation*

Disabled people
Disability Discrimination Act 1995

Ex-offenders
Rehabilitation of Offenders Act 1974

Northern Ireland
Fair Employment (Northern Ireland) Act 1989

Part timers
Employment Relations Act 1999
European Court of Justice Rulings

Racial equality
Race Relations Act 1976

Religion and belief
Employment Equality Regulations 2003

Sex discrimination
Sex Discrimination Acts 1975, 1986 and 2001
Employment Protection Act 1978
Equal Pay Act 1970
Employment Rights Act 1996

Sexual orientation
Employment Equality Regulations 2003

---

culture. Managing diversity is more about valuing the differences people have and using and celebrating these differences. This might include such diversity over:

■ qualifications	■ learning difficulties	■ gender
■ accent	■ political affiliation	■ ethnic origin
■ sexual orientation	■ spent convictions	■ age.
■ caring responsibilities	■ trade union membership	

As the CIPD (1998) points out, the reasons that managing this diversity matters in organisations are:

■ It can open up new opportunities through broadening the customer base.

■ It is part of the increasingly important ethical stand of organisations.

■ It ensures the selection, training and retention of people from the entire labour market rather than part of it only, so the organisation can attract the best talent.

- People want to work for fair employers, so having a diverse workforce may help retain good staff.
- Organisations are required to abide by equal opportunities legislation.
- Benchmarking against other organisations will show that diversity and equal opportunities are increasingly included in such things as contracts to supply.

For many well-established organisations this is still a novelty and far from achieved. For newer, small organisations, particularly in the so-called 'gorgeous' industries of fashion, hospitality and performance, there are more examples of the celebration of diversity.

Although it makes rational sense to recruit and develop staff on the basis of their ability to do the job, the judgement is easily influenced by beliefs that are not relevant. Even those committed to recruiting and developing on ability can be prejudiced in ways they do not realise. Some of the arguments that challenge stereotypical thinking in this area are (see IPD 1998):

- *Ability/disability*: performance at school is more related to the socio-economic status of the parent than to ethnic origin. Girls do better than boys. Most disabilities have no practical implications for job performance and more people acquire disabilities as they age than are born with them. We have to be very careful of 'mind sets' that lead us to make unfair assumptions about others.
- *Culture*: the non-white minority of Great Britain is about 5.5 per cent of the population, and lives mostly in London, the West Midlands and Greater Manchester. These groups have a higher proportion of young people than the white population and tend to live in larger households. In some parts of the country a significant part of the local workforce will be from these groups, in others a rare employee. The important issue is that each individual is recruited and developed for his or her individual capacity to contribute.
- *Gender*: women make up over 40 per cent of the workforce, of whom 44 per cent are part time. Men are increasingly also working part time. Two-and-a-half million men and three-and-a-half million women have caring responsibilities for elderly ependants. Approximately 10 per cent of lone parents are men. Caring responsibilities make it difficult to work conventional hours, but flexible working can suit a wide range of people who would willingly contribute their best if they could.

An important thing to remember is that focusing on the differences between people tends to group people together and assume there is something wrong. Only by concentrating on the individual and the similarities of what they can contribute can we genuinely use the talents of everyone living and wanting to work in Great Britian. In organisations with a performance-management approach to individual staff, managing diversity is less difficult to achieve than in those organisations that are set in their ways. Kandola and Fullerton (1998) researched about 500 organisations and reported that old-style, group-based equal opportunities can be developed through strategies that focus on individual performance to manage a wide variety of people with different attributes, concerns, values and needs to achieve the organisation's goals.

OVERCOMING STEREOTYPING AND PREJUDICE

In trying to understand other people we all instinctively use a short-cut method known as stereotyping. This is an essential aspect of dealing with others, but can also be a strait-jacket if we do not use it carefully. If you have lost your way in a strange place and decide to ask someone for directions, you do not stop the first person you see; you pick out someone from the surrounding crowd who looks a potential source of good information. You probably pick on someone who is not in a hurry, neither too young nor too old, appearing intelligent and sympathetic. You have a working stereotype of who would be an appropriate person to ask. At work we carry around a series of stereotypes that influence all our dealings with other people.

There is seldom time in working situations to abandon all stereotyping. As a way of approaching matters, especially in emergencies, some sort of working hypothesis is needed immediately. The danger of stereotyping is, of course, that people are not treated as individuals but as categories. This is unreasonable and can be unlawful. It also limits the ability of the person who is overdependent on stereotypes to work with others to the full extent of his or her abilities. A special form of this is the 'halo effect' – some aspect of behaviour overrides behaviour elsewhere; for example, the assistant who is always on time but does poor work is seen as an admirable member of staff. Stereotyping often occurs between teams in organisations. For example, the research staff are seen as earnest, harassed and socially ill at ease, whereas the sales assistants are seen as fun-loving and lively.

Prejudice occurs when stereotyping is taken to an extreme form where we categorise whole groups of people and see them as conforming to prejudged behaviours. Some of these prejudices can be illegal and are certainly inappropriate in the workplace.

Changing our stereotypes and prejudices is not easy. Changing other people's stereotypes and prejudices is even more difficult, but we need to try where these are inappropriate. Bringing things out into the open is certainly a help. The PC or 'politically correct' movement, despite some of its absurdities, has been helpful in allowing us to do this. The usual advice for improving our ability to perceive others accurately and therefore with less prejudice is:

- The better we know ourselves the easier it is to see others accurately. Many of the workshops on transactional analysis and assertion are about 'knowing oneself'. Intimate discussion and feedback sessions can be useful; indeed, the best appraisal interviews could include this sort of feedback – see Chapter 14.
- One's own character affects what one sees in others. Using material in the earlier part of the chapter to see how individual differences arise might help us to realise and deal with this.
- The accuracy of our perceptions depends on our sensitivity to the differences between people. Trying to develop a sensitivity about people that looks below superficial differences is the beginning of wisdom and credibility in managing people.

CAN PEOPLE'S ATTITUDE AT WORK BE CHANGED?

We have looked at three concepts for analysing individual differences, personality, perception and diversity. These might account for why individuals look at work in different ways. If people have different attitudes to work, how important is this? What do we mean by attitude? Can those attitudes be changed?

Psychologists have developed various models and theories about attitudes in general and attitude to work in particular. This chapter looks at attitudes, and Chapter 12 on motivation has material about attitudes to work. The most widely quoted definition of attitude in psychology is that of Allport (1954, p45):

> A mental and neural state of readiness, organized through experience, exerting a directive or dynamic influence upon the individual's response to all objects and situations with which it is related.

Similar is that of Krech and Crutchfield (1948, p173):

> An attitude can be defined as an enduring organisation of motivational, emotional, perceptual and cognitive processes with respect to some aspect of the individual's world.

These two classic definitions state or imply that attitudes have the following characteristics. They are related to an object – some aspect of the individual's world. They are part of the general way the individual experiences and reacts to this world. They are relatively enduring. They imply evaluation and feeling.

Katz and Kahn (1978) suggest that attitudes and motivation are intertwined. Depending on the person's motives, an attitude can provide the following:

- *Knowledge*: attitudes give a base or framework for classifying and interpreting new information.
- *Expression*: attitudes enable us to indicate what our values are, what self-concept we have, and which group values we have adopted.
- *Instrumental*: depending on our past experiences of rewards and negative experiences, we hold different attitudes to people and experiences.
- *Ego-defensive*: we may hold attitudes to protect ourselves from an undesirable truth or reality.

All of this suggests that attitudes are an important component of an individual's make-up and will account for wide differences between people.

Most social scientists agree that attitudes are a complex, multi-dimensional concept that have an emotional and a cognitive aspect to them. For this reason, attitudes can be difficult to change. Some of the techniques that are used to try to change attitudes are:

- *The rational approach*: as we experience and assimilate material in accordance with our expectations, attitudes and motivation, it is not surprising that a straightforward, rational approach which merely presents the good reasons for why we should change our attitudes and beliefs rarely has much success.
- *Social influence*: social pressure is likely to have more influence but only where the communicator has credibility and seems an attractive model.
- *The emotional approach*: emotionally toned communications tend to be more influential than straightforward, rational explanations – as long as the emotion is appropriate and does not raise feeling to a level of anxiety.

We often look at the attitude of people when we are selecting. If you look at job advertisements there is often some phrase about 'keen', 'fun-loving', 'enthusiastic' or 'hardworking'. These are indicating that some assessment about people's attitude at work is important. They are often expressions of an individual's values. Those of us managing people at work and having to deal with a problem over attitude to work might need to examine the problem more clearly. What is the problem? Is the individual's performance poor? Is it affecting others – or is it just a matter of style? Chapter 14 has a section on managing poor performance.

This chapter has briefly looked at models and concepts for analysing individual differences. Although at times this might seem a little abstract, all these concepts are useful for analysing people's behaviour at work. The most obvious examples are in the selection and training of people, but it is also increasingly being used to individualise rewards. Part 3 of this book builds on this by looking at ways of managing individuals so they contribute effectively to the work of the organisation.

ACTIVITIES

1   Can you think of three very different personalities amongst the people with whom you work?

   What does each of them do that is particularly useful at work?

   Can you think of three awkward people at work?

   Would any of the above theories suggest why they are awkward?

   If so, how would you approach them differently?

   If you are in a seminar group you might like to discuss one or two examples in groups of three or four to see how other people would handle different characters.

2   When you are feeling aggrieved by the way you have been treated, what do you feel has been misunderstood?
   How could you do something about this?

3   Do you have pet sayings about some of your colleagues? What are they?

4   How do you see other teams in the same institution? Do they have particular characteristics?

5   Get in groups of six to eight people. The better you know each other the more fun this activity can be! Follow this procedure:

   A   One person in each group is selected to be the 'psychiatrist'. This person goes out of the room.

   B   The other members of the group sit in a circle and adopt the identity of the person on their left/right/opposite, whatever you agree.

   C   The psychiatrist comes back into the room and is told that he or she has to find out who everyone is and that the group are all suffering from the same delusion. The psychiatrist can ask anyone any question.

   D   After 10–15 minutes stop the game and explain to the psychiatrist what has been happening.

   E   Discuss how each member of the group has been interpreted by the person to their right/left/opposite.

   F   Have you learnt anything about how you perceive different personalities? Which questions were most fruitful?

6   Get into a small group with four or five people. You need to do this exercise quickly without really thinking, otherwise the point will be lost. If you deliberate for too long you will not record your true views, rather something more considered and polite.

   A Write down the following:

      five or six words to describe yourself

      five or six words to describe each of the others present

      the name of an animal to describe yourself

      the name of an animal to describe each of the others.

   B Now compare results.

      This is meant to be a relatively light-hearted event so don't get too serious!

      What does this tell you about the different ways in which others perceive you?

      What does it tell you about the different ways you all understand each other?

   A similar exercise can be done when analysing people's jobs by asking those who work for, with, and are more senior to, them to describe the responsibilities of the job. This is known as a role analysis using a 360-degree analysis. It is also used in appraisal procedures.

7   Below there is a list of jobs. Each of them requires some technical skills. Each of them also requires some personal skill. Thinking of these skills, which job do you think would be more suited to an introvert? Which would be more suited to an extroverted personality?

Bar person	Hotel receptionist	Long-distance truck driver
Research chemist	Nature reserve warden	Leisure centre manager
Museum guide	IT programmer	Trader on the foreign currency market

HAVE I MET THE OBJECTIVES?

1   Can I explain some models that explain the ways in which human beings differ?

2   What words describe inherited genes and experience?

3   Can I give a sentence to describe psychoanalysis, behaviourism and humanistic psychology?

4   Can I describe six concepts that can account for how we perceive things differently?

5   What do I understand by equal opportunities?

6   What do I understand by managing diversity?

And finally ...

What would you recommend Nick does about the jamboree? Now you have looked at some of the tools to analyse individual differences, would your advice differ from what you said at first?

I would suggest that Nick tries to find a venue that would include as many people as possible, but which could also deal with a wide diversity of tastes and personalities. It may be that a day out in work time to some country estate where the active can participate in competitive activities and the gentle can stroll around the gardens is most inclusive. Having some team event during the day for speeches and jokes emphasising 'us' would be ideal. If he imposes his own taste for extreme sports, many may feel excluded.

What happened in reality was that the office group decided they should hire a coach and leave after lunch one day for a night out in Blackpool! Many of the sales people and older members of the team did not attend.

FURTHER READING

Any reputable introduction to psychology will have chapters on personality, perception and individual differences. For example:

Hayes N (2000) *Foundations of Psychology.* 3rd ed. London, Thompson. She is a well-established author of introductory books on psychology. I find her very readable and sensible.

Gross R (2001) *Psychology.* 4th ed. Hodder & Stoughton. This is a well established textbook for universities.

Pennington R ed. (2002) *Introducing Psychology.* Hodder & Stoughton. A useful collection of readings – worth a look if you really get into this area.

Pinker S (1997) *How The Mind Works.* London, Penguin. A popular, if controversial, book about some of the debates in this area. Witty and well written with lots of the detailed scientific evidence.

Learning

This chapter deals with key ideas and theories about learning. This includes the following concepts; **classical conditioning, operant conditioning, behaviour modification, the learning chain, experiential learning, learning styles** *and* **different types of learning.** *Within this chapter the practical aspects of* **learning organisations** *and the* **continuous improvement** *of organisations is discussed. Chapter 6 includes material about change that relates to learning, and Chapter 9 on training and development relies heavily on this chapter about learning theory to underpin the practical applications. The specific examples in this chapter will be your own learning.*

OBJECTIVES

When you have finished reading this chapter you should be able to:

- **describe different models of how we learn**

- **distinguish five types of learning**

- **understand individual learning styles**

- **distinguish some of the different roles that we all have at work**

- **understand what is meant by a learning organisation.**

Laura's local difficulty

Laura is the assistant manager of a busy clothes shop. The shop is not part of any chain but is owned by its manager, who comes into the shop most days but leaves the day-to-day running to Laura. There are five other members of staff on varying contracts and hours. There is no time in the week that everyone is due to come in. The owner and Laura take pride in knowing their clientele so well that customers can phone up and ask for particular kinds of clothes and the shop will send a suitable selection to them. How can they encourage this expertise in their staff?

How do people learn the names and tastes of customers? How do they remember them? Is it easier to systematise this or to rely on individuals doing it in their own way? Are some sorts of learning about customers easier than others? Are there some types of customers who relate better to some staff than others? How can every member of staff be familiarised with all the stock? Should there be evening training sessions to show everyone or can it be done more informally with each person taking a look around and deciding which clothes would suit particular sorts of customers? Should the individual differences between the staff be acknowledged and accepted? Does everyone learn in the same way?

At work we all have to learn specific skills to deal with our jobs. We also have to learn to adapt to changing circumstances. If there is one common issue that people at work have to deal with, it is change. Where change is involved in the workplace, so is learning. It may be a new skill we have to acquire, such as using a new telephone system or process. We may have to get to know new people whose company has been amalgamated with ours. Perhaps we have to learn the details of the new organisational structure so that we can follow the correct procedure for informing people about a forthcoming meeting. Whatever changes are occurring, they require us to learn something. Chapter 9 deals with the way organisations formally and systematically try to encourage particular sorts of learning to increase the performance of individuals and groups within the organisation. This chapter deals with *how* people learn. The central importance of understanding learning for team leaders and managers is that a frequent part of the job is to encourage people to change some aspect of their behaviour at work, and that inevitably means learning new things .

An important aspect of learning in organisations is the form of accumulated learning called experience. It is a crucial part of authority, expertise and effective work. It is seen in the gradual learning of better ways of getting things done that someone who has been in the job some time takes for granted, and incidentally is often overlooked when jobs are being reorganised. A more formal sort of learning in organisations is where people systematically set out to learn a different way of doing something by going on a course or to a conference. A further way of learning is the process of being coached by someone else to improve already competent behaviour, such as chairing meetings. All these examples of learning involve a change in knowledge, skills or attitude. Change in behaviour can come about through formal training, which is dealt with in Chapter 9, or by more informal processes. Most learning in organisations, and elsewhere, takes place informally and is the subject of this chapter.

HOW DO PEOPLE LEARN?

As well as the purely academic pleasure of trying to understand how people function, there are many practical reasons for trying to understand how people learn. Before we can start learning systematically or helping someone else to learn we need to know how people learn. It might enable us to reduce the time it takes us to learn something. When difficulties arise we can start analysing where the problem lies and remedy it. If organisations are to compete in an ever-changing world they need to assist people to learn the new ways so that they can retain their jobs and contribute to the new processes. Similarly, individuals need to understand how they learn best so they can adapt to a variety of environments and people. It will come as no surprise that there are several different models of how people learn. Many of these go back to the early days of systematic psychology as it was one of the earliest areas of investigation. So what models are there? The main ones are the behaviourist model, the experimental psychology model and the experiential learning model.

Behaviourist theories

Behaviourists are interested in studying observable, measurable behaviour and many of their studies have been of how learning occurs. The two classic studies are those of Pavlov (1927) and Skinner (1965).

The Russian physiologist Ivan Pavlov demonstrated how reflexes could be trained to a new stimulus. He found he could get dogs to salivate when a bell was rung, if the ringing of the bell was associated with a plate of food. This was because whenever a bell was rung a plate of food was placed in front of the dog. The dogs learned that the bell meant food and so became 'conditioned' to salivate. Anyone who has had a cat will recognise the pattern – my cats come whenever they hear a tin being opened or the fridge door being opened! This association of S(timulus) and R(esponse) is called 'classical conditioning', or S-R learning. The responses fade if the connection is not maintained. We probably all have various physiological responses to specific situations, such as raised blood pressure before a visit to the dentist.

Skinner's model was more complex. He experimented with rewards and punishment and their effects on animal learning. For example, by rewarding pigeons with corn when they showed suitable behaviour he was able to teach them to play ping-pong. The sequence starts with a stimulus to which the animal responds randomly. When an appropriate response is made it is rewarded. The behaviour can be slowly shaped from a crude response to something precise through successively conditioning the behaviour. In the pigeon example, when they approached the ping-pong ball they were initially rewarded and then finer and finer adjustments were rewarded until two pigeons were seen to be 'batting' the ball between them with their beaks. Skinner showed that a response would be learned when it was rewarded, or technically 'reinforced'. If there is no reward, no learning takes place. This is called 'operant conditioning'. He found that learning took place more quickly by using rewards for positive behaviours rather than by punishing inappropriate behaviours. His maxim is that for effective learning to take place a regime of 80 per cent rewards is needed. How many of us experience that at work?

Another aspect of learning behaviour was explained by Thorndike (1932) who was interested in the outcomes of learning. He worked with cats and other animals and observed that they learned through trial and error. He had cats getting out of complex boxes – these were called Thorndike's puzzle boxes. If an action was successful it was more likely to be repeated when the same circumstance arose again. This was called the law of effect.

These approaches to learning are called the behaviourist, or behaviour modification, approach. They have led to many examples of programmed learning at work, such as using praise to reinforce people's good working habits and the use of systematic learning programmes such as computer-assisted learning, where the task is broken into smaller sections and the learner is praised for each correct answer. The important concept to remember about behaviour modification is that learning takes place only if the individual is prepared to work for the reward offered. This model is now felt to be too simplistic to be used on its own in complex social systems such as organisations. It is worth remembering, however, as it emphasises the importance of feedback, or knowledge of results, without which learning is unlikely to be effective.

Experimental psychology model

A model that has been very influential in education and adult training is the model of RM Gagne. This summarises the findings of various experimental psychologists who have studied the behaviour of individuals in an experimental setting in order to understand the details of the learning process. In the sense that they studied behaviour systematically they are behaviourists, but not in the strict sense of Skinner's approach. Gagne (1975) has identified a chain of eight events that occur, whatever sort of learning is taking place. These are, in order:

- *motivation*. The learner has to want to learn, and to want to learn this particular thing or the final product of this type of learning. For example, a manager of a hotel may be keen to learn how to manage his or her staff well and so is motivated to learn about psychology and its application in the workplace.
- *perception*. The matter to be learned has to be distinguished from others. This involves identifying a clear objective. At first it is difficult because one has not learned the different categories in the area. With time, one learns more and more detailed ways of classifying the matter to be learned. For example, at the beginning of this course you may wonder where to start and what it is essential to learn. After a few weeks or months many of the terms become familiar, and identifiable topics that need learning become clear.

■ *acquisition*. What has to be learned is related to the familiar, so that it makes sense. For example, in this book I have tried to give examples from work settings to help to make sense of a new area of study. You can help yourself by recalling your own examples from your own experience.

■ *retention*. The two-stage process of human learning comprises a short-term memory, where items are stored first, and a long-term memory to which they are eventually transferred and where they are held permanently. Not everything needs to go to the long-term memory. For example, the anecdotes and jokes that aid the process of understanding at the time do not really need to go to the long-term memory.

■ *recall*. This is the ability to summon things up from memory when required. There are different levels. Recognition is where we know we have seen the item before and it takes less time to familiarise ourselves with it, but we could not have relied on memory alone. Recall is where we can generate the memory direct. For example, at the end of your course you may be able to recall some of the material in this book because you have learnt it thoroughly. For other parts you may need to reread sections to help you recall the material.

■ *generalisation*. This is the ability to apply the learning in situations other than the specific one in which it was learned. For example, you may generalise what you learn on this course about motivation in the workplace to thinking about motivation at the sports club or in the family.

■ *performance*. This is putting into practice what has been learned. It is the test of learning. The professional management student takes the exam, writes the essay or tries to use the materials from the course at work.

■ *feedback on performance*. This is where the learner finds out whether the performance was satisfactory or not. Sometimes it will be obvious because of the quality of the performance, particularly with physical skill learning such as car driving. But some feedback from the coach or trainer can help to distinguish more subtle levels of satisfaction or to analyse what went wrong, how it could be avoided, what needs more practice, what to do next and so on. Many professions now use the concepts of mentoring to give people the opportunity of subtle individually tailored feedback.

Learning can fail because of problems at any of these stages. The model is useful as a practical checklist when helping others to prepare for learning or when giving feedback at the end of a learning session. It is also a useful model for analysing more informal methods of learning, such as why some get the message at meetings and others do not.

Count the Fs in the following passage

Finished files are the result of years of scientific study combined with the experience of years (New Scientist 28 June 1997 p93)

How many did you see? On first reading most people see three; however, there are six. Try spelling the words out loud. Once you have seen this you will never see three Fs again. You have learnt the answer!

Experiential learning model

Another useful model of how people learn is that of Kolb, Rubin and McIntyre (1974). Figure 3.1 shows their experiential learning model. In their view, all the stages are necessary if learning is to take place.

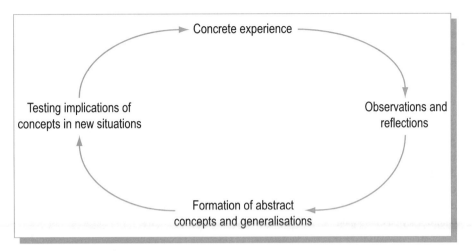

FIGURE 3.1 *KOLB'S LEARNING MODEL*

The model suggests that learning is a cycle of the following stages:

■ concrete experience, or experience that involves performance. For example, having a go at making a presentation.

■ observation and reflective analysis of the experience. This is most useful if done from many perspectives: in our example, discussing the presentation with the course tutor and friends with similar experience.

■ generalisation on the basis of experience, or doing some thinking. Such generalisations use abstract concepts to integrate the observations into the theories we have about the world – for example, discussing with others what they would have done in the circumstances of the presentation.

■ experimentation in future action based on the generalisation, or doing something similar. The application of ideas requires active experimentation. In our example, the next time a presentation is to be given, either in practice or for real, possible actions could be discussed and carried out.

■ new experience derived from this experimentation – in our example, getting the student to do another presentation.

■ initiation of a new learning cycle.

If you can imagine a spiral of these experiential learning cycles you can see how a model of continual improvement and learning could be developed, with the learner becoming increasingly confident and ambitious in his or her performance and analysis. This model of learning is very popular in higher education, where there is a growing emphasis on trying to make students do something so the cycle can actually start.

An example of how well the Kolb cycle of learning has embedded itself in British educational thinking is seen in the National Vocational Qualification boards material. They talk of a learning cycle of doing your job, thinking about what you do, using the NVQ standards, testing your perspective, and back to doing your job.

There is good theoretical evidence that a learner who uses different senses and actually does something is more engaged in the learning process than one who merely reads or listens. This is the reason there are activities and questions in this book for you to answer. Reading and listening are less effective ways to learn. This model is further developed in the next section.

WHAT ABOUT INDIVIDUAL DIFFERENCES?

So far we have suggested that everyone learns things in the same way. This may be generally true, but there are also individual differences in how we learn effectively and in how we prefer to learn. We are all aware that people differ in the speed with which they learn new things and that some learn physical skills quickly but learn theoretical material slowly compared with others, and vice versa. However, there is also some evidence that individuals differ in their preferred method of learning, whatever the subject matter. That is, they have different styles of learning.

Kolb, Rubin and Osland (1991) developed the model of a learning cycle described earlier (see Figure 3.1) to suggest that since the learning process is driven by individual needs and goals, so learning styles become highly individual in both direction and process. Each of the stages of the learning cycle can be a strength or a weakness in learning. Individuals will find some part of the cycle easier than others. Everyone will prefer different parts of the learning cycle and will attach more effort to some parts of the cycle than others will. Here are examples of four types of learner. A physicist may come to place great emphasis on abstract concepts, whereas a sculptor may value concrete experience more highly. A manager may be primarily concerned with the active application of concepts, whereas an ecologist may prize observational skills highly. Each of us will develop a personal style that has some weak points and some strong points. We may leap into experiences and fail to observe the lessons to be derived from these experiences; we may form concepts but fail to test their validity. In some areas our objectives may give us clear guidelines, while in others we wander aimlessly.

Let us try to systematise this understanding a little. There are two main dimensions in the Kolb model of learning styles: a concrete–abstract dimension, 1 and 3 in the cycle, and an active–reflective dimension, 4 and 2 in the cycle. By making a grid of the four main learning processes on these two dimensions, Kolb arrived at a grid of four basic learning styles (see Table 3.1).

Kolb's four basic learning styles are:

convergent style. The main strength of this style is in problem-solving, decision-making and the practical application of ideas. People with this style do best where there is a single answer or solution; they prefer technical rather than social and interpersonal issues.

Table 3.1 *Kolb's learning styles*

	Active experimentation	Reflective observation
Concrete experience	Accomodator	Diverger
Abstract conceptualisation	Converger	Assimilator

divergent style. This is the opposite of the convergent style. The great strength of this style is in imaginative ability and awareness of meaning and values. People with this style look at concrete issues in a variety of ways, and they are able to organise these into a pattern or 'Gestalt'. This style is characteristic of arts people, counsellors and personnel people.

assimilation style. The great strength here is the ability to create abstract models and to assimilate diverse material into a coherent explanation. People with this style have less concern with individuals and more with ideas; they tend to be researchers and planners.

accommodation style. This is the opposite of assimilation, and people with this style are good at doing things and carrying out plans. They are quick to adapt if the plan does not quite work; they simply get on with it. People with this style are most commonly found in business and are likely to be in marketing or sales.

A variation on this learning style model is that of the British writers Honey and Mumford (1992). They used Kolb's model in a slightly different way, emphasising the particular stages of the cycle that favour particular types of individuals. Such types are:

- *activists* who use concrete experience and involve themselves fully and without bias in new experiences. They tend to act first and consider the consequences afterwards.
- *reflectors* who use observation and reflection. They are thoughtful and cautious. They like to sit back and ponder experiences.
- *theorists* who form abstract concepts and integrate them into logically sound theories. They tend to be perfectionists who do not give up until everything has been fitted into a rational scheme.
- *pragmatists* who rely on generalisations. They actively seek out new ideas to see if they will work in practice. They like to get on with things and enjoy a challenge.

Whichever model of learning styles is used, both are useful in establishing that there are individual differences in how people learn from experience. Those responsible for learning, training and development of people must ensure that there is sufficient variety of learning experiences available to suit different people. The more we understand our own learning style, the more likely we are to be able to learn effectively. Just because a method works for a friend does not necessarily mean we are dumb if it does not work for us!

EFFECTIVE LEARNING IN DIFFERENT SITUATIONS

So far we have been looking at how people learn. This has attracted a good deal of attention, not only from schoolteachers but also from people involved in adult training. Other investigations have determined whether different sorts of learning material require different learning methods to optimise the learning. If we accept some of the generalisations of the previous section on how people learn, can we fine-tune them to suit different situations?

Traditionally, a distinction is drawn between cognitive (intellectual) learning, learning skills, and developing attitudes. Each of these is thought not only to be a different learning objective but also to require a different learning process. The distinction has been refined for practical use in adult learning by the Industrial Training Research Unit (1976). They took the work of Belbin to develop the CRAMP list of learning. CRAMP divides learning into five types:

*C*omprehension. This involves learning theoretical subject matter. It is learning how, why and when things happen. This type of learning is best done through methods that treat the whole subject as an entity, rather than splitting it up into bits and taking one at a time. This is usually achieved by lecture, seminar, discussion, film or video. Clarity of presentation is critical so that the main points are distinguished from the supporting evidence. An example of such a learning type would be the learning of a mathematical formula, such as how to work out the area of a circle.

*R*eflex learning. This is the acquiring of skilled movements or perceptual abilities. As well as acquiring knowledge of what to do, speed and co-ordination need to be developed; it requires practice and repetition. It is best approached by breaking the task into small steps and simplifying each step so that it can be easily learned. Even a simple piece of behaviour can actually be very complicated. Breaking a task into smaller steps is called 'task analysis' by behaviourist psychologists. If we get smaller steps right we have the opportunity to be rewarded. If the steps are too big success is unlikely, and there is no opportunity for reward and so learning does not take place readily. Examples would be learning to use a new piece of equipment, machining materials, inspecting goods for quality problems, or typing.

*A*ttitude development. This type of learning enables people to change their attitudes and social skills. It is perhaps the most difficult sort of learning to achieve. Group methods that centre on people developing better knowledge of themselves seem the most effective, as attitudes are very difficult to influence in other ways. One training example would be a customer-care course where the attitude of staff is explored by encouraging them to discuss their behaviour after doing an exercise such as 'finding the treasure' in a park. The course hopes to lead them to a better understanding of themselves, and that through such self-knowledge they will arrive at a better position from which to change their behaviour towards customers.

*M*emory training. This involves learning information by heart. It is very similar to reflex learning, where each bit is taken one at a time. All sorts of jingles and mnemonics can be helpful here; you will frequently see mnemonics such as CRAMP in student texts. Obvious examples are the methods used by actors learning their lines in a play or by medical students learning the names of the bones in the body.

*P*rocedural learning. This is similar to memory training but the items do not need to be memorised – only understood and their location known. This requires less practice. Examples are a lawyer's learning of the statutes, or an engineer's learning how to shut a plant down for maintenance. Neither person would need to know by heart what to do but both would need to know where to look for the information and to understand what they found. You have probably by now learnt to use your local academic library. If you came to visit an alternative one you would know more or less how to use it, but would probably need a few minutes in which to orientate yourself and to find the references that you need.

In practice, most learning situations require more than one of these types of learning but the categorisation is a helpful means of sorting out which would be the most appropriate means of learning something. For example, in professional exams there are some things that need to be learned by heart, others that need some understanding, and yet others where procedural learning would be most appropriate. The most effective learners are those who can classify their needs and do not waste time memorising everything.

It is claimed (Foot and Hook, 1996, p180) that the average rate of retention when learning new material is:

10 per cent of what is read

20 per cent of what is heard

30 per cent of what is seen

50 per cent of what is seen and heard

70 per cent of what the trainee says

90 per cent of what the trainee says and does.

If this is true then we'd better start saying and doing the activities suggested at the end of the chapter!

ROLE THEORY

So far we have been looking at learning from a psychologist's point of view. The sociologist's perspective on learning is to concentrate on how and why people come to belong to a group. Sociologists seek to understand the reasons behind the behaviours studied by psychologists. Only by explaining people's understanding of a situation and the methods they use to organise their attitudes and knowledge – that is, their orientation – shall we fully understand social relationships. We need to understand the meanings of actions. Why do people want to learn particular things? Why and how do they become part of the group? Which things help and which hinder membership?

To start answering these questions we need to take on some of the vocabulalry of sociology. The concepts commonly used to describe social learning – or socialisation – are given below, with some explanations:

- role – set of expectations and obligations to act in specific ways in particular settings
- status – an actor's position in a social structure which limits the roles to be played
- social structure – the result of the organisation of role, status and social institutions into a determining pattern
- institution – well established organisation of orientations, values and norms in stable patterns
- norm – one of the normal standards of behaviour that define a role
- primary group – a small, intimate group such as family, gang, group of close workmates; an important source of norms and values for individual members
- reference group – social group that provides the norms for people who want to belong to it
- significant other – a role model that the individual initially imitates in order to become part of the group that is 'socialised'
- generalised other – the other roles within a group that an individual takes into account and makes his or her own adaptation to that.

One very useful concept in answering the sorts of questions given at the beginning of this section is that of 'role'. We all have roles that we play in society. Role-playing is action in

conformity with a set of social rules. The term 'role' describes some of the effects of the continuing process of social learning. In our various roles we are driven by the pressures to learn appropriate behaviours and values in order to conform to the differing groups to which we belong, or wish to belong. This concept is used very similarly to the use of the word in drama: it describes the social interaction rather than the specific person. These social rules will be based on expectations and obligations derived from the social or cultural values of a particular setting. Any one person may have a unique set of roles to play. These personal collections of roles can come into conflict and a choice has to be made between them. For example, your lecturers may have formal expectations that require them to be teachers, writers, counsellors, researchers and administrators; they will sometimes have to choose which is the most important role when, for example, time is short.

The different roles we play are often defined by the institutions to which we belong – such as families, communities or religious groups. These institutions set norms – that is, they set expectations and obligations that go to make up a role. A business organisation is one such type of institution that sets norms for various roles. These roles in turn make up the structure of the organisation or institution.

This gives us the conceptual framework to look at various social relationships and how we adapt to them. It is a different way of looking at learning from that of psychology. It is particularly useful when looking at the informal ways we learn at work – think, for example, about how we learn to fit in when we join a new team or employer. It is also seen in one of the currently popular ways of assessing people's performance at work by getting the views of a variety of the people they come into contact with. This is discussed in Chapter 14.

THE LEARNING ORGANISATION

Dealing with change has attracted a lot of attention from writers on management, and they tend to describe organisations that cope well as 'learning organisations'. The idea of a learning organisation was first articulated by Argyris and Schon (1978) and developed by people such as Morgan (1986) and Pedlar, Burgoyne and Boydell (1991). The last group are currently influential British writers on training and development. Various lists, probably not quite well established enough yet to call them models, have been developed to describe these 'learning organisations'.

According to Marquand and Reynolds (1994), a manager wishing to build his or her organisation's capacity to learn should attempt to:

- transform the individual's and organisation's image of learning with the aim of encouraging life-long learning and a desire for continuous improvement
- create knowledge-based partnerships with people within and without the organisation in order to share ideas and information so that a real understanding develops
- develop and expand team-learning activities in order to encourage people to share questions, information, ideas, solutions and approaches
- change the role of managers so that they function as facilitators rather than controllers
- encourage experiments and risk-taking so that new possibilities emerge
- create structures and systems that allow people time to extract learning – this suggests provision of some 'soft' time for people to talk and develop

- build opportunities and mechanisms in order to disseminate learning both formally and informally
- empower people to take decisions and actions
- push information through the organisation and to external associates
- develop the discipline of system thinking – what are the implications for others?
- develop a powerful vision of organisational excellence and individual fulfilment
- root out bureaucracy.

In many ways, a learning organisation is one that manages knowledge well. This is increasingly seen as a crucial competence for organisations competing in a global market. Why new ideas are not taken up in some organisations is discussed by Marquand and Reynolds in the journal *People Management* (February 6, 2003). They identify such negative attitudes and constraints as:

not invented here

what is in it for me?

lack of leadership

lack of time

not attractively presented

lack of context sensitivity

under-investment in facilitation.

Pedlar, Burgoyne and Boydell (1991) suggest that the following features are indicative of a learning organisation, although they prefer the term 'learning company' to 'learning organisation':

- a learning approach to strategy – risks are taken and new opportunities tried, people learn about the new as well as the well-established
- participative policy-making, with consultation and participation by people from all parts of the organisation
- open information systems – nothing is hidden from members of the organisation unless it is imperative that it be hidden
- formative accounting and control – which encourages people – rather than restrictive methods
- internal exchange of ideas and information
- flexibility of rewards so people can work to their own best way
- structures that make individual contributions possible
- capacity for boundary workers to act as boundary scanners
- inter-worker learning
- a learning climate for all
- self-development opportunities for all.

DEBATE – IS THE IDEA OF LEARNING ORGANISATIONS TOO IDEALISTIC?

The lists of the types shown above can seem more like wish lists than a practical guide to the reality of most organisations. Many would feel that they are not only unworkable but also potentially damaging to the viability of the organisation as they do not deal with carrying out the main task of the organisation. It appears that when organisations are experiencing more difficult economic times they are more likely to abandon the more flexible learning organisation and institute tighter structures and more formal relations. Enthusiasts for learning organisations would argue that it is in precisely these conditions that the flexibility of a learning organisation is most important.

The advantages of the idea of the learning organisation is that it can be a useful checklist for raising questions about an existing organisation. One way is to make each of the concepts a question we can ask about the modus operandi of a particular organisation. If the answer suggests that people feel constrained then ideas from the learning-organisation approach can be used to open up the discussion and offer solutions. For example, using all the talents available to the organisation rather than simply relying on the omniscience of those at the top. Making sure we listen to those with front line experience of customer/clients' demands, as in a competitive world those close to the customer are more likely to know what the market needs than those in head office.

The concept of the learning organisation has obvious similarities to some of the underpinning ideas of Total Quality Management (TQM) and Business Process Re-engineering (BPR) – ideas with an emphasis on continuous improvement, breaking down barriers, customer supply chains and empowerment. The useful aspect of these views is that they look at the organisation as a whole and at how various functions and specialisms relate to one another. One way of looking at the learning-organisation models is to see them as a way of integrating various strands and models to do with managing people.

This chapter has emphasised models of different learning styles, objectives and roles concerned primarily with the individual. By now you should be aware that learning is not just a simple mechanical process. This concern with learning and the different models that can be used to analyse learning has also now been applied to the whole organisation and the idea of a learning organisation should now be familiar to you. The issue of learning is currently at the heart of much discussion on managing people and so recurs in other chapters in this book, particularly Chapter 9 about training and development.

ACTIVITIES

1   Use Kolb's model to analyse your own learning. Use one of the practical sessions in your course, for example an exercise, role play, case study or visit. Which part of the activity did you find most interesting? Which was most difficult? Which part seemed irrelevant and time consuming? Now can you relate these findings to the Kolb cycle?

2   Using either Kolb or Honey and Mumford, what sort of learner do you think you are? Therefore what are likely to be your learning weaknesses? How could these weaknesses be overcome?

3   What types of learning would be most effective if you wanted to do the following tasks?

- use the Internet to seek references for an assignment
- become influential in a political party
- understand organisational behaviour
- understand a balance sheet in a company's annual report.

4   Who is in your primary group at work? What norms of behaviour do you have? What behaviours did you change when you arrived in the group?

5   What was the best group learning you ever experienced? What was good about it? What was the worst group learning you experienced? Why was that? What does this suggest you need for effective group learning? Think about both the content (knowledge skills and attitudes) and process (the way you learn). If you are in a seminar group, discuss this in small groups to find three things you could do to help each other learn.

6   Using the material on roles, do a role analysis of someone you know. Ideally this would be someone at work and their work roles. To do this you interview several different people about what the person doing that job would be expected to do. Remember, it is not about the expectations of the particular individual actually doing the job but about other people's expectations of what the job should entail. I should start by talking to the person doing the job and then to people who come into contact with them, for example boss, colleagues, team members, customers/clients, and any others.

When you have collected the material, start analysing:

- Where is there consensus about the role?
- Where is there conflict?
- Where is there overload?
- Where is there an underload?
- Are there any formal/informal norms that differ?

HAVE I MET THE OBJECTIVES?

1   What is the difference between classical and operant conditioning?

2   Can I describe three different models of how we learn?

3   Can I list different individual learning styles?

4   Can I list five types of learning?

5   Am I able to distinguish some of the different roles that I have at work or college?

6   What is meant by the 'learning organisation'?

And finally ...

What would you recommend Laura do? Would any of the models in this chapter be useful? I should probably suggest looking at the individual styles of the members of staff, as the nature of the service offered is one of personal, individual attention. Emphasising individuals would make some sense. The Kolb or Honey and Mumford approach would seem appropriate.

FURTHER READING

For more on the psychology of learning, look at any introductory text on psychology – they all have chapters about learning; for example those given in Chapter 2.

The chapter on learning in either Kolb *et al* (1974) or Kolb *et al* (1991) will give you further details of their views. I particularly like the 1991 book as it offers many exercises, including one on discovering your own learning style.

For more on roles, look at any introductory text on sociology. For example, Giddens A (2001) *Sociology* 4th ed Blackwell. This is a well-established university text.

Watson TJ (1995) *Sociology, Work and Industry,* 3rd ed. Routledge is a well-regarded sociology text about how sociology can help us look at work organisations.

There are innumerable books about the change process in organisations. Pedlar, Burgoyne and Boydell (1991) is particularly well regarded in the United Kingdom.

The Changing World of Work

Factors Influencing Work, Jobs and Employment Opportunities

*This chapter is a wide-ranging one that uses a variety of theoretical and analytical perspectives. Economic theory, not covered in this book but see 'Further Reading', is an important influence on this material, with role theory from Chapter 3, politics dealt with in Chapter 7 and motivation discussed in Chapter 12 as important underpinning concepts. This chapter is about the importance of understanding the practical issues of **organisational structures, organisational culture, the psychological contract, employability and the employment environment** if we are to manage people at work successfully, with the ultimate goal of achieving the organisation's aims and a decent life for members of the team. Specific examples in this chapter come from Bisto, The Scottish Office and Shell.*

OBJECTIVES

When you have finished reading this chapter you should be able to:

- **list different approaches to analysing organisations**

- **discuss organisational culture**

- **describe the context in which organisations have to make decisions about the nature of employment**

- **discuss the importance of the customer relationship for organisations**

- **describe the psychological contract of employment.**

David's choice of management styles

David was chief executive of a waste management company. In the previous two years a raft of legislation had changed the nature of what could and could not be put into the landfill sites that the company owned and managed. The way in which the materials were handled and the documentation that went with it had also changed dramatically. Many of the employees who had worked for the organisation for a long time could not see the point of all this form filling and were loath to wear all the 'sissy' protective clothing that the company issued. What should David do?

Should he sack a token member of staff to show how serious he was? Increase the random inspections? Hope no one noticed the lapses in procedures? Offer incentives for filling in the forms and wearing the clothing? Give pep talks to the site managers? Was there a need for firm action or encouraging compliance? Would his actions change the nature of the relationship between the organisation and those who worked for it?

The dilemma for people managing in organisations is that the flexibility of what can be done is often influenced by events outside their own control, and even outside that of the organisation. These outside influences can also affect the very nature of the employment relationship. This chapter looks at the influences that affect the employment relationship. This relationship can give rise to conflict and co-operation, confusion and contradiction – and a variety of power distributions. The influence of the wider context on the relationship is mediated by the particular ways in which members of an organisation interact with each other.

THE ORGANISATIONAL SETTING

Throughout this book I have referred to the organisation as if it existed as an entity – clearly this is not the case. An organisation is made up of the component parts of the individuals and groups that co-operate with each other and comply with implicit or explicit rules to try to achieve some common goal. There are several different ways of analysing the differences between organisations. Traditionally theories were about organisational structures. More recently there has been an interest in organisational culture and the softer ways of organising work. However, there seems to be a feeling that when the economic climate is more difficult a 'back to basics' approach with a more formal approach to work is appropriate. In challenging times we see less of the blurring of work and play, more formal dress, offices looking like offices rather than cafés and people wanting bosses to give some instruction as to what is required. In other words, structures become more attractive: see for example Wooldridge (2002).

Theories of organisational structure

Theories of how organisations are, could or should be structured concentrate on one of the following: task, technology, procedures or people.

Task What is the main task of the organisation? In this analysis the emphasis is on the goals and objectives of the organisation. The nature of the inputs and outputs and the transformation that takes place is the focus of these theories. Early theories were developed by Fayol (1949) and Urwick (1952). They were concerned with the functions of management and increasing efficiency. Fayol defined the five functions of management as planning, organising, co-ordinating, commanding and controlling. This was a very influential model, and led to many managers adopting what is often called the 'command and control' mode. Another task-orientated analysis was the analysis of bureaucracy: see for example Weber (1964), which looked at the nature of hierarchies, role definition, rules and procedures.

Technology In these models the question of how the task is carried out is examined. The material, system, procedures and equipment used can affect the behaviours of people, and so the structures of the organisation will be different. The early scientific management theories, see for example Taylor (1947), were trying to find the 'one best way' of doing things. Some of his key innovations such as selection, training and job analysis still inform our approaches to managing people.

Procedures These models look at how to apportion and co-ordinate the work. Ingredients such as job descriptions, patterns of authority, formal relations between groups and communication across the organisation are important areas of study. Influential writers of management texts have been Drucker (1954) and Handy (1997). Handy gives us four ideal types of organisation. These are quite different in the way they handle power and get things done. See Figure 4.1. He explains that most large organisations will have a mixture of these structures operating in different parts of the organisation

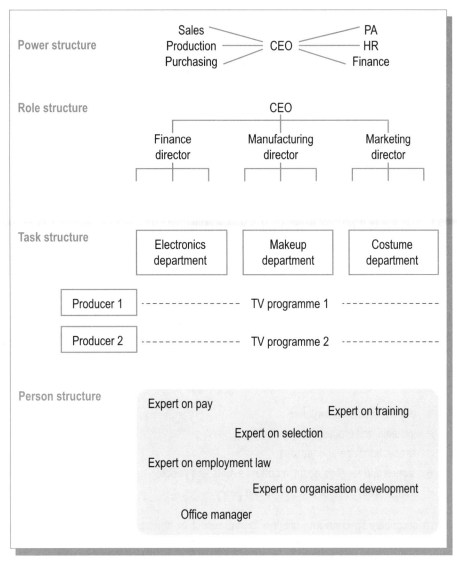

Figure 4.1 *Examples of Handy's ideal organisation structures*

People This is currently the most frequent basis for looking at organisations. The nature of the people doing the work and their attitudes, needs and relations are studied. This approach started with the early work of the human relations movement – see for example Mayo (1939) – and is the concern of much of this book.

Organisational culture

A special way of analysing organisations is the understanding of organisational culture. This is to move away from an emphasis on formal procedures and structures to an emphasis on the characteristic spirit and beliefs of an organisation. Culture is embodied in the way people treat each other and the nature of their relationships. These are the values and norms of the organisation. One of the most penetrating analyses of organisational culture is by Schein (1985). He suggests there are three levels of culture:

artifacts are the most visible level of culture and include the physical layout of the office, the language used and the behaviour of employees

values that reflect people's convictions about reality and will affect how they deal with a new task

assumptions that guide people's thinking and feeling and how they behave.

Schein goes on to distinguish two types of mechanism for organisational change, 'primary' and 'secondary'.

The primary mechanisms are:

- what leaders pay most attention to
- how leaders react to crises and critical incidents
- role modelling, teaching and coaching leaders
- criteria for allocating rewards and determining status
- criteria for selection, promotion and termination.

The first three emphasise the importance of leading by example. That is, showing people what matters. The last two are to do with emphasising people as individuals. Those who fit in and help the organisation are rewarded; those who do not go unrewarded.

The secondary mechanisms for the articulation and reinforcement of culture are:

- the organisational structure
- systems and procedures
- space, buildings and façades
- stories and legends about important events and people
- formal statements of philosophy and policy.

These secondary mechanisms are the formal aspect of management and have been the traditional areas of study, possibly because they are easier to write about. In Schein's view these formal statements come second to the informal aspects of organisational influence. The extent to which these aspects of organisational life should or could be managed is vigorously debated: see for example Smirchich (1983). As ever, it often comes down to what assumptions about the world one has. Some of these themes are further developed in Chapter 10 on leadership.

Bisto foods used to have a tradition of risk-averse management that concentrated on producing existing products, with lots of procedures about what, how and when things could be done. A culture change was made to increase innovation and staff adaptability. It was decided to increase everyone's interest in food by offering them the opportunity to spend two days in the kitchens of prestigious restaurants. A serious chef was employed to work alongside existing staff on multifunctional teams. So far the results have been encouraging – have a look for yourself on the supermarket shelves to see how far they have succeeded.

THE ORGANISATION AND EMPLOYMENT ENVIRONMENT

So far we have looked at some ways of analysing different organisations. An important influence on this is the environment in which the organisation operates. Many outside influences will affect what an organisation can actually do, and how those working in the organisation will relate to each other. A popular framework for summarising these outside factors that can influence the organisation and the employment relationship is PEST – see, for example, Marchington and Wilkinson (1996, p8). According to this framework, the following are the main outside factors:

- *Political/legal* – government stability, attitudes towards the European Union, employment and other legislation
- *Economic* – stages in the business cycle, unemployment, inflation, interest rates
- *Social* – population changes, income distribution, education and training, attitudes to work and leisure
- *Technological* – new discoveries and developments, government spending on and promotion of research, speed of technological transfer.

All of these can affect the nature of the organisation and the employment relationship. Let us look at each briefly.

Political

The attitude of politicians towards organisations and their employees varies across political perspectives and time. Legislation that has affected the employment relationship includes the Factory Acts of the first half of the nineteenth century, covering the conditions of work, and employment law covering rights to time off work, termination of employment, guarantee of minimum pay and rights of part-time staff. For many these are seen as a 'floor' of rights, a minimum that employees should expect. Many, but not all, employers give better conditions than the minimum. Another area where political influence is best seen is in the attitude to the trade union movement in the United Kingdom. One of the first priorities of the Conservative administration of Mrs Thatcher in the early 1980s was to introduce legislation covering strikes and ballots. Other political issues like the introduction of the 'Euro' affected the work of people – for example currency traders who lost their jobs as there were fewer currency transactions to be made.

Economics

How the economy is performing affects the optimism of organisations and determines whether they invest in more staff, higher salaries and new ventures. These decisions in turn affect the actual work that individuals do, as well as how many workers there are and what they are paid. Working for an expanding business is exciting and encourages innovation and risk. Money is available to develop ideas and everyone moves on. In contrast, a declining market can mean trying to preserve what one has and requires the diplomatic skills of an angel when explaining to staff that their wonderful idea for an improvement cannot be afforded. This will include aspects of the global economy as well. After decades of the economies of South East Asia, the so-called 'Tiger economies', being held up as paragons of virtue it was quite a shock to many working in the West when these tiger economies experienced sharp declines at the end of the 1990s. It affected those in the West as well, as there was a reduction in demand for many exported goods, and fewer tourists travelled from East to West. The globalisation of the economy has meant the employment relationship is now affected by global events even for those who work in locally-based concerns.

Globalisation

Globalisation is the process whereby the business environment has become increasingly international or global. One aspect derives from the improvements in telecommunications that have enabled call centres which answer queries about such things as financial matters, or airline bookings, to be based anywhere in the world. Another aspect is the increasing competition from other countries that can offer services more cheaply. For example, the software prowess of India has led to job losses in Europe as solutions are found online from India. Increasingly, large multinational organisations set the pace in their industries by transcending national practices and traditions. For example, health and safety procedures are introduced into countries with no national standards by multinationals because of company policy. Globalisation also means that organisations employ people from other countries to work alongside locals. This is particularly true in Europe with the free movement of people within the European Union for employment. Most of us will be affected by some aspect of these global trends, even if we feel we are working in a very small local organisation. For many, staying in the office late in order to talk to New York is normal. Certainly we have all experienced the slowing down in the working of the Internet in the afternoon as Americans wake up and log on!

Availability of people

Whether there is a shortage or surplus of appropriately skilled people will affect how much organisations are prepared to invest in their current staff. When there is a shortage, or one is predicted, it is worth the organisation's while to train and develop new, skilled people. When there are plenty looking for jobs, the pressure to do so is not as high. The attractions of many areas in Britain to new investors derive from the fact that there is a ready-made skilled workforce waiting.

New technologies affect the number and nature of the people required, and where there is a shortage of appropriate people there will again be a change in the balance of power between the employer and the employee. The expected problem of the change from the year 1999 to 2000 for computers (the millennium bug) ensured that those who could deal with the problem were in great demand – in reality there was not a problem. Had it been possible to buy a CD that dealt with all the problems, then these people would not have been quite so fêted.

Quality of staff

Another economic issue that is affecting many manufacturing organisations is the over-supply of goods. There is too much stuff in the market. This is because investment capital has been freely available and there is now over-production worldwide. As a result, companies are finding it difficult to make profits. This has led many companies to try to move from production to being service providers. For example, IBM in Greenock, West Scotland, used to be a manufacturer of computers. They are moving more towards service and currently, in 2003, are 60 per cent service-orientated with an emphasis on IT solutions, and hope to move even further in this direction. If manufacturing is having difficulties, how does this affect employment opportunities? As the organisations move from manufacturing to service they need good-quality staff who can reuse their skills and competencies and apply themselves to finding solutions to problems. For example, in the past cars were made and people bought what was available – in Ford's inimitable statement 'you can have any color you like as long as it is black'. Nowadays car manufacturers offer a wide range of choices so that customers can 'customise' their purchase. Indeed, Porsche allows customers to design their own combination on their website and then it is made to their specification. For all this to be possible it involves well-selected and trained staff to put into practice a high level of service and customer orientation. These staff will expect to be suitably developed and rewarded if the organisation is to keep them. Organisations that do not maintain and develop people's competencies will lose out. The weakest organisations, quite frankly, are likely to fail.

Technological innovation

Improvements in machines, processes and work layout affect our work, as do the actual methods, systems and procedures involved in carrying out the work. What work we are doing and the tools we are using will constrain the possible ways of doing the work. The machines and technologies being used can affect the following:

- the specific design of a particular job – the nature and variety of activities and the degree of autonomy for any particular worker
- the physical mobility of those doing a task – and whether they work in groups or not will affect the relationships they have with each other
- the status and pay of the operator – will depend on the difficulty of acquiring a particular skill
- the way people are dressed – people may require special clothing
- the physique of the worker – people may need special physical skills.

Managing change when new technology is introduced is important, as the workers may not only be asked to work differently but the technology may also be affecting the nature of their relationships with each other. For example, the move to teleworking at home has meant that many members of staff are isolated from the casual gossip at the photocopier and coffee machine that many enjoy and use to find out what is happening in the organisation. Some organisations set up weekly Friday lunchtime meetings to bring everyone together.

A more detailed example of the effect of new technology on work and working relationships was reported in *People Management* (9 October 1997, p44). The Scottish Office in Glasgow experimented with a variety of new ways of working. They had a staff of 70, in four teams, in a third of the space previously occupied. The aim was to create an efficient, effective and creative workplace. They used office design, technology, changes in working practices and the workplace culture to try to achieve this. They set up the following:

- telephone numbers that followed the individual at home/commuting/office
- plug-ins for laptops all over the office
- video-conferencing facilities
- wire-free workplaces for quiet work
- shared space so no one had their own spot
- hot work space/desks/worktops/cubicles/offices – all bookable
- soft areas for discussions, such as a café
- meeting areas for more formal discussions.

This was meant to lead to a status-free, creative, productive, knowledge-sharing output rather than an input culture. The emphasis changed from what people did to what they achieved. When the scheme was assessed they found the following:

- productivity was increased and not dominated by 'presenteeism' – that is, feeling that being seen in the office was more important than what you actually do
- creativity declined, as only those who knew each other got involved – the new environment was difficult for newcomers to become known
- communication declined – due to a similar problem as that restricting creativity
- it was liked by the participants but resisted by others in the organisation.

CUSTOMER AND CONSUMER EXPECTATIONS

There are two sorts of customers: those who themselves have customers, and the end-users best described as consumers. Let us first look at the effect of customer expectations.

Customers will influence what is provided by their specifications for a service or product. The nature of a contract or sale will affect what is provided and when. Increasingly, however, customers are also influencing *how* things are done because they are required to comply with various national and international standards. Influences from customers can take the form of pressure to conform to particular standards and be accredited in order that the customers' own accreditation is in place for *their* customers. This may concern such things as Quality Assurance, Investors in People or environmental auditing. Each of these standards will affect how work is done and the amount of paperwork needed to track each stage of a procedure. There is a change in the nature of the trust that is expressed in that those who require things to be written down are giving a slightly different message, 'I do not quite trust you', from those who do not. These sorts of procedure enable organisations to prove that procedures have been complied with, should a query arise. They are an inevitable consequence of the increasing cultural emphasis on 'blame'.

Another influence on the nature of the work that we do is the expectation of consumers. The effect of the 'green' lobby is perhaps the most graphic of these in the impact that has been made on pollution controls and recycling of packaging. An incentive is given to organisations to meet the required levels of acceptable environmental practice. Consumers are also becoming more differentiated and want what they want, when they want it. This means organisations have to become much more subtle and efficient in their customer services. All of this has implications for the nature of who organisations employ and how they go about this.

When Shell wanted to dispose of the Brent Spar oil platform at the end of its practical life in the early to mid-1990s they planned to sink it deep in the Atlantic Ocean. They consulted the various statutory and professional bodies about their plan, but they completely failed to consult environmental groups and they did not try to take the public along with them. Although the technical evidence was supportive of their position, they had completely failed to take account of the beliefs and emotions of the general population – particularly in Germany – concerning the need to preserve the wildness of the ocean bed. Consequently, under pressure from loss of business due to a customer boycott, Shell had to back off and reorganise the whole decision-making about Brent Spar's disposal. The understanding of the organisational context by senior management has changed completely in the light of this case. Now the consumer and general population are considered at an early stage in every environmentally sensitive project.

Organisations need to be customer-orientated for a variety of reasons. If they do not meet precisely the customer's needs then someone else will. Competition is always there. Being close to the customer enables organisations to pick up on nuances of change and to adapt gradually to these – rather than doing nothing until they find they are so far out of touch that the necessary change is impossibly big. Keeping close to the customer is important for all members of an organisation, including human resources staff who need to know how the employment market is changing and what the HRM implications are of business changes. For example, when the economic cycle is booming keeping hold of staff may be an issue, and ensuring sufficiently trained staff are available for expansion is important. When there is a depression in the cycle, however, the priority is to keep employment costs down whilst ensuring that critical skills and competencies remain available within the staff.

THE EMPLOYMENT RELATIONSHIP

The relationship between employers and their employees can be described in many ways. Any relationship is formed within a context of rights, expectations and obligations on the part of each party. Some of these are unspoken, in others there is a need for negotiation. Other aspects have a legal framework that imposes obligations and guarantees rights. Relationships are also influenced by the cultural norms of what is and what is not acceptable about the balance of power within the particular organisation. Where there are big differences of power these are more difficult to establish, and managers have to work harder to assure their staff that they matter – as we shall see in more detail in the chapters on leadership (Chapter 10) and influencing (Chapter 11).

DEBATE – THE ROLE OF TRADE UNIONS

Some people feel the relationship between trade unions and employers is unbalanced. One of the explanations for the extraordinary power of the Thatcher government in the 1980s was that many people felt the trade unions were dominating economic policy decisions in the United Kingdom and that this needed to change. Mrs Thatcher was seen as the person to do it. The general feeling in the industrial relations arena in the 1990s was that the balance of power lay with the employer. High levels of unemployment, the restrictions on trade unions, and redundancies reduced people's feelings of job security. This led to the development of more individual relationships between managers and their staff over such things as the nature of trust, openness, willingness to co-operate and acceptance of different points of view. This led to the reduction of trade union power in many organisations. What do you feel is the balance between trade unions and employers currently? What do you feel it should be?

The balance between the organisation and the individual has been summed up in the phrase 'psychological contract'. This phrase was first used by Mumford (1972) and has since been frequently used by writers on personnel management and human resource management. The psychological contract is like the implied terms of a legal contract – much of it is assumed and unspoken. It includes factors that affect feelings, motivation and loyalty. It is itself affected by the climate of the organisation and the nature of management style, which can be coercive or co-operative, or a calculated style in the middle – see Etzioni's description of this in Chapter 7. Employees differ as much as their managers in their understanding of the contract. The psychological contract between employers and the employed in the past was a job for life in return for your effort and loyalty. The new-style contract is lifelong employability in exchange for your effort. The employer is offering development, experience and maintainance of currency with modern events and methods. All of which are invaluable when seeking new employment.

As Herriot and Pemberton (1995) point out, the concept of a contract requires two people and in reality the employers are usually bullying the employees to accept what is on offer. Their model of the balance between organisations and individuals suggests that there are various dimensions in which the contract between the individual and an organisation can be negotiated. Figure 4.2 is based on some of Herriot and Pemberton's ideas.

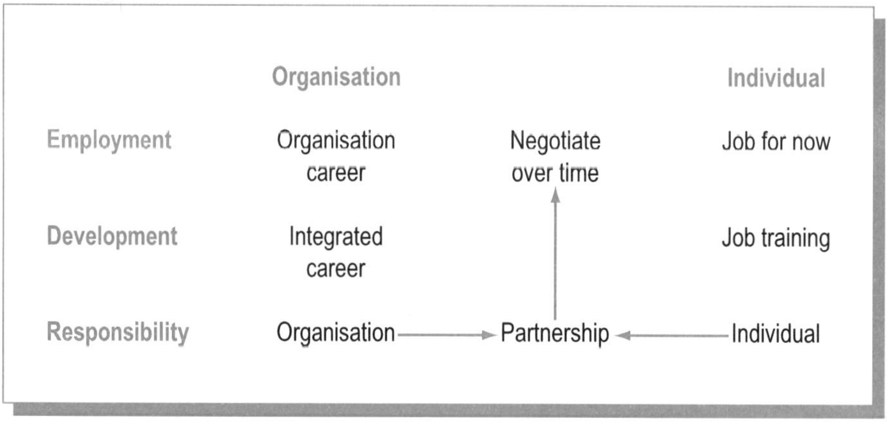

Figure 4.2 *The balance between organisations and individuals*

The concept of employability

If the psychological contract between employers and employees no longer offers security of employment in one organisation, job security will have to depend on our ability to be employable. Kanter (1989) argued the point that employability was each person's job security.

> **If security no longer comes from being employed, then it must come from being employable. In a post-entrepreneurial era in which corporations need flexibility to change and restructuring is a fact of life, the promise of very long-term employment security would be the wrong one to expect employers to make. But employment security – the knowledge that today's work will enhance the person's value in terms of future opportunities – that is a promise that can be made and kept. Employability security comes from the chance to accumulate human capital – skills and reputation – that can be invested in new opportunities as they arise.**
>
> **(Kanter, 1989, p321)**

If Kanter is right, it suggests that individuals should constantly keep their skills and knowledge up to date and learn to learn. She also implies that organisations and their managers will need employees who can take on new ideas and techniques and adapt to situations that match their core activities, and will need to encourage individuals to take on these challenges. This concept of employability is increasingly understood by individuals. One young programmer I know who works on contract will take contracts only in the up-and-coming languages to ensure his future; any that are offered in older languages he refuses, even if it means having a few days or weeks out of work. This, in turn, has implications for the organisations that have older processes and procedures: they will be seen as less favourable opportunities by the ambitious workers.

Associated with this contract is the idea of the added-value worker. This suggests that each person must add value to the organisation and to those who work with them, and this value should exceed the employee's cost. If people do not add value and are not improving they are at risk of losing their jobs. In turn, the employer is expected to make expectations clear, offer opportunities for training and development and give honest feedback. This concept of adding value as an employee suggests an individual accountability to contribute to the enterprise. As we shall see when looking at poor performance in the final chapter, an individual's contribution will be effective only if his or her personal characteristics and the organisational characteristics are well suited. Sometimes there are problems on one side, sometimes on the other. In many ways this book tries to encourage individuals to contribute and add value by ensuring that a suitable organisational climate exists for them to do so.

This chapter has looked at some of the factors that affect the work available for people to do in organisations. The relationship that develops between the individual and the organisation will depend on these and other internal factors that can be summed up as the psychological contract of employment. The final part of this book explores the nature of this contract in more detail.

ACTIVITIES

1   What outside influences in the PEST (given earlier in this chapter) terminology most affect your work? What do you do to keep up to date with this?

2   Which aspects of your work determine how and where you work? Would you want to do it differently? How easy is it for the newcomer to fit in?

3   What do you do at work because your customers/consumers ask you to? How do you find out what they want?

4   Try to collect some examples of organisations communicating with the outside – for example prospectuses, annual reports, publicity material, videos, websites, advertising. Answer the following questions in relation to the material:

   ■   What are they trying to say?
   ■   Are there any hidden messages as well?
   ■   How effective is this communication?

5   Use the debate box as a starting point to collect some material from newspapers and have a group discussion on the role of trade unions currently. The TUC conference in September/October each year may give you some materials.

HAVE I MET THE OBJECTIVES?

1   List four different approaches to analysing organisations.

2   What are the primary mechanisms of organisational culture?

3   Describe the four main outside influences on organisations.

4   How can customers influence decisions about the nature of employment?

5   What is the psychological contract of employment?

6   Describe the concept of employability.

And finally ...

What would you do about the reluctant workers at David's company? Would anything here help? I think I would consider the psychological contract and the nature of the relationship that exists. Changing the culture of an organisation takes a lot of time and effort and perhaps David has to start by emphasising the changing world outside the organisation. He may need to be tough with some of the individuals if they do not heed training and supervisory demands for compliance with regulations. In times of rapid change a combination of persuasive leadership and controls is often used. Part 3 of this book returns to this theme.

FURTHER READING

Two classic books on organisational structure and culture are those by Handy (1997) and Schein (1985). I particularly recommend the Handy book as he is very readable. It is now in its third edition.

The parallel text to this one by Farnham (1999) on the business context has sections on the economy, political system, social structure, legal framework, technology and international factors.

A standard text on consumer behaviour is MR Soloman, G Banossy and S Askegaas *Consumer Behaviour: A European Perspective* (2002) Prentice Hall.

Less academic, but very good on the general context of organisations, is the annual review published in the autumn by *The Economist* called 'The World in (next year's date)'.

A splendid novel about managing a factory is *The Goal* by EM Goldratt and J Cox (1993) Gower. It is written as a thriller but really gives a great deal of information about the issues facing managers in the context of trying to improve the running of an organisation. Many claim it is more useful than most management textbooks!

Differing Work Patterns

This chapter is underpinned by the following theories and concepts. These theories help to inform the practical applications and make them more robust. **Group theory** *is discussed here, role theory in Chapter 3, the understanding of power in Chapter 7, the concept of authority is discussed in Chapter 11, motivation theory in Chapter 12 and communication in Chapter 13. This chapter is mainly concerned with the important practical application of these theories and models to* **job design, effective teams, work patterns, planning** *and* **managing periphery staff.** *Specific examples included are Thorn Lighting, Red Arrows, BA, Lilly Industries and an NHS healthcare trust.*

OBJECTIVES

When you have finished reading this chapter you should be able to:

- **describe ways of redesigning jobs**

- **distinguish between the process and content of group working**

- **state what makes for effective teams**

- **suggest some areas that need to be considered when planning staff requirements**

- **understand and explain different types of employment and work patterns**

- **describe some of the issues associated with managing temporary staff.**

Janice's request

Janice is 33. She has been working for her boss for three years and has been with the firm for the past six years. Her work has always been acceptable but not exceptional. She has just come back from maternity leave and asks her boss whether it would be possible for her to work part time or on a job share for the next few years until her child is old enough to go to school. What do you think her boss needs to think about before giving her an answer?

What legal rights does Janice have? Should Janice's boss consult colleagues? Does her boss need to look at the precise nature of the work Janice does before deciding? Would some tasks be easier to operate part time than others? Is there a problem about which hours/days Janice works? Is there an issue of fair play? What are the implications for those who work alongside Janice? Is this an opportunity to 'lose' Janice and hope for a 'more committed' replacement? Is there another member of staff who would like to job share?

Many of us find ourselves in organisations that are reorganising departments and teams in a variety of ways, such as changing staff numbers, staff skill mix and increasingly using contract or part-time workers. We are also individually choosing to balance our lives between work and personal life in a variety of ways. It is very important, from the organisation's point of view, that someone knows what work needs doing. The work to be done needs organising into coherent jobs and into a structure that enables workers to communicate and liaise with each other. This responsibility usually falls to the team leader or line manager, as he or she is expected to know – and often is the only person in a position to know – precisely the nature of the tasks that need doing day to day. This is the heart of operational management.

WHAT TASKS NEED TO BE DONE?

Before we can design any job we need to ask what needs to be done by this job. Knowing what work is expected of the job holder is the starting point for good people management.

In general terms there are five main steps when thinking about the task to be done:

- *purpose* – what purpose in the organisation will the department, section or team serve? Does it provide a service to others in the organisation or deal direct with customers? Does it co-ordinate other people's activities or serve some other purpose?
- *activities* – what activities are needed to fulfil the purpose? What are the essential things to be done? This is not necessarily everything that is currently being done, and may include new tasks.
- *job design* – how are the activities best grouped into jobs? Which of the above activities are best done by one person because of the expertise or contacts that are required? Are some jobs best done by everyone because they keep everyone in touch with each other? This is dealt with in more detail later.
- *authority* – what formal authority do the job holders need to have delegated to them?
- *connections* – how can the activities of the job holders be connected through information systems and reporting?

The above questions are the starting points for considering what people are asked to do at work. Having a clear view of the task to be done is important. Without this, individuals will interpret the task in their own ways which may not be to the benefit of the organisation as a whole – see Chapters 13 and 14 on performance management for further discussion of how to make clear what work is expected .

JOB DESIGN

Ensuring that everyone has a suitable job has been one of the enduring themes of management thought and writing. This is usually called job design, although actually it is more often a case of job redesign. It is the process of getting the optimum fit between what the organisation requires of the individual employee and the individual's need for satisfaction in the job. This can either be done by 'dumbing down' jobs so that anyone can do them and then using a carrot and stick method, or it can be a 'holistic' approach of trying to motivate people to develop themselves and the job. Job design which takes into consideration job satisfaction is more likely to lead to sustainable work for people to do.

Hackman (1987) suggests there are various dimensions in jobs associated with good performance by the job holder. These are skill variety, task identity, task significance, levels of autonomy, and feedback. All of these affect the way people do their work. Table 5.1 shows the five characteristics identified by Hackman.

Table 5.1 *Job dimensions and their effects*

1   *Skill variety*. The way a job demands a variety of
    different activities that involve using a number of different
    skills and talents.

2   *Task identity*. The way a job requires the job holder to
    complete a whole and coherent piece of work having a   } These give meaning
    tangible outcome.   to the work people do.

3   *Task significance*. The way a job has an impact on the lives
    or work of other people, inside the organisation or outside.

4   *Autonomy*. The way a job holder enjoys freedom from   } This gives
    supervision, independence and discretion in deciding   responsibility
    how the job should be done   to job holders.

5   *Feedback*. The way the job holder receives clear and   } This gives the
    direct information about his or her effectiveness.   job holder knowledge
                                                                  of results.

Source: Adapted from JR Hackman, 'Work design', in *Motivation and Work Behaviour*, ed. RM
Steers and LW Porter, London, McGraw-Hill, 1989.

We might want to add the following further dimensions based on the human relations models of work organisation which emphasise the importance of social contact at work for motivating people at work, and so raising job satisfaction. The two dimensions are :

- dealing with others – how much staff have to deal with other people will vary, and different amounts suit different people
- friendship opportunities – establishing informal relationships at work is of varying importance to different people.

These dimensions give meaning to work, responsibility and knowledge of how they are doing to the job holders. By taking various actions according to this model – see Table 5.2 – motivation and performance can be improved.

How this might work is seen when individual team members have their own customers. This incorporates many of the ideas in Table 5.2. For example, in hospitals where patients have a named nurse, not only does the patient know who his or her carer is, but the nurse gets a whole job to do with some of the characteristics shown in Table 5.2 in the working day.

Several different ways of improving job satisfaction through redesign have been tried. The major ways of redesigning, or designing, jobs that have been described are:

- *job rotation* – moving people from one job to another to reduce boredom and increase skills. For example, in one chemical factory the operators are moved around between receiving goods from suppliers, running the process, quality control and packing the final product ready for transport to their customers.
- *job enlargement* – increasing the number of tasks done by an individual to add more variety. For example, the waiting staff at the restaurant chain TGI Fridays are

Table 5.2 *Ways of getting good results on the five job descriptions*

Action	Job dimension affected
1 *Forming natural work units* so that the work to be done has a logic and makes sense to the job holder.	2, 3
2 *Combining tasks* so that a number of natural work units may be put together to make a bigger and more coherent job.	1, 2
3 *Establishing links with clients* so that the job holder has contact with people using the service or product the job holder is supplying.	1, 4, 5
4 *Vertical loading* so that job holders take on more of the management of their jobs in deciding what to do, organising their own time, solving their own problems and controlling their own costs.	4
5 *Opening feedback channels* so that job holders can discover more about how they are doing and whether their performance is improving or deteriorating.	5

Adapted from Hackman (1987)

expected to entertain and 'host' the customers at their tables. The job is larger than just taking orders, serving meals and clearing dishes.

■ *job enrichment* – broadening the responsibilities and increasing individual autonomy for decision-making. For example, some hotel reception staff are given the authority to negotiate the price charged for a room and work out a suitable package with the customer rather than having to keep to a set price and lose the customer.

■ *autonomous work teams* – letting the team itself decide how the work is carried out, when, and for how much the work is done. This requires a skilled team and for management to be prepared to let go. It has been less common in the United Kingdom than in the USA and Scandinavia.

■ *leadership models* – where the vision of the leader is sufficient to give meaning and significance to everyone, making jobs feel more worthwhile. It is, however, difficult to achieve most of this – see Chapter 10.

■ *quality movement* – concentrating on the process of the work rather than the people, but assuming that people will be challenged and motivated by the need for constant improvement.

■ *flexibility* – working non-traditional hours. This is discussed in detail later in this chapter.

All of these potential improvements can be used successfully at team, section or departmental level. However, they can also all feel very manipulative if staff are suspicious, are feeling aggrieved over pay and conditions or are left feeling uncertain about their personal futures. Like all change, it needs sensitive management and implementation.

None of the above will be terribly effective if the department, team, section or unit is poorly organised and has poor structures. Table 5.3 gives a checklist for reviewing the organisation of a team, section or department, taken from Torrington and Weightman (1989a).

Table 5.3 *Checklist for reviewing the organisation of your department or section*

Step 1	The purpose
	Does it meet a basic business need, such as purchasing or providing?
	Or is it intended to make things run more smoothly, like HR?
	Is it necessary?
Step 2	Do the activities meet the purpose?
	What activities are necessary to meet the purpose?
	How many people, with what competencies and experience, are needed?
	Are there any duplications with other teams?
	Is there a better way?
Step 3	Grouping the activities
	How much specialisation is needed?
	How does this affect job satisfaction, commitment and efficiency?
	Have job holders the amount of discretion needed to be effective?
Step 4	The authority of job holders
	Is the authority of any job holder unreasonably restricted?
	Does everyone have sufficient access to equipment?
Step 5	Connecting the activities
	Do job holders know enough about each other's activities?
	Are there enough meetings? Too few? Too many?
	Does the physical arrangement allow suitable communication?

Based on Torrington and Weightman (1989a)

DEBATE–THE COMPETENCY APPROACH TO JOB DESIGN

There has been considerable interest in designing jobs around competencies following the national initiatives on competencies and NVQs. The design of jobs in this approach is based on analysing exactly what is required in terms of performance and then specifying the competencies required to achieve this performance and the level and standard.

The advantages claimed for this sort of approach is that it is:

- employment-led – it is about what people actually need to do
- based on the skills needed
- outcome-led – expressed in terms of things achieved
- related to national qualifications for work-based competencies.

The difficulties can be:

- Outcomes are not always easy to specify in these terms.
- It can be difficult to keep standards low enough and not over-specify jobs.
- Competency analysis can become a complex system that is an end in itself.
- It can be difficult to determine how often competencies should be measured.
- In a changing environment, flexibility may be more important than specifying precisely what people need to do.

What do you think?

EFFECTIVE GROUPS

However we design jobs, they need co-ordinating with other jobs in the organisation. One of the main ways this is done is by working in teams, sections and departments. Working in teams is an important part of most people's experience of work. Groups at work can be both formal and informal. Formal groups are where the organisation structures groups of people together to perform a particular task or function. They may be brought together to carry out a sequence of operations; they may be put together because of geography or a shared profession. These groups are deliberately planned and organised by management and would be written down in organisation charts with reporting relationships made clear through job descriptions and assessments. The formal group's main purpose is to ensure that the work of individual members is co-ordinated. These groups can be quite permanent, even if the individual membership changes. They may be short-lived for a particular purpose. The formal group will have a formal distribution of power and authority, approved channels of communication, links between sections, and be constrained by how the work is organised.

Within this formal structure there will also be people in informal groups that are based on more personal relationships. These informal groups can often cut across formal groups and can arise in a number of different ways, such as: previous working relationships, shared lifts to work, smoking outside the building, common interests and a whole variety of contacts. A very common group is the lunch group which may include people from different parts of the organisation and the hierarchy. The topics of conversation range over both work and private interests. These informal groups are an important part of an individual's network of contacts. The importance of these networks for getting things done is explored further in Chapter 11.

> Thorn Lighting in 1997 were running five-day workshops for unemployed people. The emphasis was on team-building skills to make them employable. Thorn found that people in schools and colleges were learning individual skills only appropriate to high fliers, whereas most jobs require teamwork.

Buchanan and Huczynski (1997) suggest that groups, formal or informal, take account of the following elements in how they relate to each other:

- status
- power
- roles
- leadership
- communication.

Each of these structures, or concepts, has a well-developed sociological, philosophical and political debate, and they are discussed further in Part 3 of this book. If you can analyse, describe and understand some of these aspects of the group you can appreciate their nature and how best to manage them.

As well as having various structures, groups also change over time. Tuckman (1965) suggests that there are various stages that small groups go through before they are mature enough in their relations to be able to work together consistently. These stages are set out in Table 5.4.

This is helpful in showing that groups need some time to become effective. The longer the group is expected to remain intact, and the greater the importance of its work, the longer it takes to settle down. Some tolerance of these initial stages can speed the process of getting going.

Effective teams

A formal work group is often called a team. Guirdham (1990, p374) offers the following characteristics of a fully effective team, or group:

- Team objectives are clearly understood by all members.
- All members are committed to the objectives.
- Mutual trust is high.
- Support for one another is high.
- Communications are open and reliable, not guarded and cautious.
- Team members listen to one another.
- The team is self-controlling.
- Conflicts are accepted and worked through.
- Members' abilities, knowledge and experience are fully used by the team.

Most of these characteristics concentrate on the process side of a group's working. That is the way people work together. It is also important to look at the content – what the group has

Table 5.4 *Stages in the growth of group cohesion*

Stages of development	Process	Outcome
Forming	There is anxiety, dependence on leader; testing to find out the nature of the situation and what behaviour is acceptable	Members find out what the task is, what the rules are, and what methods are appropriate
Storming	Conflict between subgroups, rebellion against leader; opinions are polarised; resistance to control by group	Emotional resistance to demands of the task
Norming	Development of group cohesion; norms emerge; resistance is overcome and conflicts are patched up; mutual support and sense of group identity	Open exchange of views and feelings; co-operation develops
Performing	Interpersonal problems are resolved; interpersonal structure becomes the means of getting things done; roles are flexible and functional	Solutions to problems emerge; there are constructive attempts to complete tasks and energy is now available for effective work

Based on Tuckman (1965)

to do. Guirdham puts this first in the list. Effective teams have both a good task orientation and cohesion amongst the group. This does not happen immediately and needs constant nurturing. This is an important role for team leaders.

> The Red Arrows are the RAF's dramatic, close-formation demonstration flying team. Have you ever wondered how they manage to do it? Clearly they are highly skilled pilots, but they also have to rely on each other to do their job correctly; otherwise everyone is in danger. Owen (1996) describes how the team concentrated on the following to build up trust:
>
> - open criticism
> - public praise
> - organisation goals
> - individual goals.

THE HR PLANNING APPROACH TO JOB DESIGN

Organisation and job design is really part of the whole planning process. A development of the traditional approach to the planning of resources has been to integrate the need for people with the planning of the organisation's goals and objectives. This planning is done at a senior level, but once the strategic plan or initiative is decided it will certainly involve line managers and team leaders in trying to propose possible ways of putting the plan into practice. The strategy may include ideas – improving services to the customers, reducing staffing costs, improving the quality of products and services, or innovations in services and interesting products.

Approaches to planning questions can occur at a sectional or team level as well as organisation-wide. For example, the common target of reducing staffing costs could be met by:

- improving recruitment techniques so that there are better employees and less turnover
- reducing absenteeism so there is less need to employ agency or cover staff
- using the skills and time of individuals better so they are more productive
- rewarding people more effectively so they are paid for performance
- having annual hours so that the work is more flexible, so there is less need to pay for overtime.

Any of these might be effective in reducing staffing costs on a unit, section or team basis.

This chapter is about the various aspects of ensuring that jobs are designed appropriately. There is also a need to ensure that there is adequate staffing for work to be done in the section or team. At the strategic level – that of the whole organisation – this would be a major aspect of the function of the HR/personnel department and of top management who control decisions about budgets. There is also an increasing expectation that the line manager or team leader is involved in human resource management. It is only at this level that particular decisions about what is needed can be integrated with the development of the particular activities, or business, of the team, section and department. The team leader or department manager is best placed to do all the prior analysis about the tasks, workloads, work methods and practices that will affect the number and expertise of staff required. He or she is also better placed than the HR department to deliver some of the softer aspects of job design, such as how people are treated, communicated with and motivated

Planning to have the right sort of people to do the job

One classic approach to these issues has been human resource planning, where an attempt is made to see whether there is likely to be a mismatch between the future needs of the organisation and the supply of suitably qualified and experienced staff. This is usually done by:

- scanning the horizon to see what likely changes are coming up and what the implications are for staffing. This involves looking at such things as the organisation's plans, government action, trends in techniques, technologies and approaches to the objective involved. Any of these might affect the nature of the work to be done in the department or team, and consequently the number and nature of staff required. For example, in hospitals the rise of less intrusive surgery has led to more day cases and fewer overnight stays – with obvious changes in staffing levels required on the wards at night. These changes need to be put alongside the demand for labour within the organisation due to current practice and future plans for contraction or expansion of the service.

- examining the supply of personnel within the organisation in terms of such factors as age, experience, qualifications, pay and conditions and personal performance of existing staff. The external supply of potential employees will vary, depending on changes in the population, competition for workers from other organisations, and the education and training available for people to qualify in particular areas.

- making a comparison between the predicted demand and supply of staff. This forecast is the basis for planning for the future. Matching supply and demand can be done manually or by computer. Except for the simplest cases, the HR/personnel department should have access to some sophisticated information systems using payroll and personnel information. The figures forecast are not an absolute, nor are the outcomes, as they can be influenced by such things as interdepartmental relations, organisational politics and the empire building of senior managers. The figures will also be affected by artificial restraints from top management, as Rothwell (1995, p171) points out. For example, the board may have put a cost limit or a headcount limit for the organisation. This could affect estimates of staff demand. There will also be arguments about how these costs are counted. Do staff costs include only the salary or the total employment costs? Are heads counted as actual numbers or full-time equivalents?

Questions to ask about an HR plan for job design

Once there are plans and a human resource forecast is available, Bramham (1989, p155) suggests that the forecast allows plans to be made. Some of the areas to ask questions about and plan for are as follows. They are listed in alphabetical order:

- Accommodation – is there a need for more or fewer rooms, desks, etc?
- Costs – where is there a need for additional/fewer resources?
- Culture – how are the changes going to affect the way people interact?

- Development – will there be different opportunities for staff development?
- Industrial relations – how will the trade unions react to the changes?
- Organisation development – do reporting relationships need to be changed or reorganised?
- Outplacements – will some people need to find new jobs?
- Promotion – what opportunities for individual advancement will there be?
- Productivity – will these changes affect the amount of work each person can sensibly do?
- Recruitment – what sort of people will need to be recruited?
- Redundancy – which groups are likely to face redundancy and how is this going to be handled?
- Retirement – is there a need to change the ages at which retirement is offered?
- Reward systems – should the salary structures be changed?
- Training and retraining – which areas of the organisation need to develop new skills?
- Transfer – should the transfer of staff be voluntary or compulsory?
- Working practices – is there a need to rethink the ways in which tasks are tackled?

This list is not only useful for major replanning but as a basic checklist when change is proposed. Decisions and practice about all of the items can affect the utilisation of people at work. Decisions about each of these will also affect how much work gets done, how well the work is done, and how many people are needed to do it. For example, if a section or team is spread across a variety of different buildings there will be a need for more staff than if they are all together, but there may be important aspects of the service that require them to be spread out. Managing the service and the people will affect the number of people required. If the service is driven by the number of people available, it is rather like having the tail wag the dog; but equally it makes some sense to ensure that the most economical use is made of staff whilst maintaining the quality of the service.

Here are some examples of the need for planning the use of staff from a Healthcare Trust with which I was associated.

- The use of operating theatres and the need to get a precise costing of them. Some consultants were overrunning their time in the theatres and the question arose as to whose budget should pay for the overtime of the porters and nurses. One way round this has been to get consultants to manage their lists by having whole days rather than half-days in the theatre.
- The maternity unit was getting regional manpower figures on the future number of midwives needed and the number of projected deliveries. The question was, how typical was the Trust's catchment area compared with these regional figures?
- One clinical directorate was looking at the workload activities of the staff and the level of dependency of individual patients – the higher the dependency of patients, the more staff are needed to look after them. This was to enable them to forward-plan what types of staff they needed and how many.
- Another directorate was collecting information on waiting lists so they could draw up plans for various initiatives such as operating at weekends and

evenings. This had obvious implications for levels of staffing and who was to pay for it.

- Looking at the case mix, including care profiles, allowed one team to manage its resources better. By having different mixes of routine and difficult cases, the specialist technical staff required for the assessment stage could be better used.

DIFFERENT WORK PATTERNS

Flexible working has become a major redesign tool for organisations. It has various meanings and implications:

- It usually refers to the hours worked – which is discussed below.
- It can also mean functional flexibility, where people can be moved around the tasks through increased training and relaxation of job demarcations.
- Numerical flexibility allows the numbers employed to fluctuate, depending upon demand.
- Financial flexibility allows the employment costs to reflect the demand and supply of people by varying the pay given to people. For example, within the public sector there are national agreements on rates of pay with little financial flexibility to vary these rates across the country.

One way of giving people greater freedom and control over their work is flexible working hours or flexitime. This usually means that there is a core time when everyone must be at work and then an agreed minimum number of hours per month to be achieved. Technological changes have meant this can be extended to include people working at home, or teleworking. This in turn has led to the use of flexibility by employers to develop core and peripheral staff. The core staff work full time and the peripheral are called in when required. For example, most retail organisations have additional part-time staff to cover the busy times – indeed, many shops have only part-time staff.

Here are two examples of companies using flexibility in an attempt to meet both staff and organisational needs:

- British Airways have 33 per cent and 50 per cent contracts for their cabin staff as well as full-time posts. People on such contracts work one month in three or one in two, with the normal rota of off and on days. This allows staff to have whole months on and off, while also enabling those managing the rotas to treat everyone equally within a month.

Lilly Industries have a 'worklife programme' which includes the following options:

- part-time working – of varying lengths
- job shares – for two people to share the same full-time job
- teleworking – people work from home
- term-time working – people work only when their children are at school

- paid paternity leave – for fathers in the first year of a child's life
- career breaks – for parental care
- sabbaticals – for a variety of reasons
- periods of reduced hours – again for a variety of personal reasons.

Additional options for staff within the scheme also includes health insurance, share options and pensions.

The aim of these flexible working programmes is to retain skilled staff in whom the organisation has invested through training and experience. They also help to deal with skill shortages, to lower sickness rates and to reduce 'burn-out' and enhance recruitment.

The examples show how flexibility in job design, and particularly in job hours, can benefit both employers and employees. Indeed, when the economy is tight, offering flexible working can be one of the few ways available to reward staff. They can then get the balance between work and home that suits individual situations. However, not all such schemes are so equally balanced. Flexibility is too often a one-sided bargain with intolerable insecurity for individuals who have to take on the risks of the organisations. An example is the zero-hours contract. In these contracts there is no guaranteed work or income but the employer can call the person up when he or she is required to come and work. Other examples are those of full-time staff who are compulsorily made part-time, or of employees forced to become self-employed, with the loss of their unfair dismissal and redundancy rights. All these have been common practice in British organisations in the 1990s and 2000s. These practices may help the short-term survival of the organisation and enhance profits, but they do little to engender commitment over the long term.

Managing temporary and contract staff

A particular aspect of managing flexible working hours is planning for temporary or contract staff. Nursing, particularly, has always used 'bank' staff to cover for absent colleagues, but increasingly organisations at all levels are using peripheral workers to manage the ebb and flow of work and income. Temporary, part-time and contract staff – or peripheral staff – need a different sort of managing from full-time permanent staff – or core staff.

- Core staff are full-time, permanent, career staff mainly in managerial, professional and skilled technical positions. They are offered relatively secure employment with an expectation of training and development, and career moves when appropriate.
- Peripheral staff are part-time and/or temporary staff usually employed on a contract basis. They have fewer opportunities for training and promotions within the organisation. Some services have become entirely staffed by peripheral workers, as they are contracted out.

The benefits to the organisation of employing peripheral staff include improved flexibility and productivity, reduced employment costs, increased resources for core tasks where contracting out is used, and enhanced job security for core employees. Contracting can also be attractive to individuals such as professionals with high earning capacity and scarce skills, and is convenient for some others such as parents of school-age children. However, the great majority of people seek the security of core employment. There are a number of disadvantages in the widespread use of contract staff:

- Cost – the short-term gains may be offset against longer-term costs if the contractors are employed at premium rates for a long time.

- Quality and reliability – it is more difficult to monitor work and the safety standards of contract staff.

- Employee relations – the contract staff may upset agreements with trade unions and with core staff about terms and conditions.

Another group of part-time staff are those permanently on part-time contracts or permanent staff who are temporarily part time. Increasingly organisations are finding flexibility suits people and allows the organisation to hold on to experienced staff in this way. Usually these people are treated as core employees and offered training and development. However, many of the issues of managing peripheral staff still apply.

There are some particular management issues associated with managing peripheral staff:

- There is a greater need for clear instructions and procedures if things are to be done consistently. This is better done by specifying 'what' is required rather than 'how' it is. Staff gain in confidence, and the contribution of people is better, where they feel as if they have some say in how they do something.

- Whole jobs are better than bits and pieces. Give the temporary or part-time members of staff something to complete rather than merely assist with, no matter how tempting it is to get them to do all the little things that no one else has got around to doing. This will ensure a more committed contribution.

- Peripheral staff are nearly always more detached emotionally from the organisation than core staff. As a result, they are willing to fit in with your requirements. Many do not want to be more involved, which can come as a surprise to the very involved core co-worker and team leader.

- It is necessary to ensure that peripheral staff have access to all the housekeeping information, such as when breaks are taken, where lavatories are and what dress standards are, as well as health and safety information and disciplinary procedures.

- No matter how rare and mysterious the skills brought in on the periphery are, those people in the core must themselves have sufficient expertise to specify and manage the contribution. Otherwise the peripherals begin to determine and dominate the organisation. This has happened in some of the uses of management consultants and early uses of computer staff.

- There is a need to recognise that the core staff are involved in helping the peripheral staff and this can mean extra work for them.

- If senior staff devote all their time to the peripheral workers, core staff can feel ignored and aggrieved.

- Many of the peripheral people will work for more than one organisation at any one time and can be a useful source of opinions on the reputation of a particular unit. They can also be your best, or worst, PR department!

- The Employment Relations Act 1999 ensures that part-time and contract workers must be treated fairly. This means they are entitled to similar holiday allowances and training.

Peripheral staff are widely used in such industries as retailing, education and nursing. All of these have large numbers of people employed and staffing is a major part of the organisation's budget. Other industries – for example aircraft building and chemicals – operate with much a smaller workforce, often with confidential processes. Here peripheral staff are really of only marginal use. For many individuals, a portfolio of several peripheral jobs can lead to a secure and sustainable career, as they never lose all the jobs at once and can balance their own work. Ensuring that they keep current by taking the risk on new trends with one employer whilst continuing with an old one can often mean that they have skills that employers seek out.

Ensuring that the work of the team, section or department is done is the responsibility of the team leader or manager. Breaking this work up into suitable, co-ordinated chunks is at the heart of the team leader's or manager's responsibilities. This chapter has looked at some of the well-established ways of doing so and some of the issues associated with the process.

ACTIVITIES

1   Are there any jobs in your team/section/department that could do with being revamped? Would any of the above approaches help?

2   Using the Tuckman sequence, where do you think your seminar group is up to? Do you all agree with the diagnosis?

3   Do you have any flexible working in your workplace? Should you have? Whom does it benefit? What are the problems with it?

4   How do you ensure peripheral staff in your organisation know what to do? Do you give them enough support to make them feel welcome? Who looks after their queries? In which of the following activities do you include part timers and temporary staff – meetings, staff development, appraisal procedures, coffee clubs, staff outings, the Christmas party?

5   When do you use external consultants? Do you do it to save time or to take advantage of their expertise? How do you monitor what external experts are doing? How do you control external consultants?

HAVE I MET THE OBJECTIVES?

1   Can I describe four ways of redesigning jobs?

2   What is the difference between the process and content of group working?

3   What are Tuckman's stages for group cohesion?

4   What makes for effective teams?

5   Can I describe different types of employment and work patterns?

6   What areas must be considered when planning what staff are required in the future?

7   What particular things must be considered when employing temporary staff?

And finally ...

What would you recommend Janice's boss to think about, based on the material in this chapter? Under the Employment Act 2002 Janice's boss has to formally hear the request and give a formal response. Parents have the right to request flexible work. The answer does not have to be yes. I would suggest her boss systematically looks at the work of the section to see if this is an opportunity to redistribute the work. There may be opportunities for enhancing some other people's work to give them more satisfaction as well as acceding to Janice's request for part-time work. By allowing Janice to go part time her boss is also giving the message to everyone that home matters. However, there will be implications for her co-workers and it is important they do not feel put upon.

FURTHER READING

Stredwick J *and* Ellis S (1998) *Flexible Working Practices*. London, IPD. This is a substantial book with many examples on this topic.

You will also find material in most personnel and HRM books: see for example those listed in Chapter 1.

Mullins LJ (2002) *Management and Organisational Behaviour.* 6th edition. Prentice Hall. This is a standard text in this area and has a very impressive section on group working.

High Performance Teams (1996), a video from The Industrial Society which includes some of the material about the Red Arrows mentioned in this chapter.

The Management of
Work-Related Stress

This chapter uses some of the theoretical models we have already looked at to inform the practical material that is discussed in this chapter. Psychology and sociology, see Chapter 1; personality theory, see Chapter 2; learning and role theory, in Chapter 3; and motivation which is dealt with in Chapter 12 are the main influences. This mainly practical chapter looks at various strands dealing with **stress at work, the role of managers** *and* **leaders, managing change and time, counselling and mentoring.** *Specific aspects of* **flexible working** *and* **Health and safety** *are also dealt with. Chapters 13 and 14, on performance management, have additional related material. Specific examples are intensive care units; aid workers; train drivers; and The Royal Bank of Scotland.*

OBJECTIVES

When you have finished reading this chapter you should be able to:

■ **understand some of the causes of work-related stress**

■ **describe symptoms of work-related stress**

■ **explain possible prevention and treatment strategies for work-related stress**

■ **understand some of the issues associated with using the term 'stress'**

■ **describe ways of managing change**

■ **understand the need for time management and prioritising demands**

■ **describe a sequence for counselling.**

Trish's concern with staff morale

Trish is head of department in a further education college. She has ten full-time members of teaching staff and seven part timers working for her. Whenever more than two are gathered, they all say how stressed they are. The talk is of how much work they all have to do and the constant demands from the various agencies with which they come into contact. Moaning about the hours and pay are endemic. What should Trish do?

Remind them that they are relatively well paid, on national pay scales, compared with the surrounding area? Remind them that they have longer holidays than most? Ask colleagues in other departments what they think? Analyse whether their moans affect the work of the individuals? Consider whether it is just a habit that has grown up? Investigate whether there are particular individuals who are having a bad time? Talk to senior management about the problem of morale? Look for symptoms? Change the way work is done or allocated? Organise for a stress counsellor to be available?

These feelings of being stressed are not typical just of teachers. There is a current belief that we are subject to constant, everyday, barely tolerable stress. Anti-depressants outsell all other types of prescription drugs, and lists of best-selling books include soothing volumes on how to deal with stress. Stress is frequently described as an epidemic of modern times. A few decades ago it was unknown. The word in its current meaning has been used only for the past 30 years. Stress is blamed for physical and mental illness as well as costing industry millions of hours in lost work time. So what is stress?

WHAT IS STRESS?

Psychologists have for a long time looked at the balance between strain and boredom. As early as 1874 Wundt, referred to in Scitovsky (1976), postulated a curve of pleasure versus novel stimulation that goes up in pleasure with the initial stimulus of novelty but then sharply dips into unpleasantness if the intensity is very strong. For a satisfactory life we all need a balance of novel experiences and others that give us comfort or stability. How each of us wishes to balance these will vary, as will the interpretation of novelty and comfort – your comfort may be my novelty. The stimulation of novelty and change usually means we shall put effort into something. However, if the stimulation becomes too great we are less able to make a contribution. It is at this point that stress is experienced, with all the associated feelings of increased uncertainty and the possibility of failure.

The word 'stress' is very widely used these days and has come to mean a variety of things, so some definitions are required. Stress can refer to pressure applied to someone, for example: 'The manager was putting a great deal of stress on the new salesperson and she resented it.' Stress can refer to the individual's response, for example: 'The GP felt very stressed because of the number of patients who had been discharged early from hospital who needed seeing.' Stress can also be applied to the interaction between individuals and their environment, for example: 'Working in the offices that faced on to the main interchange for the city's road system meant they felt stressed.'

There can be good and bad stress, over- and under-stress. When people talk about being stressed, they usually are referring to being over-stressed with bad stress. The consequences of too much of this sort of stress are, in the long term, damaging to health and well-being. Research – for example, Mestel (1994) – suggests that there is a link between the brain and the immune system. The research describes how chronic stress from work or insomnia can be bad for us, as the activity of the immune cells goes up or down according to our different moods. If this is so, no wonder some illness is explained by the stress experienced by individuals.

Symptoms of over-stress include:

- short temper and impatience
- emotional outbursts
- lack of attention to duties
- decreased productivity
- increase in number of accidents
- increased absenteeism, lateness and turnover of staff.

In varying degrees of seriousness, all these should set alarm bells ringing that things in the workplace may not be running smoothly – some investigation of the problem is necessary.

STRESS AT WORK

In the United Kingdom in the years 2001–2002, 40 million days of sick leave were taken. Of these, 33 million were defined as occupational ill health and of these, 13 million were due to stress, anxiety and depression. That is, more than a quarter of the days taken off work were due to stress-related illness. Is it any wonder that the head of the Health and Safety Executive (HSE) published a booklet (2002) on stress? The HSE has put reducing stress in the workplace as a major priority for its work. It suggests that there are seven key workplace stressors:

- culture – the nature of the organisational climate
- demands – the kinds of expectations people have of people
- control – how much individuals can manage their own work and outcomes
- relationships – with those we work with
- change – how much, and how it is managed
- role – that an individual has and how this competes, conflicts with others and their own values
- support and development and individual factors.

These are all dealt with in this chapter and elsewhere in the book. The HSE is looking for ways of tackling the continuing rise of stress-related time off work and improving employee health. Currently, unfortunately, there is no firm evidence for what interventions on the part of organisations are best for preventing and dealing with work-related stress.

So what are the identifiable stress factors at work, and what can be done about them? The overwhelming conclusions of behavioural studies of stress are that it is experienced in all occupations, especially manual work, and particularly where there is routine repetitiveness and lack of autonomy – see Cooper and Earnshaw (1996). This lack of control over what we do and how we do it appears to be the most stressful experience. Perhaps this is one reason why so many people in work are claiming to be more stressed now as they feel more controlled by financial considerations. Individual members of professional staff feel as if they have less personal autonomy than previously, as managers have become more powerful.

Other areas at work in which to look for stressors include:

- the work environment – for example, a culture of never saying you are overworked
- internally – for example, being anxious all the time
- interpersonal relationships – for example, thinking other people are not trustworthy
- communication – for example, always insinuating and never getting round to saying anything clearly
- workload – for example, working five shifts can be more stressful than four shifts even if the hours are the same, because there is less time 'off work'
- noise and physical conditions – for example, working close to noisy machinery, or in over- or underheated conditions, is especially stressful if precise judgements are being made.

Intensive care units often have a high turnover of staff, which is associated with stressors such as grief, anxiety, guilt, exhaustion, overcommitment and overstimulation.

Aid workers often feel guilty about looking after themselves and have a 'tough guy' culture. The 'Save the Children' charity now includes in its staff appraisal something about 'looking after yourself'.

Train drivers have to deal with the sudden death of members of the public with what they call 'one under' suicides. London Underground uses a process of traumatic incident reduction where the driver is asked to review the incident silently and then talk about it until the memory is no longer active.

COPING WITH STRESS

There are various strategies for trying to cope with the stress, aside from the longer-term need to reduce the pressure. The main responses tend to be:

- emotional or mental – crying, drinking alcohol, praying
- physical – dieting, exercise, meditation or other relaxation techniques
- retreat – into hobbies, distractions or holidays
- reliance on problem-solving – confrontation, assertion, action-planning
- reliance on personal and social support – from family, friends and colleagues.

It is up to individuals to choose the strategy that suits them best, and there are well-established self-help groups in most localities. If we are going to help our staff cope with their stress we clearly also need to cope with our own stress by using some of the above strategies.

Merely attempting to calm down everyone who is feeling stressed is not a suitable strategy in the long term as it does not deal with the underlying cause of the problem. Indeed, it can be counterproductive, as it often encourages a passive response in the individual and a learned helplessness that acts as a sort of anaesthetic; people become less likely to help themselves. Stress should be seen as an alarm, not as the problem. Working out what you are worried about in such situations as having to deal with tomorrow's presentation, your sick cat, or when to make that difficult phone call, gives you some strategies for sorting things out. This is better than merely saying: 'I am feeling stressed, I had better light a sweet-smelling candle and have a warm bath.' Pleasant though they might be, they will not address the underlying problems of feeling stressed.

DEBATE – THE BALANCE OF WORK AND LIFE

In the past decade or so it has become a badge of modern life that we consider ourselves stressed. Is this because we are no longer making such clear distinctions between work and home? The phrase 'work/life balance' is often used to describe this. We communicate with our pals at work on phones and e-mails, we go on 'away days' and have fun activities and then work longer hours than previously. Or are we confusing the work/life balance issue with a felt work pressure that is not easy to admit for fear of losing out in the career stakes? Or are we being pathetic, as Angela Patmore pointed out in the *Independent* (24 May 1998, p26) and that the argument that we are more stressed in the modern day because of a few phone calls is insulting to our predecessors who lived through periods of famine or war. Surely we are not that vulnerable. Or do we have greater expectations of personal freedom and happiness these days? What do you think? What are we to do about managing work-related stress? Currently there are lots of ideas and suggestions on this, but no firm evidence on what is best practice. So your ideas are worth exploring.

WHAT IS THE ROLE OF THE TEAM LEADER OR MANAGER IN SUPPORTING STAFF?

Although it is still not clear which interventions are best for reducing stress for staff, there are some general indications of actions that might help. The first difficulty for many people is admitting they are feeling stressed at work as they feel to do so may damage their career prospects. This may well be so as many employers – reported in *People Management* 23 Jan 2003, page 5 – say they would not promote people they felt could not deal with the pressure.

This chapter tries to answer the question 'How can we help staff to keep things going when all around things are changing?' By its very nature it is a more practical chapter than some others. People at work are often good at looking after the well-being of their customers and clients, but looking after the well-being of the staff is often left to others or not done at all. Usually the argument is something like: 'Well, we must put the customers first.' If we are looking for a sustained period of effort from ourselves and others, we cannot expect it unless we ensure that staff are well. All of us can keep working like crazy for a few weeks, or indeed a few months in crisis, but this is not sustainable indefinitely – we shall burn out. If we are investing in expensive selection and training of staff it is absurd to then risk losing them because they are too exhausted or worn down to do their best work. Increasing the stress in people so they are no longer productive or motivated to work is counterproductive. If this becomes routine, problems of recruiting and retaining staff can develop. Sustaining staff is a management and leadership role.

This need to look after the staff is best seen in the overall context of managing people at work. The current thinking about the role of team leaders and managers often refers to the need to combine traditional skills with the ability to maximise the individual contributions of the team. The aim is to bring the skills of analytical thinking and a sound financial approach into a softer approach to people. This includes the leader having an ability to listen well, give useful feedback, and serve as coach and mentor to staff in order to enhance their satisfaction with, and performance in, the job. The systematic HR approach to this is to establish accountability systems to support team leaders and managers, set standards, arrange training, give feedback on achievements and assess individual performance, and give appropriate rewards. There is emphasis on systematically deploying and paying people whose performance determines the success of the organisation. This is discussed further in Chapter 14.

The Royal Bank of Scotland (Rick, 1996) has established a framework for all human resource policies and practices with the idea of creating a high-performing and capable organisation. The Royal Bank of Scotland model includes the following, some aspects of which are discussed in this book in more detail:

- job and organisation design
- selecting for success, using a competency-based approach
- continuously managing performance, using appraisal and coaching as a key responsibility for all managers and supervisors
- developing individual capability with individually agreed development plans
- business and resource planning
- rewarding performance by using clear performance standards and rewards.

The idea behind these trends in management is to improve standards. No doubt they can all be very useful and can enhance the effectiveness of any organisation. Unfortunately they have been used in a cost-cutting environment in many organisations, and so are seen negatively by some for whom 'best practice' is interpreted as meaning 'most competitive' rather than anything else. Another irony is that these newer approaches usually mean devolving responsibilities for managing people to team leaders and line managers at a time when substantial numbers of these very same people are facing being made redundant. It could be argued that the negative associations of some of these methods come from the environment in which they have been introduced. The techniques themselves can in reality be about improving the organisation of work for all of us.

If team leaders and line managers are seen as responsible for the work of the people in their teams, they are also responsible for ensuring that the work they are asking people to do is not going to harm them and that the work is sustainable. If they do not do this, their staff will feel stressed.

HANDLING CHANGE

Changes in the organisation and in the technical aspects of work have meant that most people experience change in their working practice. To some, these changes mean excitement and the thrill of being part of the action. For others, they feel like a threatening dismantling of the stable order of things. Although there is actually less change generally in society and industry in Britain now than at the end of the nineteenth century, we all feel as if change is an everyday part of our lives. Where the change is unwelcome or excessive, we can feel stressed. Where change is prolonged, health problems can arise with all the associated effects on productivity and motivation.

Types of change in organisations

There are several different kinds of change, which can be put into four broad categories of experience:

- *imposition*, where the initiative comes from someone else and we have to alter our ways of doing things to comply with outside requirements. This may undermine our sense of being able to handle things and we worry about the implications. If there is too much imposed, many feel very stressed as they have little control. New rules and laws are the obvious examples.
- *adaptation*, where we have to change our behaviour or attitudes at the behest of others. This can be very difficult, and if too extreme can lead to people leaving or

retiring from the organisation. Examples are changes in taking on a business orientation rather than a public service one, or a relocation.

■ *growth*, where we are responding to opportunities for developing competence, poise and achievement. Examples would be 'acting up' for one's boss or job changes.

■ *creativity*, where we are the instigator and in control of the process. Examples would be introducing new standards at work, developing a new technique or trying something to see whether it will work.

Most of us resist the first, are uncertain about the second, are delighted with the third and excited by the fourth kind of change. As a team leader or line manager you will undoubtedly experience all of these and have to sustain your staff through periods of such change. How can you help?

Managing change

As well as helping people to cope with change so they do not become stressed, we also have to manage change at work. The normal sequence of steps for managing change goes something like this:

■ establish the project – what are we going to do?

■ set goals – what should we target for, and by when?

■ identify a solution – how are we going to get there?

■ prepare for implementing – what resources do we need?

■ implement the project – how do we influence people and deal with the unexpected?

■ review progress – how are we doing?

■ maintain the project – are there any problems?

This sort of list is useful as a checklist to prepare for change, but the important point is that ownership of a project by the staff builds and develops over time. It comes through working to improve something. It makes sense to give a firm push at the beginning of a project to ensure that it really gets started. Don't do so much planning that you never get on to the action! It is also important to offer plenty of help and support to your staff – and this help is better done after the initial planning. There is plenty of advice in the literature about how to manage change – see, for example, McCalman and Paton (1992). It is not my intention to deal here in any detail with the subject of introducing change. However, there are some useful questions to ask about managing people involved in change.

There are several questions you must ask when trying to persuade people to change. These include the following:

■ What is in it for them? If people can see that the new behaviour, procedure or technology will make their work more satisfying, they are likely to be enthusiastic. If they cannot see any benefit, they are likely to be resistant or at best not co-operative.

■ Have they had a say in the change? If people help to create a new scheme they are more committed to trying to make it work. This needs to be a genuine opportunity to participate in the introduction, design, execution and feedback of the new programme. If people are not involved at all, or the consultation is a sham, then they may well use their innovative and creative behaviours to demonstrate just why the scheme will not work.

■ Is it clear what change is envisaged? We need a clear vision of what we are trying to achieve if we are to persuade others to become involved. It needs to be put into terms that others will understand, because not everyone speaks in management terms!

These questions are given to help you think through some of the issues that will affect how people react to a change. Partly they may help you to manage the change better, but they are also offered to help reduce the amount of distress felt by those involved.

Keeping something stable in a period of change

As long ago as 1970, Toffler recognised that we can cope with a great deal of change, pressure, complexity and confusion if at least one area of our lives is relatively stable. We can rely on this stable part of our lives and so risk change elsewhere. If we have nothing stable, everything becomes turmoil and we begin to experience stress. He suggested that 'stability zones' were all-important to each of us, but that each of us had different ones. The main stability zones described by Toffler are:

■ ideas – moral, religious, political beliefs

■ places – home, town, pub, place of work that we know well

■ people – spouse, partner, parents, old friends with whom we share our lives

■ organisations – church, employer, clubs that we belong to

■ things and habits – possessions we know how to use, routines that we recognise.

We all need at least one of these zones to be secure. Working out what they are and maintaining them helps us to cope with stress in other areas.

Schein (1978) applied this idea of stability zones to the workplace. He coined the term 'career anchors' to suggest that there are distinct categories of stability zone at work and that individuals use them to evaluate themselves. Each of us will have one of these as the most important in his or her working life:

■ managerial competence – seeking out opportunities to manage and take responsibility

■ technical competence – enjoying the technical activity of engineering, IT or medicine, for example

■ security – working for job security, income and pension are foremost considerations

■ creativity – important for those who want to build or invent something of their own, such as a new process, theory, technique or product

■ autonomy and independence – valuing freedom from the constraints of other people's rules and regulations. Having your own lifestyle in a self-determined setting is the most important thing about work for people with this career anchor.

There are various other strategies for keeping one's balance when there is a period of rapid and unsettling change. In addition to the long-term strategy of trying to keep something stable – such as using the stability zones or career anchors listed above – there are also the smaller strategies, such as trying to calm the pace at which one works by breathing slowly for a second or two. You might also try to remember that you do not have to deal with something on your own. Asking for help can bring new insights, companionship and learning. Even just unloading your fears and frustration can make it easier to cope. But beware the danger of becoming an advice junkie!

MANAGING TIME

As a manager or team leader, one aspect of supporting staff in periods of high demand is to help them manage their time more effectively and thereby help to reduce stress levels. It is also necessary for you to manage your own time well so as to make as much time available as possible for 'having a chat'. One way to start this is to keep a simple activity diary for a few days listing all the things you do as you go along. Then have a look at it and see how much you are doing to please others. Also look to see where and when you have a real choice about whether to do the task or not, and what it is you should do. Jobs vary enormously in the degree of choice there is about what to do. People vary enormously in their interpretation about what is essential. Some people see all demands and requests of them as essential: they never prioritise or say no – no wonder they feel stressed.

It is also worth making a list of all the demands that come to you over a couple of days. Then ask yourself the following questions. Where could you say no? Which tasks could be done differently? Most people experience too many demands in their jobs at the moment. This means making choices: some things clearly have to be done and some things can be left. The bulk, in the middle, are important things that need doing, but not all of them can be done within the resources available. The normal advice is to prioritise these into 'must dos' and 'hope to dos' with possibly some consultation with one's boss or co-workers. However, it is not always at all clear how one should go about this. Frankly, if it is impossible to discriminate between equally important things that need doing, and if you cannot do them all, you might as well do the interesting ones and leave the others. You cannot do everything. Nowadays most of us are having to choose not to do things that appear to be worth doing. It is learning to let go of some of these that can lead to greater job satisfaction.

A particular aspect of managing time that creates stress is the balance between work and private life. Increasingly organisations are agreeing individual flexibility for working arrangements. The home/work balance is increasingly an area of individual negotiation. If an arrangement can be agreed then people are more likely to be motivated and committed to the work that is required, and hence be less stressed.

COUNSELLING STAFF

Working with different people who are experiencing stress often means guiding them and trying to make them see things in a slightly different way. Sometimes we do this by telling them specifically what needs to be done. Sometimes we try to sell the idea to them by demonstrating how much better it would be to do it in a particular new way. A third way is when the outcome is less certain but a problem or potential problem has been identified and we need some sort of joint problem-solving. When we are trying to encourage others to take responsibility for this problem-solving, we may wish to use the counselling method for guiding them. Where the problem is severe we should be well advised to refer them to professional counselling services.

Counselling is not the same as giving advice. It is part of the leader's or manager's art to enable other people to develop their skills and effectiveness by helping them to find solutions to problems and develop strengths of their own. The role of the counsellor is to provide a different perspective from which to try out ideas. Those being counselled need to find their own solutions and exercise their own responsibility. Neither the counsellor nor the counselled knows the 'answer' before the interview begins: it emerges from the process itself. This process can be effective only if the counsellor is willing to listen. Listening requires more than just allowing the other person to talk. There must be a willingness to believe that the other person has something to say and to make sure that you have understood it. This requires the counsellor to pay attention to the other and not to be distracted. It has to be clear that there is plenty of time for the discussion, with no furtive glances at the watch. The meeting must be private and free from interruption.

The style, warmth, integrity and authority of the counsellor are going to be the key to how effective the process is. There are several different formats or sequences for counselling that seem to work – one such sequence is shown in Table 6.1. Counselling is not just about getting someone to feel better or less stressed, it is also about getting people to perform better so they can contribute effectively to the work process. By finding a genuine solution to a problem there is a better chance of the solution being permanent.

Specialist counselling services can also offered by organisations. This may be in-house, with its associated issues of confidentiality, or outsourced to a separate institution, which may send someone to the place of work on a regular basis or when required. Organisations with occupational health departments tend to do it in-house; the nurse has historically often played this counselling role alongside his or her other duties.

MENTORING

Mentoring is another way of guiding people and may reduce the stress experienced by individuals trying to take on new work. Mentoring is a form of coaching that reproduces in a modern organisation the working relationship of skilled worker and apprentice by attaching a new recruit to an established member to induct, guide, coach and develop the recruit to full competence and performance. It is a particularly useful device for encouraging new recruits from different backgrounds or experiences, such as young people, those with disabilities, or those with no previous employment experience such as graduates. Mentoring can also be used to help someone think about and develop their career, become expert or to try to develop a creative team. Mentoring means:

Table 6.1 *Stages in a counselling interview*

---

1 *Factual interchange.* Focus on the facts of the situation first. Ask factual questions and give factual information. This provides a basis for later analysis.

2 *Exchange opinions.* Ask their opinions and feelings but do not offer any criticism or decisions, as you both need to understand the position more clearly.

3 *Joint problem-solving.* Ask them to analyse the situation described. Help by questioning and focusing, but it must be their analysis. Do not give answers.

4 *Decision-making.* The counsellor helps to generate alternative actions for the client to consider. Both are involved in deciding which to follow, but only the client can behave differently.

Based on Torrington and Weightman (1991)

- **m**anaging the relationship
- **e**ncouraging the protégé
- **n**urturing the protégé
- **t**eaching the protégé
- **o**ffering mutual respect
- **r**esponding to the protégé's needs.

Mentoring is increasingly used to ensure a diverse workforce. Mentoring people so they can be promoted has become a widely used method for encouraging those from minorities to reach senior levels within organisations.

ENSURING HEALTH AND SAFETY

Through ignorance, carelessness or neglect, an employer can endanger the health of those working in the organisation, as well as that of customers, visitors and local residents. Protecting both the physical and psychological well-being, including reduction of stress, of those whose lives the organisation affects is an important aspect of managing people. There is extensive legislation about health and safety matters that grows ever more extensive as new inventions, and new findings about old materials, create fresh hazards not covered by existing laws. The basic protection for many years was a series of Factory Acts, which were mainly directed at shielding workers from long hours and unsatisfactory space, ventilation and heating.

A development of the Factory Acts is the Control of Substances Hazardous to Health (COSHH) Regulations of 1988, which comprise 19 different regulations and at least four codes of practice. The Regulations require employers to:

- assess the risks to employees' health
- identify what precautions are needed to limit these risks
- introduce measures to control or nullify the risks
- ensure that control measures are used
- make sure that the appropriate procedures are followed
- ensure that equipment is regularly maintained
- carry out health surveillance
- inform staff of risks
- train staff to deal with hazards to health.

There is a danger that this system can become very bureaucratic and use up a lot of resources without really concentrating on the actual safety and well-being of the people at work. However, there is a real responsibility for each team leader and manager to ensure that all the staff working in their section, whether core or peripheral, are aware of any hazardous substances or procedures.

Many of these protections are now part of the EU's Social Charter on the rights of workers. The UK has not signed up to this charter but its recommendations are being introduced by many multinational companies, and so are likely to become the norm for British organisations.

Health and safety legislation has also been used in legal cases to do with employee stress at work. In 1994 Walker, a senior social worker, successfully took his employers, Northumberland County Council, to court. He was given compensation for the stress-related illness he suffered due to the unreasonable pressures at work. His work was not adjusted to his needs after he returned to work after a nervous breakdown. He then had another breakdown and was dismissed on health grounds. As he had already had a breakdown it could reasonably have been foreseen that his workload needed changing. Since this case there have been several more. The HSE booklet mentioned earlier may well lead to some more formal edicts on the responsibilities of organisations to prevent ill health through stress.

This chapter has tried to point out that stress is really an alarm bell indicating that something is felt to be wrong. Team leaders and line managers are best advised to deal with the underlying problems rather than offering soothing unctions. Solutions are likely to be longer-lasting and encourage more independent action from staff. It may be that staff are overworked, with long hours that allow little time and energy for the other parts of their lives. The wise employer and manager understands that, for sustainable performance, life has to be in balance and that requiring too much of employees will lead to burn-out. In terms of cost-effectiveness, the constant cost of recruitment and training new staff to replace 'worn out' employees is difficult to justify, to say nothing of the human cost.

ACTIVITIES

1   What are the main causes of stress in your department? Does everyone have something to call their own in their jobs? Is there someone in your department people can talk to, either formally or informally, when they are feeling overwhelmed? Do you encourage staff to develop life outside of work? Do you give them enough time to do so? What about yourself?

2   In the past year, which sorts of change have you experienced at work?

    First, think of the way individuals have coped. Can you think of someone who responds well to change? What about someone who responds badly to change? What characteristics would you say describe each of them?

    Second, think of the outcomes. Which of these were successfully achieved? Does anything distinguish these from the more problematic? When you want to introduce some new aspect to the work of your team, will you try using the questions above?

3   What are your stability zones? What are those of the people who work for you?

4   What are your career anchors? Have any of the people who work for you got unreasonable career anchors?

5   To whom could you go for advice and succour with problems at work?

6   Have you carried on doing some things through habit even though they are no longer strictly necessary? If so, is there some good reason for doing them – such as because you like doing them?

7   When would you use a counselling model to discuss something with a member of staff? Are there other times when it could be used? How would you ensure a reasonable amount of time and privacy?

8   Have you tried mentoring someone?

9   Have you ensured that all the rotas are within the permitted hours?

10   What are the hazardous substances and their associated procedures in your work? Does everyone know about this, including students and placements?

11   Peter Warr (2003) states that on average British managers spend 100 hours a month in meetings. What do you think consequences of this, in terms of stress, might be for them, their colleagues, the organisation? What can be done about it? If you are in a seminar group you might like to take this activity and really tease it out – many organisations would like to know the answer!

HAVE I MET THE OBJECTIVES?

1   What are some of the causes of work-related stress?

2   Describe symptoms of work-related stress.

3   How might an employer prevent work-related stress?

4   What are the difficulties associated with using the term 'stress'?

5   Can I describe some way of managing change?

6   Describe a sequence for counseling.

And finally ...

What would you do in Trish's position? Would you use any of the ideas in this chapter? I should probably try to get the members of staff together to discuss what is really irritating them and get them to suggest what we could do about them within the obvious limits of our resources. In trying to encourage a joint problem-solving approach, I should be aiming to bring about a more active approach to their moans. If there were specific members of staff who were particularly unhappy I should probably see them separately in a problem-solving or counselling mode.

FURTHER READING

My colleague Cary Cooper has a well-established reputation in researching, talking and writing on stress in organisations, so I would recommend his books.

Cooper C and Williams S (1994) *Creating Healthy Work Organizations*. Chichester, John Wiley.

The more personal Cooper C and Palmer S (2000) *Conquer Your Stress,* CIPD, is a small self-help booklet that is easy to use.

I would also recommend books by the clinical psychologist Dorothy Rowe, who writes very wisely and readably about various aspects of the human condition, from depression to the meaning of money. Try Rowe (1996) *Dorothy Rowe's Guide to Life*. London, Kogan Page.

Health and Safety Executive (2002) *Tackling Work-related Stress: A manager's guide to improving and maintaining employee health and well being.* This is the current state of debate within Britain for managers and team leaders. It is seen as a priority for the HSE.

Optimising the People Contribution

The Move from Compliance to Commitment

This chapter depends on political theory, particularly that dealing with the **control/participation dilemma** *and* **theories of power**. *The motivation theories examined in Chapter 12 are also relevant. The main practical applications discussed are* **managing conflict, teams, empowerment, valuing** *and* **morale**. *Material from Chapter 4 on organisational structures, Chapter 10 on leadership and Chapter 14 on performance appraisal are also relevant to these discussions. Specific examples in this chapter are the NHS, Hitler, and a coffee shop.*

OBJECTIVES

When you have finished reading this chapter you should be able to:

■ **describe a continuum from powerful leaders to powerful groups**

■ **understand the use of power in organisations**

■ **list possible sources of conflict within organisations**

■ **classify different power relationships in organisations**

■ **recognise several different sources of power in organisatons**

■ **discuss the factors that influence whether compliance or commitment is sought**

■ **describe several different ways of empowering people at work**

■ **name four ways of valuing people at work.**

Fiona's difficult decision

Fiona is 29 and runs the Bath office of a medium-sized PR agency. She has three people working for her in the office. Dave, who is slightly older than Fiona, was recruited three months ago. Fiona finds she has to spell everything out to Dave. He takes no initiatives. When given specific tasks his work is excellent, but Fiona sometimes feels it would be quicker and easier to do it herself rather than tell Dave what to do. Sometimes the Bath office is very busy and Fiona feels she could do with a more committed colleague. What should she do?

Should she wait for him to become more experienced? Assume he lacks confidence and boost him up? Delegate specific tasks and hope he fails, giving her the opportunity of replacing him? Have a serious talk with him about his work? Tell the boss at head office about her difficulties? Carry on giving the detailed job tasks to him?

The difference between compliance and commitment from one's colleagues is easy to distinguish. The dilemma for the manager or team leader is how much to use control and how much to seek participation from team members to ensure a committed and appropriate performance.

THE PLACE OF POLITICS IN ORGANISATIONS

As we increasingly depend on less formal kinds of influence in organisations it becomes more and more important to understand power and how it is used. Indeed, the very popularity of the phrase 'empowerment' in organisations shows the importance of this – see later in this chapter. Power is a property that exists in any organisation or system; politics is the way that power is put into action. Those who understand the subtleties of power in relationships are better able to get things done than those who are ignorant of them. Or, as the political theorist Robert A. Dahl so trenchantly puts it:

> The graveyards of history are strewn with the corpses of reformers who failed utterly to reform anything, of revolutionaries who failed to win power ... of anti-revolutionaries who failed to prevent a revolution – men and women who failed not only because of the forces arrayed against them but because the pictures in their minds about power and influence were simplistic and inaccurate.
>
> Dahl (1970, p15)

Organisations have power as one of their crucial dimensions, and only by understanding how power is distributed and deployed can members get things done. Leading and managing people inevitably includes an understanding of the use of power. The innovative idea or accurate diagnosis is insufficient without the means for its implementation. The analysis of power is an important part of understanding how groups work and how leadership is exercised.

Dahl is one of the political theorists who help us to an understanding of organisational politics. As he points out, this political behaviour comes from conflicting aims:

> If everyone were perfectly agreed on ends and means, no-one would ever need to change the way of another. Hence no relations of influence or power would arise. Hence no political system would exist. Let one person frustrate another in the pursuit of his goals and you already have the germ of a political system; conflict and politics are born inseparable twins.
>
> Dahl (1970, p59)

Pfeffer (1981, pp67–8) specifically looked at power in organisations. He suggests that the following elements produce conflict and the use of power in organisations:

- *interdependence* – where what happens to one person affects another, such as in joint activities. My work affects your work.

■ *inconsistent goals* – where there are different aims within an organisation. My aim might conflict with what you are trying to do.

■ *technologies* – differences will lead to conflict. For example, if you have one IT system and I have another, who should pay to make them compatible? Incidentally, this is often an underestimated cost of joint ventures and the amalgamation of organisations.

■ *scarcity of resources* – the greater the scarcity compared with demand, the more power and effort will be put into resolving the issue. If we both want to use the same piece of equipment we shall spend time trying to resolve a suitable rota of use.

All organisations have limited resources for their members, so we compete with each other for promotion and career development. On an everyday level, we shall be competing for a bigger budget, more space, newer equipment, more staff and a greater say over the direction of organisational policy. This competition causes the nature of political activity to vary according to the state of growth or decline of the organisation. With growth, there is more opportunity for individuals than in a stagnant state so the politics is likely to have more winners in a state of growth than in periods of stability or stagnation.

The control–participation dilemma

A useful model for trying to analyse the behaviour of team leaders and managers is that of Tannenbaum and Schmidt (1973), which suggests a continuum of behaviour by leaders and those who work for them. The continuum is given below, starting at one end and finishing at the other end of the balance of behaviours:

■ At one end, the leader makes all the decisions and announces them. Everyone is expected to comply.

■ The leader sells the decision.

■ The leader presents ideas and invites questions.

■ The leader presents tentative decisions, subject to change.

■ The leader presents problems and asks for suggestions and makes the decision.

■ The leader defines the limits and asks the group to make the decision.

■ At the other end, the leader permits the group to function within limits defined by others.

Variation along this continuum depends on the amount of control that the leader has over the led. It is also about the level of participation of the led. Individuals in the first half of the continuum would be team leaders and managers of a unitarist perspective. In the second half would be the leaders and managers of a pluralist perspective.

This type of model has given rise to the use of four defining words which differentiate the range of leaders:

■ tells

■ sells

■ consults

■ joins.

This brief summary is often used informally in organisations to describe a boss's behaviour. It simply describes the movement from enforced compliance to commitment.

Conflict

The reality of working in organisations is that conflict will appear. Whether this is seen positively or negatively depends on the nature of the conflict and on an individual's perspective. Those who hold a unitary perspective believe that organisations should be an integrated harmonious whole, one happy team. Those who hold a pluralist view believe that conflicts between sub-groups within an organisation are inevitable and can lead to useful discussion and innovation. Radicals with a Marxist view believe that conflict reflects the difference in power and control between the leaders and the led, and the struggle for power and control.

The possible sources of conflict have been summarised by Bryans and Cronin (1983) as:

- differences between organisational and individual goals – for example, seeing priorities differently
- differences between different teams, departments or groups – where they need to co-operate but feel the other group is not pulling its weight
- differences between the formal and the informal – for example, a felt violation of territory which may be formally given or developed over time
- differences between leaders and led – for example, a felt inequality of treatment
- differences between individuals and their job – for example, there may be a role conflict in the expectations of others
- differences between individuals – for example, when one person is dependent on the other to get their work done and the standard is not felt to be appropriate.

Possible ways in which team leaders and managers may deal with conflict, depending on the nature of the conflict, are to:

- clarify the goals and reinforce those that are agreed
- renegotiate the use of resources
- clarify the work of individuals by having a serious appraisal, redesigning the job and changing their level of responsibility
- change the nature of relationships to a more co-operative structure
- re-examine the formal structures of the organisation to see if they are appropriate, changing them where they are not and reinforcing them where they are. Examples are such things as organisation charts, communication channels, reporting relationships, and co-ordinating devices such as meetings.

Serious conflicts in organisations are often the starting point for change and can indicate the need for change. If you experience frequent conflict at work, it is worth having a good hard look to try to analyse why it occurs and what to do about it.

Power and control in organisations

In the past, management was seen as having to control what happened in the organisation, with careful control of the minute detail of each individual worker – see, for example, the early scientific management work of FW Taylor. More recently the management task is seen as leading, and has taken into account some of the humanistic psychology approaches to encourage staff to take more power and control of the details of their jobs. There is still, however, central management control of budgets and objectives. There is less control over the methods used to achieve the desired results. Organisation structures are about who should control what. Power is the extent of the real influence that people have in the organisation.

> An overwhelming characteristic of the British is a desire for fairness, see Morgan (1993) *History of Britain*. An example is the way the National Health Service (NHS) treats patients fairly and equally at the point of treatment. Similarly, the NHS has treated staff reasonably fairly with, for example, similar increases of pay across the country and professions. Morale and commitment is undermined when this felt fairness is eroded by vastly different increases in pay, changes in degrees of autonomy or misuse of small privileges such as rotas, breaks and types of work.

Etzioni (1975) compared a wide range of complex organisations and classified the nature of relationships within them, based on the differences in power and involvement.

Members of organisations differed in the way in which they complied with power:

- Coercive power relied on threats, sanctions and force – such as reduced food and comfort.
- Remunerative power involved manipulating rewards such as wages.
- Normative power relied on manipulating symbolic rewards such as esteem and prestige.

Members of organisations varied in their degree of commitment and involvement:

- Alienative involvement occurs when individuals are present against their wishes.
- Calculative involvement is where attachment is due to extrinsic rewards such as cash.
- Moral involvement occurs when individuals believe in the goals of the organisation.

Etzioni suggested that a particular kind of power usually goes with a particular kind of involvement:

- Coercive power goes with alienative involvement – for example, in prisons.
- Remunerative power goes with calculative involvement – for example, in many businesses and manufacturing.
- Normative power goes with moral involvement – for example, in charities and religious organisations, and businesses like the Body Shop.

Etzioni suggested that organisations that have matching power and involvement structures are more effective than those in which they are mismatched. This may account for the difficulty that some organisations have in implementing the current fashion for empowerment and facilitation. They may really be command and control organisations beneath the apparent new management style.

Sources of power available to organisation members

So far we have looked at the large-scale, organisation-wide aspects of power. What about the individual working in an organisation who wants to influence events? There are four main sources of power available to individuals and groups to exercise political influence: position, expertise, personal qualities, and political factors. The most obvious is the control of resources. Those who control what others need are in the position of relative power.

The bases of power were described in a classic study by French and Raven (1958). These are:

- reward – being able to give the other what he or she wants
- coercive – forcing him or her to do it
- referent – having desirable attributes that make people wish to refer to the leader
- legitimate – as opposed to illegitimate in the eyes of the followers
- expert – having an expertise that others want to use.

They argued that all these depend on the beliefs of the followers, they are interrelated and a leader can operate from a multiple base of power.

Using French and Raven's list as a starting point, the sources of power available to anyone in an organisation are listed in Table 7.1. Understanding these and using them to change what is decided or done is part of working in an organisation. Power is sometimes felt to be a

Table 7.1 *Sources of power*

1 Position	
Resources	Controlling access to what others need
	It includes materials, information, rewards, finance, time, staff, promotion, references
Delegation	Whether jobs are pushed down the hierarchy, are rights of veto retained?
Gatekeeper	Controlling information, relaxing or tightening rules, making life difficult or easy depending on the loyalty of individuals
2 Expertise	
Skill	Being an expert – having a skill others desire or need
Uncertainty	Those who can deal with a crisis become powerful until it's over
Indispensable	Through expertise or essential part of process
3 Personal qualities	
Motivation	Some seek power more than others
Physical	Being bigger or stronger than others. Statistically, leaders tend to be taller than the led
Charisma	Very rare indeed. Usually control of resources accounts for charisma
Persuasion skills	Making the most of other powers
4 Political factors	
Debts	Having others obliged from previous favours
Control of agenda	Ensuring meeting runs as you wish
Dependence	The power to remove oneself

Based on Torrington and Weightman (1989a)

negative thing in organisations, but access to resources and getting things done is, after all, what a leader or manager is being paid to do. This does not necessarily mean putting others down but it does mean maximising the power available to them to influence events appropriately. Examples of using one's power to influence things within the organisation are:

■ trying to increase the team's allocation of the budget and so keep extra facilities open

■ increasing the profile of the team or department so that the service is used more

■ trying to get the security staff to help with unwanted visitors

■ attending the meeting and being prepared to demonstrate why your action plan is more appropriate than the proposed one

■ through careful preparation, being able to argue your team's point of view in policy-making meetings.

John Stuart Mill, in his book on Liberty (1859) said:

The only purpose for which power can be rightly exercised over any member of a civilised community, against his will, is to prevent harm to others. His own good, either physical or moral, is not sufficient warrant.

Trying to understand who has power and how it is used will also enable people to work better in their organisations, since there is a constant shift of power as new partnerships develop. For example, joint ventures with other organisations shift the locus of power from the traditional hierarchy to those who can effectively influence the partners and represent the home organisation's agenda. An estate manager can suddenly rise in importance when land is being sold. Similar changes can happen when there is a change from having a central supply unit in an organisation to new supplier–customer partnerships. Instead of routine administration, the purchasing department has to develop collaborative webs of relationships across the departments and teams to negotiate appropriate supplies from a variety of suppliers.

EMPOWERMENT

All members of organisations need to understand the use of power to influence others. It is not just the prerogative of the mighty. With increased responsibility and accountability being devolved to the small team, section and individual, we all need to be able to influence what is going on. Everyone needs to understand how to manage people. This is often summed up in the concept of 'empowerment'. Increasingly in organisations there is talk of empowering individuals to take initiatives and responsibility. Empowering must include providing the resources to carry out an initiative and having the power to say no. Otherwise it can often feel to people as if the bosses are just asking them to do more, for less. Those who feel most empowered are those who are confident that they can influence others and have the power to get things done.

HITLER EMPOWERS HIS STAFF

Hitler believed in allowing his generals and ministers to get to put the bones and details on the strategy set by Hitler. He empowered them. They could solve the problems of implementation as they came to them without having to consult Hitler. He thought that as he was usually sitting in the Alps he would not see the real detailed problems that needed resolving to push the strategy forward. He had total trust in his staff at first and they were successful. Once this trust was lost, following the invasion of Russia when he felt the generals were unsympathetic to the war in the East, he did not allow them to make such detailed decisions. He consistently replaced the earlier generals and ministers with 'yes men' and this created problems. Hitler now got poor intelligence and was too remote to deal with the detailed problems of war. I have deliberately given this example to show that successful techniques of managing people are effective even where the objective is ghastly.

Source: Andrew Roberts *The Secrets of Leadership,* BBC2, 7 March 2003

If there is one concept from the human resources field that has become popular with senior managers, it is 'empowerment' – see, for example, Foy (1994). This simple idea means that employees at all levels are responsible for their actions and should be given the authority to make decisions about their own work. This is not just to make people more satisfied with their work but also to enable organisations to respond quickly. The advantages claimed for an empowered workforce are better services, flexibility, speed, cross-team and department links, improved morale, and compensation for limited career paths.

Empowerment is about ownership of the problem and the solution. True empowerment means that employees have the discretion to take decisions about what they feel it is appropriate to do at a particular time. This empowerment, presumably, also includes the right to be consulted about the nature of the empowerment proposed, and indeed the power to say no to empowerment.

One coffee shop has empowered each member of staff to give away some coffees every day. There is an allocation for each team member. They may choose to give it to someone if there is a mistake, a problem or where there is a personal celebration. The organisation has benefited because the customers feel personally treated and there has been a reduction in staff turnover, a constant problem in this sector. The staff have benefited because they feel empowered.

Typical elements of a system likely to ensure the success of an empowered workforce, from a management perspective, include:

- tolerance of errors
- enhanced communication
- generalist managers and staff
- giving yourselves time to develop confidence in each other
- sufficient resources to deliver some of the solutions that are generated
- performance evaluations drawn from a variety of sources
- variable rewards, including some group element.

Empowerment can really happen only where there are sufficient resources to take on any training that is necessary for individuals. Too often empowerment procedures are initiated as a substitute for sufficient resources to get on with the job. It also requires roles to be clearly defined and previous managers to give up some of their power.

It is worth thinking about what is in it for each empowered person. It could include such things as:

- a team bonus
- increased recognition
- security of employment
- the satisfaction of developing new talents.

Very often, claims to have empowered the staff fall well short of these ideals. The difficulties with empowerment from the organisation's point of view are a greater potential for chaos, a lack of clarity, breakdown of hierarchical control, and demoralisation of those staff who do not want more responsibility. But without there being something in it for the staff they will feel very put upon, the whole initiative will sink in a flurry of accusations about the latest fashion and fad, and it will not work. Empowerment should not feel like dumping! Hyman and Cunningham (1996) found that empowerment in several UK organisations was in many cases little different from earlier prescriptions for job enlargement, or at best job enrichment. Where employees could exercise discretion and influence over their immediate tasks, the overall parameters within which they operate were in many cases not so flexible.

VALUING: CONSIDERATION, FEEDBACK, DELEGATION AND PARTICIPATION

If staff are to work so they willingly contribute their efforts and commitment, there has to be something in it for them. Clearly, the salary and interest of the work are important parts of this. But where extraordinary commitment is given there is usually something more. This may be because the work itself is seen to matter, because of the unusually effective leadership of the manager, or because the individual member of staff feels valued, or all of these.

DEBATE – RELATION BETWEEN STAFF MORALE AND CHANGE

'Dealing with change' and 'frequent change' have become common expressions within organisations. Another common phrase is the term 'staff morale'. The relation between morale and change is debated. Some maintain 'morale' is too vague a term to be useful. Others feel it expresses all the softer aspects of commitment.

Most organisations are suffering from innovation overload. This is often happening just when staff morale is lowered because of redundancies and a general levelling of staff differentials. Staff respond to this in different ways. Some withhold commitment – see Scase and Goffee (1989) on how middle managers remove their commitment; some withdraw from extra work; some increase their militancy; some simply bow their heads and resolve to work harder – again – like Boxer the horse in George Orwell's *Animal Farm*.

So what can a team leader or line manager do about it? It is not usually possible to reduce the innovation overload. But perhaps there is something that could be done about morale. What do you think?

Where people are feeling valued there seems to be a strong, positive morale amongst the team. How does this come about? There are several ways that people can help to improve the morale of their team by valuing each other. It is a complex social interaction and has something to do with valuing people as individuals as well as for the jobs they do. We (Torrington and Weightman, 1989b) found four types of valuing. They are consideration, feedback, delegation, and consultation.

- *Consideration*. People tend to feel a lack of consideration from their colleagues when the organisational culture is one of keeping to oneself rather than one of talking to one's colleagues. Even at the simplest level such things as making eye contact in corridors, saying 'Good morning' and smiling can make a difference. Evidence from our research in a variety of organisations suggests that most people would welcome more of these small gestures at work. Lack of consideration may be one of Hertzberg's dissatisfiers – see Chapter 12.

- *Feedback*. All too often the exhausting effort that people put into their jobs seems to lack any perceptible output. People need feedback from their colleagues. This can take the form of a formal performance appraisal, dealt with in Chapter 14. It can also be informal, such as taking an interest in what a colleague is doing. It is not hierarchy-bound; a junior saying 'That's great! How do you do it?' can be very pleasing.

- *Delegation*. Members of staff are valued when responsibility is delegated to them, but this involves delegating real responsibility, not just giving people jobs to do. Individuals must be trusted to make decisions about when, whether and how to do things, not just given the job of completing tasks. Otherwise they are likely to work to rule and feel like machines. Responsibility cannot be delegated and then taken away without devaluing confidence and future effectiveness. They also need sufficient resources actually to do the task.

- *Consultation and participation*. Due to the innovation overload it is difficult to create the conditions in which people will respond with enthusiasm to change. However, if they are to respond with commitment rather than stoical compliance then some sort of participation in at least the 'how', even if not the 'what', will help. Although it takes longer to reach a decision if more people are involved, they are at least committed to trying to make it work if they have been involved in the decision-making process. Whereas, if you do not include people in the decision-making process it will take much longer to persuade them afterwards and they will often use all their creative powers to prove it cannot be done.

Another principle that reflects these issues is trust. Where people trust each other they are more likely to take a risk with each other and accept the other's word. The enemies of trust, according to Galford and Drapeau (2003) are:

- inconsistent messages
- inconsistent standards
- misplaced benevolence
- false feedback
- ignoring difficulties
- rumours in a vacuum
- consistent organisational underperformance.

Any and all of these factors can reduce the level of trust between people. The reverse of these factors leads to increased trust. Trust has to be two-way. The leader and the led have to trust each other before the quick informal methods of communication and action can be relied upon. Where there is little trust, people have to rely on the formalities and this is always more cumbersome. This is further explored in Chapter 11 under the heading Credibility.

This chapter has looked at some of the political concepts that can be used to analyse behaviour in organisations and then manage people. Using this sort of analysis alongside the psychology and sociology models gives a fuller picture. It is like using different probes to come up with different evidence on the same subject. In practice the different models can be used to analyse different problems. For example, if you are having problems with the boss, you might use material in Part 1 of this book to understand his or her individuality, or use material from this chapter to analyse his or her use/abuse of power. The balance of power between the manager and the managed, the leader and the led, has a great deal to do with whether people comply with demands or commit themselves to finding better ways of working.

'Leadership' is currently a popular word in HR and management circles. There have been many studies of leadership behaviour but it is still a confused area – as we shall see in Chapter 10. Some of this confusion is because of the aspects of power, authority and control implicit in the relationship of leader and led. The control–participation dilemma mentioned at the beginning of this chapter shows the interdependence of the leader and the led and the balance of power between them. Compliance or commitment is the result.

ACTIVITIES

1   What conflict at work have you experienced recently?

    Does it happen over the same things, or similar things, each time?

    Does something need changing?

    If so, what?

2   Which of the sources of power in Table 7.1 have you used?

    Which others do you think you might use in the future?

3   JM Barrie wrote the play *The Admirable Crichton* in 1902. It tells the tale of an aristocratic family shipwrecked on a desert island. The authority of the head of the family rapidly deteriorates and the role of the leader is gradually taken on by Crichton, the family butler. When they are rescued the roles revert back to their original positions. What do you think might have been Crichton's sources of power on the island? What were the sources of power of the family father back home?

4   See if you can answer all the 'Have I met the objectives?' questions below.

HAVE I MET THE OBJECTIVES?

1   Describe a continuum from powerful leaders to powerful groups.

2   What do you understand about the use of power in organisations?

3   List possible sources of conflict within organisations.

4   What are Etzioni's three types of power?

5   Name three different sources of power in organisations.

6   What is empowerment?

7   Name four types of valuing people at work.

And finally ...

What do you think Fiona should do? Could she use any of the ideas in this chapter? I should probably look at some of the ideas about empowerment and valuing if I were Fiona. It might be useful to have a discussion with her boss to see if there are any specific development opportunities within the organisation that would help Dave. I might also seek the help of the HR department, if the organisation has one.

FURTHER READING

Pfeffer J (1981) is a classic discussion of this area. Another classic is Lukes S (1975) *Power: A radical view* (Studies in Sociology). Macmillan.

Peter LJ (1969) *The Peter Principle*, New York, Morrow, is a classic humorous take on the subject. The author suggests that people get promoted to their level of incompetence – according to the 'Peter Principle'.

It is also worth looking at the currently fashionable management books to get a flavour of up-to-date thinking. Airport bookshops are usually a good source.

There are various readable novels about the abuse of power in organisations. See, for example, *Disclosure* (1992) by Michael Crichton, which was also made into a film, about sexual harassment. *Anonymous Primary Colors* (1996), also a film, is a fictitious account of Bill Clinton's rise to be President of the USA.

Finding and Selecting People

This chapter relies on psychology theories, Chapters 1 and 2, and the concept of socialisation, see Chapter 3. This is a practical chapter that deals with **selection, recruitment, interviewing, induction** *and* **peripheral staff**. *There are specific examples from the New Scientist, Harry Ramsden, Pret à Manger and the Hawthorne studies.*

OBJECTIVES

When you have finished reading this chapter you should be able to:

- **list ways of identifying vacancies**

- **describe different ways of selecting staff**

- **discuss the nature of letters of offer and contracts of employment**

- **discuss the importance of initiating new employees**

- **understand and explain the basic elements of recruitment and selection.**

Gita's announcement

Gita, the reception manager for a large hotel, came into the office on Monday to say she was giving in her notice to leave. She has got a job at a nearby hotel which, although it pays no better salary, fits the weekly hours of work into four day shifts rather than five. This rota suits Gita rather better, because she is attempting to gain a further qualification to improve her basic training and the college-based course runs all day on Wednesday and the new hotel can guarantee her that day off.

As her immediate boss, what do you think is the appropriate next step? Questions such as do we want to fight to keep her? Usually not, in the public sector, because there is a tradition of individuals' deciding their own career moves. But things are different in other organisations, where some individual negotiating may go on at this point. If we want to keep her, can we find the flexibility? If we decide not to try to keep her, what are the procedures for handing in notice? Who should be asked? Then comes the task of thinking about whether and how to replace Gita. Questions such as does this job need doing? Do we want it done in the same way? Do we want to reorganise the team? What sort of person do we want?

This chapter is about what to do when there appears to be a vacancy in the organisation. This is usually when an existing staff member leaves, but it can also be when there are plans for expanding or changing a service. Very few of us ever have the task of selecting a completely new team from scratch. Most of us experience the selection of people as one-off events. Although the HR/personnel department will have tried and tested procedures for dealing with this, there are important aspects of the procedure that involve the line manager or team leader. Only the line manager or team leader can know in detail the work that needs doing. It is also an opportunity to bring in changes if they are required. The team leader needs to be involved for another important reason. When we apply for a job we all expect to meet the people we shall be working with. At the very least, an interviewee for a job would expect to meet his or her immediate boss before accepting a job.

IDENTIFYING VACANCIES

The business of replacing or recruiting someone is an opportunity to rethink what we want the content of the job to be. Do we want the same work or something different? Do we want to split the job into a different combination with other members of staff? Is this an opportunity to move people around? The process of recruiting and selecting someone is also the point at which strategic ideas of restructuring and change can be put into effect. It can mean reducing one aspect of the work and increasing the commitment to other parts of the job. For example, a move from servicing existing customers to looking for new ones in a sales team may be easier to implement with a new member of staff specifically recruited for this purpose.

Many organisations have an overall strategy on staffing that whenever someone leaves a post the question is raised by senior staff as to whether that post really needs refilling. In a climate of cost-cutting and reducing staff numbers the strategic question is often received at the operational level as: 'How can you justify this post? Surely you can manage without him or her or with someone less qualified or experienced by reorganising and managing more efficiently.' This can be very irritating, to say the least, for busy staff who see a colleague leaving.

How do I start?

Once you have decided there is a need for recruitment, how do you get started? The HR/personnel approach to selection is to try to be as systematic as possible and to reduce the costs of doing so as far as possible. Traditionally this has been to look at a systematic description of the tasks required in the job and then to specify the personal attributes of the individual as applied to these tasks. This does rather make the assumption that the work to be done, and the individual to do it, will not change very much over the years. Some organisations using HRM have tried to overcome the difficulty of predicting the future requirement for change in the job by looking at the personal attributes of individuals to see whether they have the potential for change and development. This approach assumes that these attributes are measurable and predictable. Like so many aspects of working with people, there is no perfect system and each of us is likely to prefer a slightly different model. What I have given here is the tried and tested personnel approach to selection with some of the more frequently used HRM methods. Testing personal attributes is a more sophisticated and less assured process, which is probably best devised by the psychology professionals. Certainly many of the techniques require specific training – for example the well known personality questionaire MBTI. A review of the issues involved in selection is provided by Iles and Salaman (1995).

What do we need?

The first tasks in appointing new staff are to work out what the job requires and what sort of candidiate would be suitable to carry it out. This involves the following:

- Consider the longer-term aspects of the job, such as future plans for the organisation and section and the distribution of competencies and age within the organisation. Will there be a permanent need for someone doing this sort of job?
- Decide what work needs to be done by reviewing the job description or using a competencies approach. Having a vacancy is a good opportunity for introducing

change, so it is worth having a good think at this point rather than rushing in to appoint another person just like the one who has left: Gita in our example. Indeed, anything other than another Gita maybe what you are looking for!

■ When drawing up the job specification, it is better to include phrases like 'To do ... and to carry out ...' rather than 'responsibility for ...' or 'to assist with ...'. If you use the second two alternatives, you imply that the job does not really stand on its own.

What do we want from this job?

The second task is to draw up a job description. The conventional way of drawing up a job description, well described in ACAS (1994), would be to consider the following points:

■ the main purpose of the job – written in one sentence. If you cannot find a main purpose, then the job needs reviewing

■ the main tasks of the job – using active participles like 'cleaning', 'writing', 'repairing' to describe what is done rather than vague terms such as 'in charge of' or 'deals with'

■ the scope of the job – the importance of the job to the organisation. This can be done by describing the value of equipment or materials handled, the degree of precision required and the number of people supervised.

This format, sometimes called job analysis, is well suited to using a competencies approach – where the statements lead on to descriptions of the behaviours that the job holder would need to exhibit in order to do the things described.

What sort of person do we want?

The third task is to draw up a person specification, which is where the knowledge, skills and abilities of the ideal candidate are described. The simplest method of drawing up this specification is to think in terms of the technical skills and knowledge the job holder will need in order to be able to do the things listed in the job description. Then think of the interpersonal, generic competencies he or she will need to be able to function in the job. The important thing is to set an appropriate level for these characteristics for a particular job. Too high a specification may lead to no suitable candidate being found. Too low a specification may underestimate the problems associated with the job being done badly. Two well-established classifications exist to help this process: Rodgers' seven-point plan and Munro Fraser's five-fold grading system – see Table 8.1. For jobs where lists of competencies exist, these can be very useful for drawing up a person specification.

How are we going to reward them?

Fourth, you need to make decisions about the terms and conditions associated with the job. In most instances, this will be done in consultation with the personnel or HR department, whose task is to ensure some comparability across departments and institutions.

In a rational, systematic organisation there would be a logical examination of the real needs of the section for the work to be done, perhaps using some of the methods given above. This would be followed by an assessment of how many people there were doing the work and some decision about whether there was a need for further staffing. However, nowadays the whole issue can become more political. Management in all its various guises has so emphasised the need to cut staff numbers that a backlash is developing of defending jobs. Sometimes it is necessary to point out what would not be done if a post were not refilled or retained.

Table 8.1 *Person specifications*

The seven-point plan

1 *Physical make-up*: health, appearance, bearing and speech
2 *Attainments*: education, qualifications, experience
3 *General intelligence*: intellectual capacity
4 *Special aptitudes*: mechanical, manual dexterity, facility in use of words and figures
5 *Interests*: intellectual, practical, constructional, physically active, social, artistic
6 *Disposition*: acceptability, influence over others, steadiness, dependability, self-reliance
7 *Circumstances*: any special demands of the job, such as ability to work unsocial hours, travel abroad, etc

Adapted from Rodger (1952)

The five-fold grading system

1 *Impact on others*: physical make-up, appearance, speech and manner
2 *Acquired qualifications*: education, vocational training, work experience
3 *Innate abilities*: quickness of comprehension, aptitude for learning
4 *Motivation*: individual goals, consistency and determination in following them, success rate
5 *Adjustment*: emotional stability, ability to stand up to stress, ability to get on with people

Adapted from Munro Fraser (1950)

As an example, one organisation that I visited had a decision at top level that all posts with 'assistant' or 'deputy' in the title would be abolished. This led to all sorts of ingenious retitling and the drawing up of lists of major responsibilities and tasks that would not have been performed if the people in these posts were lost. The most astute operators used the stated aims of the institution as the starting point for their list of tasks that could not be done without the 'assistants' and 'deputies'.

Is this job suitable for flexible working?

The fifth consideration is of core and peripheral issues, such as whether a full-time, permanent core worker is wanted or a part-time, temporary peripheral member of staff is to be considered. There are management issues associated with these decisions. Many organisations have become very enthusiastic about employing part-time, temporary or contract staff, as it allows the organisation to have the staff at busy periods with the minimum of financial cost. However, there are other costs – the less commitment one makes to a member of staff the less they will make in return. A peripheral member of staff can require more managing and organising. This burden often falls on those who work alongside the temporary member because they know where things live, who needs what sort of attention, and the details of working practice – and also because they are there when the question is asked. So the management of peripheral staff is often through default done by the more junior, permanent staff. However, the peripheral appointment maintains flexibility over future changes in demand or type of work that may be done.

At the end of this sequence you should have made some decisions about whether to recruit and what sort of job and person you are looking for. It is important that the process does not unfairly discriminate on the basis of gender, marriage or race, as this is illegal. It is not good practice, and is illegal, to discriminate on the basis of age, sexuality, disability or religion, as this will reduce the number of suitable people you have to choose from.

RECRUITMENT METHODS

Recruitment is the business of attracting sufficient suitable candidates for the job at a reasonable cost. There are various methods of recruiting people, which are listed in Table 8.2. The best method is the one that produces the most suitable candidate within reasonable cost restraints.

This early stage of the recruitment process involves both the organisation and the individual sending messages to each other, so there is a mutual exchange and negotiation (Herriot, 1989). We can probably all remember examples of job advertisements that attracted us to apply, and others that were very off-putting. The nature of the recruitment literature does influence who applies for the job. It deserves careful attention if we want to attract the right sort of people.

It is worth considering using word of mouth methods of recruitment, such as phoning contacts or acquaintances who might know of someone looking to move jobs or return to work. This can often lead to a good fit of personal qualities. It has also been established that people recruited by word of mouth tend to stay longer (Jenkins, 1986). However, there is a danger of selection being based on 'like' recruiting 'like' and of ending up with a department of clones. It can also lead to discriminating against those who are not part of the network – and it may be illegal.

The HR/personnel department usually deals with the administration of recruitment – such things as placing advertisements, sending application forms and job descriptions to potential candidates, receiving the completed forms, and answering general telephone enquiries. Line managers need to ensure that the HR/personnel department knows of any special recruitment considerations for this post, such as the necessity of advertising in a particular trade journal well known for job advertisements.

Table 8.2 *Methods of recruiting candidates*

Commercial employment agencies
Headhunters
Internal advertising
Job centres
Local newspapers, radio, TV and cinemas
Local schools and colleges
National newspapers
Notice for public to see
Recruitment consultants
Recruitment fairs
Specialist and professional papers
The Officers Association
Trade unions
University appointment boards
Web

The *New Scientist* carries many advertisements of vacancies for research assistants and technicians in the laboratories of hospitals and universities. *The Economist* has adverts for jobs in international agencies.

The advantages of the HR/personnel department dealing with the administration of recruitment is that some sort of consistency between departments can exist, with a corporate approach for differing posts. HR/personnel, moreover, actually have people to deal with the phone calls and paperwork as part of their jobs – whereas you as a team manager might find that you were constantly called away from work if you tried to do it yourself.

DIFFERENT WAYS OF CARRYING OUT THE SELECTION PROCESS

Having compiled a list of candidates who are interested in the job, the task now is to select one of them. The complexity and permanence of the job will be reflected in the nature of the selection procedure. For a straightforward job, a simple selection interview usually suffices. For more complex jobs, a variety of selection procedures are used – some of which are listed below. The important thing is always to involve the immediate supervisor in the selection procedure to ensure that he or she is committed to welcoming the new worker and that the new worker has the opportunity of assessing whether he or she could work with the supervisor.

Harry Ramsden, the fish and chip restaurant company, gave pre-interview training to long-term unemployed people because they found that such people were very committed when taken on in Manchester. The five-day course involved food hygiene, customer care and confidence-building mock job interviews at the local college. When the real interviews were held the managers were not told which applicants had been on the course.

Here is a list of some of the most common types of selection procedures, with some of their associated advantages and disadvantages.

Application forms

These provide the basic information needed for an initial trawl prior to short-listing. They can also form the basic starting point of the personnel record. They need to be designed for easy use, with the opportunity for individuals to offer additional material where they want. Usually there is a standard organisation-wide form for you to use. Check you are not asking illegally for information – for example marital status, number of children or race. It is important that you ask for the information that you are going to use to make the initial sifting. For example, if some particular qualification or experience is required it needs to be asked for.

Assessment centres

This is where a number of short-listed candidates undergo a range of selection procedures, activities including group exercises, and individual interviews. The value lies in the variety of evidence collected; but assessment centres are expensive to run both in time and in money so are usually reserved for critical senior appointments such as chief executives or where selection for expensive training is being considered – for example management training.

The ultimate assessment centre is practised by the sandwich chain Pret à Manger which has a job-experience day where all candidates come and work for a day and are then judged on their performance. Indeed, all those working alongside the candidate are given a vote after it has been explained what the consequences of selecting on various criteria may be. This was established to reduce staff turnover and proved successful.

Curriculum Vitae (CVs)

These are similar to application forms, except that the candidates select their own ways of presenting data about themselves and their careers. There are now commercial companies and websites offering help in the presentation of career experience, emphasising the competencies demonstrated at work. There can be real differences between people, but sometimes the only difference is in the quality of presentation in their CVs. It can be helpful to candidates if you indicate what you are looking for, so they can tailor their CVs to your needs and save a lot of reading on your part.

Health check-ups

There are various kinds of health checks that can be asked for, from simply asking whether there are any health problems to the full-blown, detailed health assessment that the Premier division football clubs order before signing a new player. The decision is usually based on how physically fit the individual needs to be, how crucial the post is, how long the job is expected to last, and how much it will cost to get a replacement.

Interviews

Whenever research is done on evaluating whether selection interviews are effective in selecting the right candidate, they are found to be unreliable – yet most selection processes include an interview. They remain popular partly because they are an important part of the initiation ritual. Is anyone really going to offer or take a job without some sort of face-to-face conversation? It is also important for everyone involved in the decision to gather in one place to see how the decision falls. This aspect of ritual is ignored at one's peril!

How can you get the best from an interview?

- Preparation – compare the candidates with the job and person specification. What do you need to ask more about? Prepare some questions; these should concern abilities or experience and be related to the job rather than being personal questions. What questions are the candidates likely to ask? Can you answer them? Look after the housekeeping: make sure you have a quiet room, free from interruption, as well as someone to greet the candidates and give instructions on how to find you.

- Conducting the interview – the key is to strike a balance between formality and friendliness. Describe what is going to happen. Start with easy questions for the candidate to reply to, such as what does he or she do in the current job. The flow of the interview is the interviewer's responsibility. To encourage the flow, use approaches such as 'I was particularly interested in …'; to discourage the flow, use phrases like 'I should prefer if we could move on to …' Eye contact and nodding will keep candidates talking; looking at your watch or your papers will shut them up. It is worth taking notes openly during the interview. Towards the end ask the candidate if there is anything he or she would like to know and try to answer any questions that arise. Tell candidates when they are likely to hear the outcome of the process and ensure that someone sorts out travel expenses and provides a tour of the workplace if this has not been done before.

■ Immediately after the interview, make notes of your impressions. To what extent do the candidates meet your specification? Have their career patterns shown appropriate development and progress?

Recruitment agencies

These agencies are sometimes called 'headhunters'. They can handle some of the preliminary recruitment and selection processes, such as advertisements, application forms and testing. They are often very helpful in recruiting peripheral staff. In specialised fields, such as sales and computing, they are particularly useful as they maintain contacts with individuals over periods of years. However, the final stage of selection should be performed in-house, except for a very temporary post, as the individual does need to 'fit in'. They are also informally called 'headhunters' as they approach people who are currently employed in other organisations to see if they would wish to make a move.

References

This is where some previous boss or educationalist writes a testimonial about the candidate. Sometimes referees are asked to answer specific questions, sometimes references are completely open-ended. They are frequently used in public sector employment, but are almost unheard of elsewhere. They often tell you more about the writer than the written about. Their main purpose is to confirm judgements and information formed elsewhere. Perhaps their most useful function is with young candidates who have had little or no work experience, where some judgement about their potential from those who know them, such as schools and universities, might inform the selection procedure. They should be taken up, or used, only with the candidate's permission.

Selection tests

These are tests of attainment and performance related to the skills necessary to do the job. It is important that a prescribed test really does test the skills that are needed to do the job and does not discriminate unfairly. The tests need to be selected very carefully as many are out of date. More controversial is the use of psychological tests – psychometrics – which look at general intelligence, personality and attitudes. They may be useful for young people with no track record to assist in judging potential. B&Q use an online recruitment system with psychometrics, including immediate feedback, to generate a database of potential recruits. This type of testing should be done only by carefully trained people.

SELECTION DECISION-MAKING

Having generated the written evidence about the candidates and in almost all cases conducted interviews, you now need to decide to whom you will offer the post. Some system of comparing the results with your original criteria needs to be set up either formally or informally. The advantage of having a slightly more formal system is that you can defend yourself against claims of discrimination more easily than if you have just said something like 'I really liked her because I think she'll fit in.' This is not to say you should not consider the informal 'feel' about the suitability of a candidate, but you do need to be able to demonstrate to another that your selection decision is reasonable and not just prejudiced. One way of doing so is to prepare a sheet of paper with the main criteria for selection along one side and the names of the candidates across the top, and tick when you have evidence that they have the necessary competence. Another method is to sort candidates into 'possibles' and 'probables' and then have a good look at the 'probables'.

It is obvious that the selection must be done fairly. In addition to the social and legal obligations there are increasing economic and demographic reasons to avoid unfair bias. You may not get enough suitable people if you do not select from a wide section of society. The areas where discrimination most commonly occur are in job advertisements, recruitment procedures, promotion, training and transfer policies. It is the responsibility of the HR/personnel department to monitor these, and help with specific problems.

The most important legal edicts on gender discrimination are the Equal Pay Act 1970, the Sex Discrimination Act 1975 and the Sex Discrimination (Indirect Discrimination and Burden of Proof) Regulations 2001. The Equal Pay Act was designed to stop discrimination in terms and conditions between men and women. 'Equal pay for equal worth' is how this is interpreted. This means that the two parties quoted in a legal case have to be working for the same employer, at the same establishment. The Sex Discrimination Act aimed to remove discrimination in non-contractual areas of employment and the indirect discrimination seen in such areas as advertising – for example 'Those under six foot need not apply'. This means you cannot prefer to promote one gender, or to develop only men or women, and there has to be demonstrably equal access to experience.

The Race Relations Act 1976 and the Fair Employment (Northern Ireland) Act 1989 follow very similar lines. The Equal Opportunities Commission and the Commission for Racial Equality are specialist organisations that provide help in this area. Your HR/personnel department or local Citizens' Advice Bureau can all help with advice in these areas. It is important to ensure that the selection procedures give people a genuine opportunity to prove their worth, including those with disabilities. The decision-making in selection happens at three main points: first, when drawing up a short-list for interview from the initial application forms and CVs; second, when testing and interviewing; third, the final selection at the end of the procedure. All three stages need to comply with the anti-discrimination laws and should be fair.

DEBATE – MANAGING THOSE LEFT AFTER A REORGANISATION

Reorganisation, mergers and takeovers lead to some very particular types of selections. Very often there is redundancy, early retirement and relocating of staff. There may also be the reselection of existing staff for the future organisation's structure, and everyone has to reapply for jobs. As well as the normal need for systematic selection there is the need to address the insecurity and sheer frustration that many individuals feel during this time. This selection process needs a different period of induction to deal with those who are left after a period of redundancies and early retirements. Those who take a unitarist view will emphasise the importance of the team and the leader and pulling together in the new organisation. Those with a pluralist view will ensure that individuals feel supported. What do you think would be the difference in how those with a hard management approach, 'command and control', and those with a 'transitional' leadership approach would be to getting things going after a period of redundancies?

DRAFTING LETTERS OF OFFER AND CONTRACTS OF EMPLOYMENT

Usually the HR/personnel department sends out the formal letters of offer of employment. When an offer is accepted they will usually deal with all the administration. This involves areas such as the formal contract of employment, health and safety regulations, pay scales, pensions and starting dates. Everyone needs to have a formal contract of employment under Part 1 of the Employment Protection Consolidation Act 1981 amended in the Trade Union Reform and Employment Rights Act 1993. The Employment Relations Act 1999 is about fairness at work and particularly covers part-time and fixed contract employees to ensure they have similar treatment to full-time permanent staff. Table 8.3 lists some of the usual items in a contract of employment. Some people choose to send out more informal stuff about the department with this mailing. However, in large establishments this may not be advisable as the bureaucracy can get very bogged down. The important thing is to ensure that the selected person knows when, where, and to whom to report on starting the job.

INDUCTING THE NEW MEMBER OF STAFF

The first few days or weeks of a new job are usually bewildering and amazing. Remember the mixture of excitement and terror? This needs to be picked up on. There may be a formal induction programme or handover period but there are also informal housekeeping matters that need attention, particularly in a busy workplace. If this is a person's first job he or she has everything to learn, and not very much will be expected in the initial stages. More experienced people will also need support as they have no familiarity with the new workplace and so will not know very simple things about systems and procedures. Make sure that someone is named to take them round, introduce them, answer any questions and accompany them to coffee and lunch breaks. This person is sometimes called the mentor.

Table 8.3 *Contract of employment*

Basic facts
Name of employer
Where work will take place
When to start
How much will be paid
When it will be paid
Job description

Conditions
Hours of work
Holiday entitlement
Holiday and sickness pay
Pensions
Length of notice employer and employee need to give
Length of job for temporary posts
Disciplinary rules

Foreign travel more than once per month
Period of work outside UK
Currency of pay
Terms and conditions of return to UK

Most employers will not include all these, but they are typical of good practice. An
employee has the legal right to receive a written statement of the terms of employment.

'Induction' is the term used to cover the more formal introduction to the organisation and would usually be arranged by the HR/personnel department. It would normally include an introduction to the organisation, with a senior member of staff reiterating the main goals of the organisation or department. Aspects of health, safety and conduct would also be covered. Then comes the more specific introduction to the tasks the individual will be doing and how these fit in with other people's work. Depending on the complexity of the task and the number of people involved, this induction process can last anything from an hour to a month. For very senior posts this is often called 'handover' rather than induction.

As well as the induction of the newcomer there is also more informal socialisation, which deals with aspects of coming to belong to the group. It is worth remembering that a great deal of learning that takes place at work takes place in the informal setting of the group, where members nudge each other into behaving in particular ways. For example, there will be norms about dress codes that are subtle variations on the formal rules – and these need learning. There will be norms of how to speak to one's colleagues, what sorts of coffee breaks to have and when to go home. All will need learning. The balance of formal and informal induction leads to an individual fitting in with the new workplace as soon as possible.

In the Hawthorne experiments, which looked at various ways of improving productivity within an electrical factory in the 1930s, referred to in Chapter 1, group pressures were found to be stronger than financial rewards for changing the behaviour of individuals. The group developed its own pattern of norms that were:

- not to be a rate buster – not to produce at too high a rate compared to others
- not to be a chiseller – not to produce at too low a rate compared to others
- not to be a squealer – not to say anything to supervisors or management that might harm other members of the group
- not to be officious – of those with authority, such as inspectors, not to take advantage of their seniority.

This chapter has looked at the conventional advice about a systematic approach to recruiting new staff. Frequently the actual experience of recruitment is less systematic and can be based on an immediate response to a need, or some fascination with current fashion for psychometric testing, handwriting analysis, measures of compatibility or technique. All of these may well help the process, but in the long term taking a systematic approach using a variety of techniques probably results in a more robust employing organisation.

ACTIVITIES

The following questions can be used as an exercise or applied to a real situation such as selecting someone to join your seminar group, shared house, sports team, work team, or to appoint an essay writer for your course!

1   Do we need an extra person in our team or can we rearrange the work between us? What future plans do we have for this section? What work do we want doing? What sort of person would we need to do this sort of work? Do we want a full-time, permanent person or a part-time, temporary appointment?

2   Do we need any special skills from the person we recruit for this post? Do any of us know someone who might be interested and appropriate?

3   How much time and effort can we give to this selection? What are the consequences of a wrong appointment? Who should be involved in the selection procedure? How can we match our findings with our specification?

4   Are we discriminating unfairly? Are we unintentionally discriminating by the contacts we have? Is what we are doing legal?

5   Who is responsible for administering the letter of appointment and contract of employment in our place? Do I want to contact the person before they start work?

6   If we are expecting a new member of staff, have we thought of the following: What day and time are we expecting them? Have we arranged for someone to be free for a suitable length of time to explain things? Who will be the new member of staff's named mentor for the first few weeks'?

HAVE I MET THE OBJECTIVES?

1   What are the five steps to take when identifying vacancies at work?

2   Can I describe five different methods of selecting staff?

3   What is the nature of letters of offer and contracts of employment?

4   Why is it important to induct new employees carefully?

5   Can I explain the basic elements of recruitment and selection?

And finally ...

What would you do about Gita? Could you use the process described in the activities? I should probably start by asking how critical Gita is to the team. How hard should we try to keep her? If she is difficult to replace and we need her skills then what can we offer to keep her? Would Wednesday as a day for training be sufficient? Does this cause problems for others? Does it set some difficult precedents or is it a good example of individual flexibility?

If we assume that Gita is leaving it is necessary to ensure that all the right procedures for handing in notice are complied with and that a suitable acknowledgement of Gita's service is made. Would you use the material in this chapter to respond to Gita leaving? If so, what? I feel that, as this is a very practical chapter, most of what is here could very easily address the question of what to do about replacing Gita. I would start at the beginning and work through the chapter until we either had decided not to replace Gita, or had done so.

FURTHER READING

ACAS (1994) *Recruitment and Induction*. London, ACAS. Available from ACAS, PO Box 16, Earl Shilton, Leicester LE9 8ZZ. Tel: 01455 852225.

IPD (1996) *IPD Guide on Recruitment.* London, Chartered Institute of Personnel and Development.

These booklets give practical, sensible advice on how to ensure fairness in the recruitment process. Both organisations are set up to encourage a reasonable approach to the contract between individuals and employing organisations.

There are also some very good, free pamphlets produced by The Consumers' Association for the Community Legal Service, a public service. Number 2 is about employment rights, Number 15 is about equal opportunities, and Number 16 is about racial discrimination. The organisation can be contacted by phoning 0845 3000343.

You will also find chapters on selection and recruitment in any human resources or personnel text, for example Marchington and Wilkinson (2002).

Leighton P and Proctor G (2001) *Recruiting within the Law,* CIPD, gives the legal implications of the whole process and what should be considered. This is a useful book as there is a lot of legislation in the recruitment area.

Video: *It's Your Choice* (1993) Video Arts, is a clear explanation of the recruitment process on video. Video Arts have a well established and strong reputation for videos about management techniques.

Nurturing People at Work

*Many would argue that managing people at work is about developing them. This chapter is about how to do so. It is based on the theories of psychology, sociology and learning which we looked at in Chapters 1, 2 and 3. Motivation theories covered in Chapter 12 are also important for this chapter. The practical applied concepts covered are **competencies, training and development methods, evaluation, lifelong learning** and **career management**. You might also want to look at Chapter 14 on appraisal and Chapters 13 and 14 on performance management. There are no boxed examples in this chapter as there are lots of small examples built into the text.*

OBJECTIVES

When you have finished reading this chapter you should be able to:

■ **describe how to maximise performance through training and development**

■ **identify training needs**

■ **describe some of the methods used for training and developing people at work**

■ **understand the need for evaluation of training and development**

■ **discuss the role of lifelong learning in organisations.**

Toby's ambition

Ben is the store manager for a medium-sized branch of a national supermarket. He has five section managers working for him. One of them is Toby, who is in his mid-20s and has been in the store for two years. At the annual appraisal interview Toby said he was wanting to leave because there did not seem to be any prospect of promotion and he was getting rather bored. At the moment there are no immediate prospects for promotion, because the supermarket chain is not expanding. Toby is well thought of, bright and an excellent manager. What would you advise Ben to do about Toby?

Should he try to arrange for him to act up whenever Ben is off duty? Should he arrange for a secondment to head office so Toby can learn some different skills? Is there some specific project that would be worth carrying out? Should Ben accept that Toby's career might be better served by going to one of their competitors? Would it make a difference to your advice if a new supermarket was opening up in the neighbouring town?

Training and developing staff is seen as an important part of managing people at work. However, finding the time and the money to pay for resources can be tricky. So why bother? There seems to be a wide consensus in Britain that training is a good thing. It is certainly felt to be at the heart of managing change. The government exhorts us to train through initiatives such as National Vocational Qualifications (NVQs) and Investors in People (IiP). Employers' organisations see training as the way to upgrade the skills of the workforce in order to meet new challenges from overseas. Trade unions see training and development as a way of helping members to keep their jobs – indeed, trade unions have become one of the major suppliers of workplace training. All agree that encouraging people to undertake training and development is one of the main tasks of managing people. It may be the induction and training of a junior, the development of an experienced member of staff, or the 'switching on' of a jaded member of staff to adapt to the changes sweeping through the organisation. Training and developing is also a way of ensuring one is up to date and employable.

Training and development is also an important part of motivating people to give a committed performance. Most people want to be stimulated by their work. They want to have the appropriate skills and competencies to be able to perform well. With the increasing emphasis on managing performance through managing people, ensuring that they have suitable training and development is a critical part of the job of leading or managing.

DECIDING WHAT SKILLS TO TRAIN AND DEVELOP

The technical skills associated with training systematically are increasingly described in terms of identifying the competencies required, measuring the competencies of the post holders, seeing if there is a gap between the two, identifying training needs, and then developing those competencies that are less well developed. Identifying training needs for the people whom one manages is done in a variety of ways. The most systematic way is to compare the planned needs of the department with the assessed competencies of the people in the department, and to attend to the difference between these. Reality, fortunately, is never quite as mechanical as that!

Training needs are commonly identified in the following ways:

- at appraisal sessions when the team leader or manager and the individual discuss what training would be appropriate over the next year to help improve and develop the individual's contribution and career prospects
- as a result of changes that the team or department is taking on that may involve a training and development programme for the whole department
- at the instigation of the individual who wants to improve and develop his or her abilities, either for current work or for career purposes
- as part of the systematic process of induction and initial training of new members of staff
- as part of a recovery programme after the identification of poor performance of an individual or group.

These needs can be for training in skills, knowledge or understanding. Increasingly, they are expressed in competency terms.

Competency is something you can demonstrate – for example, 'change gear whilst driving a car' or 'slice bread'. It is clear when the behaviour is successful. These behaviours in turn can be analysed into smaller steps when the overall competency is difficult to achieve. However, not all necessary work behaviours or competencies are easy to describe and analyse. Many of the most useful behaviours require subtle application and experience to be effective. This means many statements and lists of competencies include knowledge, understanding and personal attributes as well as strictly behavioural descriptions.

Lists of competencies appropriate for a particular job, profession or qualification can be drawn up. This is done by analysing and describing the behaviours and associated activities necessary to perform specific aspects of a job. To this list are added the other behaviours that are likely to be required in the foreseeable future. Then appropriate assessment procedures can be devised for individuals to be assessed for selection, qualification, training and development purposes. Training specialists have led the way in the use of these competency lists. Implicit in the whole competency approach is that line managers are really involved in ensuring that the people they manage are given appropriate opportunities to develop their competencies.

With a list of the competencies required in the job and a measure of the competencies of the post holder made, a comparison between the two is carried out and the areas for development or training needs are identified. Then a programme of development can be agreed for the following period.

DECIDING HOW TO TRAIN AND DEVELOP

Having decided what needs training and developing, the next question is how to go about it. A lot of the professional literature debates the niceties of different methods: two useful books on this subject are Bee and Bee (1994) and Reid and Barrington (1999). Like most management decisions, those about training and development have to be made on the basis of resources and opportunities available. There is no point in planning a perfect but impracticable programme. This pragmatism also needs to be applied to what makes sense. There is absolutely no point in sending people off on a long course if there is no prospect of their implementing the newly learnt skills when they come back. Equally, there is no point in trying to learn a new technique at work if the necessary equipment does not exist. There is also a cultural aspect to this. In the more centralised organisations, staff are told what they need to learn and are given training experiences to deliver this; whereas more self-managing organisations will expect the staff to identify their own learning priorities and find the resources available to achieve them.

A choice of methods

Many different methods for training and development exist, and I have included a brief description, in alphabetical order, of some of the more common ways of training and developing people's competencies and some of the associated advantages and disadvantages. This is to help you think of something when faced with finding a training and development opportunity for one of your people. Remember that sending people on courses is not the only way to train and develop them.

'Acting up'

Acting up is doing a more senior job temporarily to cover for absence or vacancy – for example, maternity or paternity leave. It gives individuals the opportunity to broaden their experience and skills in positions of greater responsibility. The difficulty can be that returning to the original post after the acting-up period can be demoralising and this re-entry needs sympathetic managing by the returning senior post holder.

An example is a catering manager acting up for a hotel services director whilst he or she is off having a major operation.

Action learning

This involves the linking of a real, structured task and action within the learning process using action learning sets. Action learning sets are groups of people who discuss the problems associated with the task using an identified facilitator. It can be difficult to keep the group on the task as individuals develop, but it is a technique found particularly useful by senior staff, who enjoy being part of a group, as they can feel very isolated in normal day-to-day operations.

A true-life example involves a group of six personnel directors from two regional health authorities who came together to develop a personnel auditing form. The six originally met on a course but continued meeting occasionally with a facilitator over two years to complete the task.

Audio-visual presentations

These include slides, films, DVDs and video. They are similar to lectures in what they can achieve, but video has an advantage over lectures in that it can be stopped and started as required and also can be taken home to study at leisure.

Examples are the numerous marketing videos promoting new techniques and apparatus. Similarly, many journals now present their material on audiotape and CD so you can listen in the car on the way to or from work.

Blended learning

This is the current term for using a mixture of methods. It is particularly associated with a blend of e-learning and others. This has been found necessary as most people learn better if they look, listen and do.

Examples are found on many higher education courses. A variety of methods are used. You are probably experiencing a blend yourself.

Case studies

This is where a history of some event is given and the trainees are invited to analyse the causes of a problem or to find a solution. This provides an opportunity for a cool look at problems and for the exchange of ideas about possible solutions. However, trainees may not realise that the real world is not quite the same as the training session.

An example is the use made of case studies for people on business development courses and particularly to get them to take on the notion of financial control. This might involve looking at various scenarios for a business, or case studies of individual managers and the decisions they need to make in order to allocate financial resources. Another example of where case-study presentations are frequently used is in the clinical development of doctors.

Coaching

This is a technique to improve the performance of someone who is already competent rather than establishing competency in the first place. It is usually done on a one-to-one basis in the everyday work situation and is a continuing activity. It involves gently nudging people to improve their performance, to develop their skills and to increase their self-confidence so that they can take more responsibility for their own work and develop their career prospects. Many of the attributes of credibility, dealt with in Chapter 11, are useful for the coach. If the advice is sought it is more likely to be followed. Similarly the personal skills of influencing, also dealt with in Chapter 11, are useful for the coach so that appropriate behaviour can be nudged into place. Most coaching is done by the more senior person but the subordinate position of the person coached is by no means a prerequisite. What is essential is that the coach should have the qualities of expertise, judgement and experience that make it possible for the person coached to follow the guidance.

An example can be found in almost any contact between professionals. Just think of some of the best interactions between lawyers and their juniors.

Delegation

Delegation is not just giving jobs to people to do – it is giving people the scope, responsibility and authority to do the jobs in their own way. It allows individuals to test their own ideas and to develop understanding and confidence. This is often called empowerment. The more specific the instructions and terms of reference, the less learning will be achieved as a result of the activity. With the assignment delegated, the individuals start to work on their own. The decision about when to seek guidance and discussion on progress from the manager is also in their own hands.

An example is the director of estates handing over a portfolio of buildings to a junior who is given the autonomy, and budget, to decide how to maintain the buildings.

Discussion

This is where knowledge, ideas and opinions on a subject are exchanged between trainees and trainer. This is particularly suitable where the application of some idea is a matter of opinion. It is also a starting point for changing attitudes and finding out how knowledge is going to be applied. The technique requires skill on the part of the trainer, as it can be difficult to keep the discussion focused or useful.

One actual example of this technique involved the staff of an intensive care unit who at the end of a day's training about performance appraisal discussed with the trainer and the senior staff how to go forward with an action plan.

Distance learning

This method involves the individual using a range of printed, audio-visual and other teaching materials outside the traditional course environment. It is self-learning, requires high levels of personal discipline, and can be difficult to sustain in isolation.

The Open University is probably the best-known example of a teaching institute using the technique.

e-learning

This refers to the various types of material available on websites and through e-mail. Some of them are specific in-house material, others are generally available to the public. It usually involves individuals working on their own through a programme already written. As the process has developed it has become clear that different programmes are needed to reflect different learning styles. Some people do not like to follow something so structured, some want more information, some want to challenge the assumptions and some will want it precisely geared to their particular situation. So e-learning cannot meet all training needs.

An example is a real-life course to learn Spanish which is entirely delivered by e-mail, with each learner having a personal tutor who responds to e-mail and sends questions to be answered in a suitable structure. The learner and tutor can be anywhere in the world. It is all conducted in Spanish. The downside is the lack of spoken practice.

Empowerment

This is similar to delegation, which is described above. Empowerment is giving people the opportunity to do things their own way. By trying things out they will learn from the experience. If you look back at Kolb's cycle of learning in Chapter 3 you will understand why empowerment can be a powerful learning method.

An example is a group of technical sales people who could visit and contact their customers as and when they felt appropriate rather than having set targets of visits.

Exercises

This is where the trainees do a particular task, in a particular way, to get a particular result. This is suitable when trainees need practice in following a specific procedure or formula to reach a required objective. The exercise must be realistic.

Most of us have had to do exercises to master the latest electronic technology such as PCs, faxes, answerphones, video and DVDs.

Feedback

Any precise and accurate feedback is going to help people develop their competencies. Leaders can provide this. The feedback needs to be given in a form that the receiver can accept and act upon.

Examples are appraisals and 360-degree feedback from a variety of people one comes into contact with, or the more common coaching and mentoring feedback team.

Group dynamics

Using this method, trainees are put in situations where their behaviour is examined. The task given usually requires them to co-operate before they can achieve the goal. Observers collect information on how the trainees go about this and then feed back to the group and the individuals after the task is completed. Trainees learn about the effect they have on others. This may be threatening, and anxieties need to be resolved before the end of the session. This sort of developing is very dependent on the quality of the trainer and can be dangerous if entered into too casually. Usually the task is relatively remote from work.

The most common examples of group dynamics training are found in outdoor activity centres offering leadership training courses for managers.

Job rotation

In job rotation individuals do different jobs within the section or organisation over a period of time. By setting up flexible working patterns within the organisation, individuals can be facilitated to broaden their experience and skills. The disadvantage can be the loss of the experience of highly specialised staff and their commitment to ensuring that things are right.

One example is the reorganisation of operators on a chemical plant who perform every part of the process – including packing – rather than specialising in particular types of work.

Learning contracts

These are usually agreed between individuals, their bosses and whoever is providing the learning experience. They specify what learning opportunities are expected, when these will occur and what outcomes are expected. The aim is to ensure that everyone agrees and the individual is then expected to monitor his or her own performance against this contract. Contracts can also be used in conjunction with informal learning and to generate learning opportunities at work.

An example is the case of second-year psychology students from a university, who had contracts agreed between themselves, tutors and the placements they were going to for work experience.

Learning opportunities

Many opportunities come up in the normal working environment that can be used to develop oneself or others. Look around and see what already exists before using time-consuming outside opportunities. The difficulty is that these workplace learning opportunities can be missed, or that by concentrating on the learning the task is not carried out as efficiently. An example is 'walking the floor', a classic way in which managers learn about what are current concerns in their patch; they can also pick up on new ways of working and the relationships that exist in the department. By using these to ensure that individuals learn how to be more effective, useful development takes place.

Lectures

A lecture is a talk given without much participation by the trainees. The method is suitable for large audiences where the information to be imparted can be worked out precisely in advance. There is little opportunity for feedback, so some in the audience may not get the point. A lecture requires careful preparation and should never be longer than 40 minutes; otherwise there is a risk of losing the audience's attention, as they are not able to give feedback and question the lecturer.

A lecture to quality assurance managers about the new European Directives at a conference is an example.

On-the-job training

With this method, trainees work in the real environment with support from a skilled person. This gives the trainee real practice and it does not involve expensive new equipment. However, not all skilled people are skilled trainers. The essential ingredients are briefing, feedback and support that help the individual to achieve the objectives in a structured way. An example of on-the-job training is the case of a new business manager who was in the office for two weeks before the old business manager moved to a new job; this overlap allowed for a smoother handover of procedures and commitments.

Programmed instruction

This can also be called Computer-assisted Learning (CAL). Trainees work at their own pace using a book or computer program which has a series of tasks and tests geared to teaching something systematically. It is suitable for learning logical skills and knowledge. However, it does not allow for discussion with others, which may be important where the application is debatable.

An example is libraries that have computer programs on how to use their services. There are also several such programmed instructions on how to work out budgets, taxes and business planning.

Projects

This is similar to an exercise, but a project allows greater freedom to display initiative and creativity. Projects can allow feedback to be given on a range of personal qualities as well as on technical abilities. They need the full commitment and co-operation of the trainee, and specific terms of reference.

Many courses for post-experience management students have projects as part of their studies. These are expected to be work based and practical, and usually are an opportunity for doing a more detailed study of something that needs to be done anyway – such as a business plan for a new development within the unit.

Role play

In this training method people are asked to act the role they, or someone else, would play at work. It is particularly used for training for face-to-face situations and is suitable for near-real-life situations where criticism would be useful. The difficulties are that people can be embarrassed and the usefulness of the exercise is very dependent on the nature of the feedback given.

An example is offered by the staff of the intensive care group mentioned above, under Discussion, who practised interviewing each other using different techniques. They then role-played by conducting a mini appraisal interview about each other's work in the previous week.

Secondments

This involves organising a placement in an alternative department or organisation for the achievement of a specific purpose. It is often used for management and professional development. The individual may of course choose not to come back!

A common example of the use of secondments in the public sector is the case of mid-ranking managers who go on secondment to a particular, similar institution, often abroad, to learn specific techniques and standards. An example is police studying what their colleagues in the USA are doing for three months just before taking up a more senior post in the UK.

Simulations

This training method involves the use of mock-ups of real-life situations and equipment. It gives people experience before they encounter the real thing. It can be used for initial training, updating, keeping in practice, or introducing new techniques. The expense of creating a realistic mock-up is really justified only where practising on the real thing is totally impossible or where a mistake would be catastrophic. The increasing sophistication of computer graphics has enabled all sorts of simulations and 'virtual reality' to be created for workplace training and development to take place.

An example of the use of computer simulation teaching is a training programme for airline pilots to use a new system before actually flying the real aircraft. Another example is the use of artificial bodies for surgeons to practise various procedures on before operating for real.

Skill instruction

Here the trainee is told how to perform an action, is shown how to do it, and then does it under supervision. This is suitable for teaching skills, as long as the task is broken down into suitable parts. What is considered manageable will vary with the task and the person receiving the training. Breaking things down into small steps is not suitable for all skills, as some are better learned as a whole.

The teaching of any of the mechanical skills would be a good example here, such as learning how to service machines or stripping down air-conditioning units.

Talks

A talk allows participation by the trainees, providing an opportunity for questions to be asked. It is useful for getting over a new way of looking at things which involve abstraction. It is appropriate for up to 20 people, but can be used only where people are willing and able to participate. Where people do not want to participate it becomes a lecture.

Examples are when ideas about management or the future are being explored. Management consultants usually report their findings to the board by giving a presentation and then individuals ask questions and test out their understanding of the findings.

EVALUATING TRAINING

If organisations and people are to spend time, effort and money on training and development it is important to evaluate whether it really has been useful. 'Validation' is the word used to describe the process of seeing whether the training and development has achieved its objectives, and evaluation is the process of ascertaining whether the training has affected the performance of the job. It may be that the Outward Bound leadership course has met all the objectives – validation, but we cannot see any change in performance at work – evaluation. Evaluation is much more difficult because of the problems of deciding, defining and measuring performance or competency. I lamblin (1974) suggest five levels at which evaluation can take place:

- reaction – trainees give their personal view and impressions of the experience
- learning – the amount of learning is measured
- job behaviour – work behaviour is looked at six to nine months later to see if it has changed
- organisation – productivity, time taken to do things, absenteeism, turnover and labour costs are examined to see if there is a difference after the training
- ultimate level – the effect on profitability and growth over a period of years.

At a line management level you probably do not want to get involved in elaborate evaluation of any training you use, as the cost-effectiveness of doing so may well not be justified. However, it is worth having some simple sort of evaluation – if only at the level of asking 'Do we think this has been useful?' or 'Would we do this again?' It is an important legal obligation that training and development is not discriminatory, and that those who work part time are given appropriate training and development.

ENCOURAGING LIFELONG LEARNING OR LIFETIME PERSONAL DEVELOPMENT

Increasingly, organisations, professional bodies and the government are emphasising the need for individuals to develop and learn throughout their lives so they can cope with the rising speed of change in society. The argument is made that the more learning that is undertaken, the easier it becomes, and the more confident the individual will be in facing change and moving from one employer to another now that lifetime employment with one single organisation is rare. This emphasis on lifelong learning or lifetime personal development is enshrined in two formal developments.

- Continuous Professional Development (CPD) – many professional bodies are emphasising CPD and expect their members to fulfil a minimum training requirement every year to maintain membership. Some of this CPD experience is credit-bearing, leading to further qualifications and higher ranking within the profession.
- Investors in People (IiP) is a government-backed initiative to encourage organisations to train and develop their staff. Where there are suitable systems of identifying training and development needs, and carrying out the required programmes of training and development takes place, organisations are entitled to a certificate as

'Investors in People'. It has proved popular with organisations both in the private and public sectors as a demonstration of their comitment to quality.

There is a parallel emphasis on the 'learning organisation' which is able to encourage individuals to take on change and new tasks by a process of continuous learning. This is discussed in Chapter 3.

Another aspect of encouraging lifetime personal development is the management of individual careers. Team leaders and managers have to learn to manage talent, and this includes developing staff so that they build careers to suit themselves. This is increasingly important if Kanter's (1989) comments about security of employment coming from being employable rather than from being employed by a particular employer are true. It is part of many people's motivation at work to feel that they are developing into skilled players at the forefront of the profession. All of us need opportunities to develop skills and a reputation. This involves ensuring that people have a variety of opportunities and experiences. As Handy (1989, p104) puts it, managers have to be:

> **teacher, counsellor and friend, as much or more than he or she is commander, inspector and judge.**

DEBATE – NURTURING PEOPLE'S CAREERS

My colleague Valmai Bowden (1997), looking at the careers of bench scientists, has pointed out that this nurturing of people's careers can be compared to parenting. Some team leaders and managers are very strict and dogmatic – 'Do like me'; others are more facilitating and encourage self-direction and assessment. Those who are lucky enough to have good 'parenting' are likely to develop into the confident, learning, self-developing individuals who are likely to have rewarding careers. Those who feel ignored and rejected can become embittered. Maybe this facilitating of people's careers is at the heart of the relationship between team leaders and the led in the new empowered climate, whereas the previous manager and managed relationship was about ensuring current performance. What do you feel is the distinguishing feature of leading compared to managing?

Nurturing people at work is important for the organisation and the individual. The organisation needs to keep people up to date and skilled for the job. It is also an important part of the employment contract that people are kept up to date in their skills so they are employable if the organisation has to make them redundant. Keeping skills and knowledge developed keeps an individual more flexible and employable as well as increasing the job satisfaction due when a job is done appropriately. Nothing is more alarming than trying to do something when one does not have the appropriate competencies. This chapter gives some of the well-known approaches to enabling this development and training.

ACTIVITIES

1   How do we identify what training we need in our team? Do we leave it up to individuals to volunteer or is there another method as well? What opportunities for development on the job do we encourage? Are there any others in the team we could use for development purposes? Have we started using a competency approach? Should we?

2   Which of the following list of training and development methods would be best suited to short-term, less than six months, training and development? Which would be better suited to longer-term goals, more than six months? Which of the methods are appropriate for introducing new working practices where everyone needs to do it? Which methods require a degree of self-confidence and motivation? Which methods would you find it easy to resource, and which require major expenditure?

Acting up		Action learning	
Audio-visual presentations		Blended learning	
Case studies		Coaching	
Delegation		Discussion	
Distance learning		e-learning	
Empowerment		Exercises	
Feedback		Group dynamics	
Job rotation		Learning contracts	
Learning opportunities		Lectures	
On-the-job training		Programmed instruction	
Projects		Role play	
Secondments		Simulations	
Skill instruction		Talks	

3   Thinking back to the learning theories in Chapter 3, which of the methods listed in the previous question would fit with Kolb's learning cycle?

Acting up		Action learning	
Audio-visual presentations		Blended learning	
Case studies		Coaching	
Delegation		Discussion	
Distance learning		e-learning	
Empowerment		Exercises	
Feedback		Group dynamics	
Job rotation		Learning contracts	
Learning opportunities		Lectures	
On-the-job training		Programmed instruction	
Projects		Role play	
Secondments		Simulations	
Skill instruction		Talks	

4   What sort of evaluation do we use on our training courses and development programmes at work? Would it be cost-effective to do some more?

5   In what ways do I encourage my staff to develop careers appropriate to each of them? Do I expect them to want the same things that I do? Do I encourage learning in all the staff, including the established members?

HAVE I MET THE OBJECTIVES?

1   Can I describe how to improve performance through training and development?

2   How can an organisation identify training needs?

3   What are some of the methods used for training and development of people at work?

4   Why is there a need for evaluation of training and development?

5   What is the role of lifelong learning in organisations?

And finally ...

What would you advise Ben to do? Would you use the material in this chapter to respond to Toby? If so, which part of it? Can you think of a particular move that could be tried so the organisation would keep his enthusiasm?

I feel that since this is a very practical chapter, most of what is here could very easily address the question of what to do about Toby. I would probably try some sort of special project or secondment to allow other people in the organisation to see what Toby is made of. If he makes a mark, other managers as well as Ben will then be looking for opportunities for Toby.

FURTHER READING

The Chartered Institute of Personnel and Development has a large selection of books about training at work. I suggest having a look at:

Reid MA *and* Barrington H (1999) – this has, for a long time, been the standard text in this area. It is good, sensible stuff.

Harrison R (2002) *Learning and Development.* London, Chartered Institute of Personnel and Development. This is really the third edition of what used to be called *Employee Development.* It is a detailed, well-considered text aimed at students specialising in this area. It covers both theory and practice, with plenty of examples.

Hackett P (1997) *Introduction to Training.* London, Chartered Institute of Personnel and Development. This is probably the easiest to read of the three but (as the title implies) has less detail.

Leadership

*The concept of leadership is much debated in management circles as well as elsewhere. The academic disciplines involved can include theology, politics, history, psychology and sociology. Particular theoretical models covered in this book, which are relevant, are the control–participation continuum, Chapter 7, individual differences, Chapter 2, and socialisation, Chapters 2 and 3. This chapter deals with the applied aspects of leadership by looking at **management, the roles of leaders, the traits of leaders, styles of leadership** and **the behaviour of leaders**. Specific examples are Nelson Mandela, Sven-Göran Eriksson, BT Challenge yachts and the Heathrow Express.*

OBJECTIVES

When you have finished reading this chapter you should be able to:

- **distinguish between leadership and management**
- **understand and explain the various attributes of leadership**
- **describe different models of leadership style**
- **discuss the criteria for effective leadership.**

Ali's little local difficulty

Ali is the IT manager of a medium-sized retail organisation in the UK. The company has taken over several small British companies in the past few years and it is wholly owned by a large American retail organisation. The American boss came over to address the whole staff at the UK head office on the plans to integrate all the parts into 'one organisation, one product, one team'. The occasion had something of a religious atmosphere, with messianic messages and grand statements of confidence pouring from the American boss. One of Ali's team fell asleep in the meeting. Not only that, but after the meeting several IT team members discussed how they were shaken by the lack of attention to the details of exactly how and when the integration of the IT was going to happen. Some felt the big American boss was completely wrong in the facts given to the audience. Integrating the IT was central to the planned development of the single organisation.

What should Ali do? Explain that there is a different culture in American leadership talks, where there is a taste for the theological, inspirational peptalk? Try to influence the senior managers to be more precise in such talks? Get his own team together to discuss the implications, anxieties and progress for the IT department? Reprimand the sleeping team member? Make some jokes about the 'happiness drug' of 'one organisation, one product, one team'? Being a leader is not just about being the boss of the organisation. It is a complex social role.

For any team there are two main aspects of their functioning that need to be considered: content and process. First, content: is there something for them to do? If so, is it clear what that is, who is going to do it, and how? Is there a consensus about what the task is, and is it accepted not only by those within the team but those outside who may overlap or need to co-ordinate with the team? Second, process: how are the people within the team going to work together? Are they complementary and do they aid each other to get the best out of the team? Are there some processes that are hindering the team? Are there some tasks that the team is better at than others?

To answer these questions about particular groups or teams we often end up asking questions about how the team is managed or led. Questions such as: how much autonomy does the group have? How much do they feel as one about what they are doing? What pressures are on the team members to conform? It is these questions, amongst others, that we shall be looking at in this chapter. The answers to them often indicate the style of management or leadership being experienced within the group or team. The currently preferred approach in management circles is to talk of a style of leadership that – it is claimed – is different from management in that it is about enabling others to perform rather than making them perform.

WHAT IS LEADERSHIP?

Leadership is one of the holy grails of management writing and presentations. Everyone would like to claim it as a personal attribute, but it is very difficult to get any consensus on quite what it means. Although we find it difficult to agree quite what leadership is, it is useful to have some sort of definition. It is usually said to include the ability to get people to do different things from that which they would have done otherwise, and to do these different things with some degree of commitment and enthusiasm. Surprisingly, it is quite easy for a manager without any particular skill or personal charm to get people to obey orders at work. On the whole, when people are being paid to do something they get on with it. However, if we want something more from the performance of duties than a mere minimum contribution then something else is required.

A popular distinction between leaders is that made by Burns (1978) and Kuhnert and Lewis (1987), amongst others. They distinguish between transactional and transformational leaders:

- Transactional leaders clarify the task requirements by using analytical techniques to break the task into appropriate chunks and then communicating these requirements clearly. They ensure that there are appropriate rewards when the task is completed. This is sometimes called a 'command and control' type of leadership.

- Transformational leaders are those who articulate a mission. They create and maintain a positive image in followers and superiors in the way they communicate and encourage others. Rewards are tailored to individual needs. These leaders are sometimes called visionary leaders.

The latter has become the more accepted definition of what leadership is about.

Leadership traits

All the early studies that looked for the personality traits that make up a leader failed to find any conclusive evidence, except that leaders on the whole were taller than the led! In a review of the evidence, Davies (1972) found the four general traits related to leadership success were:

- intelligence – leaders usually have a slightly higher general intelligence than their followers
- social maturity – leaders have self-assurance and self-respect. They are mature and able to handle a wide variety of social situations

■ achievement drive – leaders have a strong drive to get things done

■ human-relations attitudes – leaders know that they rely on other people to get things done and are therefore interested in their team members.

This traits model of leadership concentrates on the person leading rather than on the job that has to be done.

Nowadays you will hear phrases about leadership competencies rather than leadership traits – such phrases as:

■ maintain the trust and support of colleagues and team members

■ set up collaborative and consultative working arrangements

■ provide the environment for people to excel

■ nurture individual development

■ recognise success

■ encourage enthusiasm through teamwork.

None of us would disagree with these as worthy ambitions for leaders; they are what are called 'motherhood terms', in that you cannot really be against either motherhood – or the above phrases. But it is quite difficult to see exactly how a team leader should go about doing it. The two essential responsibilities of leadership seem to be clarifying the tasks to be done and establishing suitable enthusiasm and expertise in the people to undertake the tasks effectively. However, there are, as ever, several different approaches to analysing leadership and we shall look at different approaches in the following sections.

Nelson Mandela (1994, p583) writes:

I saw the garden as a metaphor for certain aspects of my life. A leader must also tend his garden; he, too, sows seeds, and then watches, cultivates and harvests the result. Like the gardener a leader must take responsibility for what he cultivates; he must mind his work, try to repel enemies, preserve what can be preserved and eliminate what cannot succeed.

The roles of the leader

After the early studies had failed to come up with any useful common personality traits or qualities that were associated with leaders, another more pragmatic approach was taken: to look at what functions a leader fulfils for a group. There were various studies that investigated the work done by managers and leaders – see, for example, Mintzberg (1973) and Stewart (1967). This sort of research led to a description of the various roles that leaders could or should fill in organisations.

A useful summary by Krech, Crutchfield and Ballachey (1962) suggests the following possible roles for the leaders:

■ co-ordinator – of the various functions and work of others

■ planner – to identify and realise the goals of the organisation

■ policy maker – to work out how to achieve the goals

- expert – in the technology or processes of the organisation
- external group representative – to customers, suppliers and other agencies
- controller of internal relations – between groups and individuals, often by chairing meetings
- controller of rewards and punishments – salaries, promotions, developments and careers
- arbitrator and mediator – where conflict is unresolved
- role model – of what is acceptable behaviour in the organisation
- symbol of the group – embodying the culture of the organisation
- ideologist – having a strong articulated mission
- parent figure – who can always cope with the unexpected and take an interest in individuals
- scapegoat – someone to blame for the ills of the organisation.

No one is suggesting that every manager or leader plays all these roles, but they are typical roles filled by leaders within organisations.

Sven-Göran Eriksson, team manager of various football teams, including England, is a high-profile example of a successful, modern leader. His leadership is based on the following types of behaviour and attributes:

Concilliatry	Creates empathy and trust
Understated	Not too close to people
Diplomatic	Makes tough decisions
Cosmopolitan	Looks after individuals rather than teams
Values the work of others	Listens
Supports others	

Styles of leadership

An early influential model of leadership in Britain was first described by Adair (1982). Adair used his model to develop leadership skills among army officers training at the Royal Military Academy, Sandhurst. The methods have since been adopted in a wide variety of organisations. He argued that people working in groups have three sets of needs, two of which are shared with all group members, the third being related to each individual. The three are:

- the task to be accomplished together
- maintaining social cohesion of the group
- individual needs of team members.

These three sets of needs are interdependent. If the task fails, there is diminished satisfaction for the individual and the group tends to fall apart. If the group lacks unity, this will affect performance. If the individual is discontented, then he or she will not give his or her best performance. These three sets of needs, or leadership functions, can be seen as three overlapping circles – see Figure 10.1. This model emphasises the essential unity of leadership, so that a single action by a leader may have an influence in all three areas.

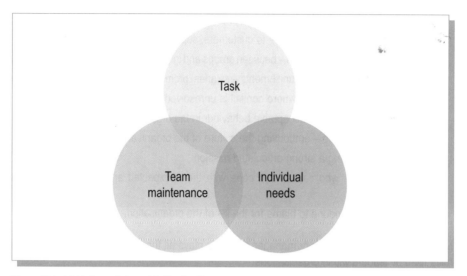

Figure 10.1 *Adair's three-circle model of leadership*

Another well-tried device for identifying the leadership style of an individual is Blake and Mouton's (1969) managerial grid. This can be used as an exercise in finding one's current leadership style with the hope that it can be modified, at least slightly, to become more appropriate to the situation in which one is working. The managerial grid identifies concern for production and concern for people as the two axes of a grid – see Figure 10.2.

The result is a grid of different types of leader. For example, at the extremes:

- At the lower left-hand corner is a 1.1 management style, which is the style of managers with a low concern for both people and production, who try to stay out of trouble and simply do what they are told.
- In the upper left-hand corner is the 1.9 style of high concern for people but low concern for production. This is the utterly delightful leader, full of charm and consideration who never quite gets round to making anything happen.
- The bottom right corner is the 9.1 style, with high concern for production and little concern for people. They are full of ideas on what needs doing but are very frustrated when no one pays any attention – nor do they get others to co-operate with them.
- The style of 9.9 of high concern with both people and production is the obvious goal.

This emphasis on style, rather than personal characteristics, is probably the secret of the success that grid methods have enjoyed, as it provides useful criticism of a kind that most people can live with and hope to modify. This grid could also be used as a way of analysing the general culture or behaviour in organisations, and whether the concern for people and tasks is in balance or not, and whether some changes are required.

Contingency models of leadership

So far we have looked at leadership in various ways, but with no consideration of the conditions in which the leader is performing. Clearly, to lead in a period of expansion and wealth is quite different from leading in times of hardship and fear. The contingency approach emphasises the importance of the situation in which leader and group find themselves.

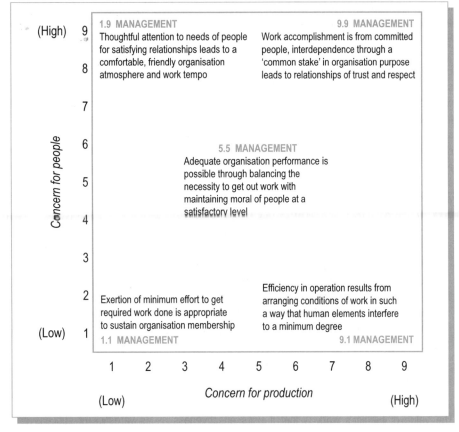

Figure 10.2 *The managerial grid*

Fiedler (1967) was the first to use the phrase 'contingency' in the context of leadership. He argued that any leadership style may be effective but it depends on the situation, so that the leader has to be adaptive. He also appreciated that it is very difficult for individuals to change their style of leadership as these styles tend to be relatively inflexible: the autocrat will remain autocratic and the free-wheeling laissez-faire advocate will remain free-wheeling. As no single style is appropriate in all situations, effectiveness can be achieved either by changing the leader to fit the situation or by altering the situation to fit the leader.

Three main factors will determine the leader's effectiveness:

- leader–member relations – how well is the leader accepted by the other members?
- task structure – are the jobs of the members routine and precise or vague and undefined?
- position power – what formal authority does the leader's position confer?

Fiedler then devised a novel device for measuring leadership style. It was a scale that indicates the degree to which people describe favourably or unfavourably their least preferred co-worker (LPC). Those who use relatively favourable terms tend towards permissiveness and a human-relations-orientated and considerate style – he calls them high LPC. Those who use an unfavourable style tend to be managing and task-controlling, and to be less concerned with the human-relations aspects of the job – he calls them low LPC.

It is then possible to combine all these elements to show how the style of leadership that is effective varies with the situation in which it is exercised. Table 10.1 shows the results from Fiedler's study of 800 leaders.

High LPC leaders are likely to be most effective in situations where relations with subordinates are good but task structure is low and position power weak. This would work well, for example, in many professional and creative teams. They do reasonably well when they have poor relationships with the other members but there is high task structure and strong position power. Both of these are moderately favourable combinations of circumstances. Low LPC leaders are more effective at the ends of the spectrum, when they either have a favourable combination or an unfavourable combination of factors in the situation. This would be in circumstances where personal relations have broken down or where the tasks are routine.

A practical example of team leadership engendering commitment was the Heathrow Express construction project. Lownds (1998) describes how the project managers faced indefinite delays following the collapse of a number of tunnels. They changed the way of working by emphasising that all the different organisations and contractors – including BAA, which had commissioned the work – were a single team. They ran development courses for staff on the frontline with an emphasis on 'soft' skills for supervisors, engineers, tunnellers and support staff. These were seen as crucial to the change away from blame and confrontation. The project was soon back on track and in 1997 it won an award from the Institute of Personnel and Development for changing the way the construction industry worked.

The value of Fiedler's work is that it uses effectiveness as its yardstick of success and demonstrates the fallacy of believing that there is a single best way to lead in all situations. It is interesting that the majority of situations he describes appear to call for a generally less attractive type of person as leader. We should, however, remember that he was examining a range of situations for the purpose of explanation and that situations at the extremes of his continuum may not be very common in organisational life. In many respects this model supports the current fashion for leaders rather than managers as the preferred way of

Table 10.1 *Leadership performance in different situations*

Condition	Leader–member relations	Task structures	Position power	Which LPC leader more effective
1	Good	High	Strong	Low
2	Good	High	Weak	Low
3	Good	Low	Strong	Low
4	Good	Low	Weak	High
5	Poor	High	Strong	High
6	Poor	High	Weak	Similar
7	Poor	Low	Strong	Low
8	Poor	Low	Weak	Low

Based on Fiedler (1967)

managing people. Fiedler's low LPC is the manager and the high LPC is the leader in current parlance. Not everyone agrees with Fiedler's view that leaders cannot change their style.

That there is no one right way of being a leader is also evident when we consider the variation in those being led. Different groups in different situations may demand different leadership. Support for this comes from the work of Clarke and Pratt (1985), who found that different stages of the business cycle required different types of leaders. The champion was needed to fight for and defend the new business. The tank commander was necessary to develop a strong team and drive into exploitable markets. A housekeeper ensures efficient and economic leadership of the established business, and the lemon-squeezer extracts the maximum benefit at the declining end of the business. No one leader can fulfil all these roles. Indeed, for many start-ups the difficulty comes when the organisation is up and running and needs to move into a more mature phase and the founder/owner is still in champion mode.

THE DRIVE FOR LEADERSHIP IN ORGANISATIONS

Since the 1980s there has been increasing emphasis on leaders rather than managers. Several people have addressed the distinction. Watson (1983) used a well-known organisational framework, based on management consultancy, known as the Seven S's – of strategy, structure, systems, style, staff, skills and shared goals. Watson suggested that managers tend to rely on:

- strategy
- structure
- systems.

Leaders, on the other hand, use the softer S's of:

- style
- staff
- skills
- shared goals.

Kotter (1982) made a more detailed distinction. He saw management as predominantly activity based, whereas leadership means dealing with people rather than things. Management involves the following:

- Planning and budgeting. This involves target setting, establishing procedures for reaching targets and allocating the resources necessary to meet plans.
- Organising and staffing. This is setting the organisation structure: it means recruiting the right people and giving them incentives.
- Controlling and problem-solving. This means monitoring the results compared with the plan and involves identifying problems and working out solutions.

Here everything is concerned with logic, structure, analysis and control and, if well done, it produces predictable results on time.

Leadership, on the other hand, is about:

- creating a sense of direction. This is usually as a result of dissatisfaction with the status quo: it is challenged, and out of this challenge a vision for something different is born.

- communicating the vision. The vision must be the realised or unconscious needs of other people, and the leader must work to give it credibility. In the British context it is also important not to make too many mission statements that are remote as they can be met with cynicism and scepticism.

- energising, inspiring and motivating. These words encapsulate much of what a leader must be seen to do. People must be kept moving, enthusiasm must be bred and maintained, and when the going is tough they must be supported and helped. Part of this is developing talent in team members.

If done well, and with passion and commitment, it will produce impetus for change. If no change is necessary, frankly, management might be better! Where change is necessary management will be found lacking, and the need for leadership will be paramount.

In management circles, and in human resource management circles in particular, there is at present a great deal of emphasis on developing leadership in those with responsibilities for managing people. The idea is to move from management to leadership. The factor prompting this move is an ideal of moving from compliance to commitment based on the humanistic approach of many working in this field – see Chapter 1 for discussion of this. There is also a feeling that as organisations become less hierarchical and more team- and project-based, individuals will increasingly belong to several teams and will be required to offer their contribution rather than have it demanded of them.

DEBATE – EMOTIONAL INTELLIGENCE OR TOUGHNESS?

One phrase that has been linked with ideas of leadership is that of 'emotional intelligence'. Emotional intelligence is, in Goleman's (1995) view, about four things. Self-awareness and recognising your feelings. Self-management, which means keeping disruptive feelings under control and deferring pleasure. Social awareness or empathy for others' feelings. Managing relationships by guiding, motivating, working with, and living with others. The idea is to suggest that emotional intelligence is more important than intellectual ability. This is very much the soft approach to leadership and management.

Stern (2003) argues that hard times call for tough leaders. He argues that leaders need to have self-belief, resilience, focus, drive, control, resolve, nerves of steel, independence, competitiveness and what he calls 'chill ability' – the ability to be remote and unattached. What do you think?

Mobilising this commitment through effective leadership has become one of the buzz words of management at the beginning of the twenty-first century. There is a particular emphasis on the visionary leadership and the ability to inspire others through a suitable statement of the purpose and mission of the group. Words about how people can be taken out of themselves and achieve more than they imagined are often bandied about. It remains to be seen whether this will work and whether criteria for effective leadership behaviour can be distinguished. It is also worth remembering that leaders can lead only as far as followers allow them to – unless some coercion is involved.

A study (Dulewicz, Higgs and Cranwell-Ward, 2002) of the 12 identical yachts in the BT Global Challenge to sail round the world found that the difference between the winning and losing boats was the nature of the leadership which led to better teamwork and consequently more skilful navigation. It was not a matter of luck, starting at different times or technical differences between the boats. Managing people well, in this study, makes the difference between winning and losing.

CRITERIA FOR EFFECTIVE LEADERSHIP

If leaders are seen to be so important to the success of organisations, we need to ensure that we select and develop the best for this role. How do we judge who are, and who can be, effective leaders?

One approach is to look for the competencies that are associated with leadership and then use these as a basis for selection and development. Several lists of generic management competencies look very much like leadership competencies. For example, the list of the Management Standards Centre, which is the NVQ body for management, includes such phrases as:

- establish organisational values and culture
- inspire people
- establish integrity and ethics
- communicate sensitively.

These competencies can be judged only by seeing people in action. For many people, the only way to do this is to set up some specific exercise, as their working day is remote or confined to specific roles. Outdoor programmes are frequently used as they encourage individuals to cope with unusual situations, especially if there are no designated leaders for the group. In these sorts of activities it is clear whether issues such as communication, delegation and motivation are being tackled. Others use role-playing activities to create similar opportunities to observe and analyse – and usually give feedback to develop skills.

Hall (2002), in a plea for organisations to develop their own leaders, lists some of the currently popular phrases describing leadership behaviours that are valued. Leadership includes the following behaviours:

- self-management – organising oneself to perform
- role modelling – setting an example of the required behaviours
- coaching and mentoring – nudging others' performance to improve
- formal support – giving people resources to get things done
- internal exposure – being seen around and championing the team
- expressing a vision – what is the aim and goal for the team, but based in reality
- communicating – clearly and regularly
- trusting people – assuming they will do it right
- giving praise – informally and formally
- spotting talent and stretching it – developing the next leaders and excellent performers

■ taking responsibility – both when things go right and when they do not. Dealing with other people's uncertainty in difficult times is perhaps the most important role.

■ walking the talk – do it, do not just talk it.

Organisations increasingly use the vocabulary of teams and leaders to describe the people who work together. Some of the leaders have not changed from the previous management approaches. Others are genuinely trying to be leaders. Those who acquire the vocabulary without the change of behaviour are perhaps the least likely to succeed as everyone just cringes and the senior person seriously lacks credibility, which makes it even more difficult to get things done.

ACTIVITIES

1   Whom have I worked for who seemed a good leader? Whom have I worked for who was not a good leader? What characteristics distinguished them from each other? Could I use any of these characteristics to lead others more successfully?

2   Which of the roles in Krech et al's list do I fill? Is there any conflict between these? Are there any roles I should be filling? Are there any roles I would like to add or subtract?

3   Can you think of different examples of leaders to fit into the Blake and Mouton Grid? Can you use the three circles model as a basis for your work?

4   What sort of boss do I work for? Is he or she a leader? If so, do I find the leadership appropriate? Is there anything in his or her behaviour I could use?

5   Over the next week see if you can collect ten examples of behaviour that you consider demonstrate leadership. You might find examples among your friends when you are deciding what to do, or among your colleagues, or it may be an emergency, or strangers observed, or you might see an example of leadership on television. You may like to compare your examples with other people's.

Do you all agree that each other's examples demonstrate leadership?

Are there different degrees of leadership demonstrated?

Try to group the examples using either Adair's model or Blake and Mouton's grid. Do they fit ? Are there any difficulties?

HAVE I MET THE OBJECTIVES?

1   Can I distinguish between leadership and management?

2   What are some of the attributes of leadership?

3   Can I describe two different models of leadership style?

4   What are some of the criteria for effective leadership?

And finally ...

What would you do if you were Ali? Would you use any of the material here? I would probably use the Adair and Blake and Mouton models to remind me that the 'task' and 'people' orientation need to be in balance. Too much emphasis on either 'people' or 'task' is seen as absurd by those working in teams. With too much emphasis on the inspirational and people aspect everyone wonders what they are supposed to do. With too little of it, people feel irritated that they are not regarded as people. I would try to arrange a meeting of the IT team to emphasise what we as a team are trying to do. This does not necessarily have to be a very long meeting.

FURTHER READING

Sir John Harvey-Jones was chairman of ICI and has written several very readable books about management which are really about leading people – for example, *All Together Now* (1994) published by Mandarin.

Lownds (1998) is a practical example of something that has actually been done – and in the UK.

Mandela N (1994) *Long Walk To Freedom*. London, Abacus. The autobiography of perhaps the most famous leader of the late twentieth century. An extraordinary story, quite long, but well worth reading.

Hamel G (2002) *Leading the Revolution*. Boston, Mass., Harvard Business School Press. This is by a very well-established writer and is addressed to those who would be leaders. A good example of the managerial approach to leadership.

Goleman D (2002) *The New Leaders: Emotional Intelligence at Work*. Little, Brown. This is by a well-known current writer on leadership and typical of the genre. He is perhaps most responsible for the concept of emotional intelligence.

Influence and Persuasion

*This chapter deals with a central aspect of social life. Consequently there are several academic theories that have models to inform this area. Psychology and sociology, Chapters 1 and 2, group theory, Chapter 5 and power theories, Chapter 7. There is also specific **political theory about authority** which is very influential in this chapter. The applied aspects of these theories dealt with here are **delegation, legitimising, credibility, delegation, networking, meetings** and **presentations.** Material on organisational culture, Chapter 4, and empowerment in Chapters 7 and 9 are also relevant to a discussion of influence and persuasion. There are no specific organisations named in this chapter but several anonymous, real examples are given to illustrate the concepts. You are also asked to generate your own examples.*

OBJECTIVES

When you have finished reading this chapter you should be able to:

■ **distinguish between 'in' authority and 'an' authority**

■ **discuss the importance of credibility**

■ **understand and explain how those lacking significant degrees of hierarchical authority can influence and persuade others**

■ **describe the importance of networking for individuals within organisations**

■ **describe how to delegate tasks**

■ **understand how to organise meetings.**

Hans' three systems

Hans is the technical manager for product 'XL' with a large multinational chemical company. He is responsible for co-ordinating technical effort throughout Europe. There are manufacturing plants in Holland, France and Great Britain and a research laboratory in Belgium. It has been decided that all four sites should use the same machinery and methods for testing their materials so that the results are directly comparable. The Dutch have one system and think it terrific, the French have another on which they have just spent a good deal of money, while the Belgian and British sites both have a variety of old machinery which they are happy to replace but can only agree on a third system. What should Hans do?

Should he ask everyone for their proposals? Should he call a meeting of interested parties? Perhaps he could set up a working group with representatives from all sites? Alternatively he could decide himself which system to go for and fund the changes from central budgets. He could implement a job rotation for people to try all the different systems hoping a consensus arises. He could tell top management that the change is too costly to be worth doing. He could go on holiday and hope it is all sorted out when he gets back. Influencing and persuading people to do things they would not have done otherwise introduces all sorts of issues about how much to use authority and how much to consult.

At the heart of working in an organisation is the desire to influence others into some decision or behaviour that would not otherwise have taken place. The main question is how can we do this when there are so many different personalities involved? We need to take their different desires and points of view into account. We need to understand how these different people can be understood and influenced. Part of the answer is to use the models and theories of the social sciences which we explored in Part 1 of this book. These discuss how we are complex and how we all have a different point of view. This needs to be appreciated if we want to influence each other's behaviours. Only by tailoring our requests so that others can understand and be enthusiastic are we likely to be influential.

There are many reasons for trying to understand the differences between people. Among those we work with, we are more likely to put requests, demands and expectations in a way that is appropriate to them. When we are experiencing difficulties in influencing someone it can be helpful to have a range of analytical models to understand his or her behaviour and suggest alternative approaches. When we have a difficult piece of information to give to those we work with we can think of different strategies and decide which is most likely to succeed with the particular individual if we have some sort of understanding of the person. Most of us do this instinctively: the social science models can help to systematise our thoughts and perhaps suggest new approaches when everything else has failed.

PERSONAL QUALITIES THAT ASSIST INFLUENCING

As well as understanding the individual differences, there are other important aspects of influencing. There are questions about power (see Chapter 7), authority and delegation. There is the balance between the legitimate demands and claims made by the parties involved. Also, different organisational cultures will accept differing levels of influence from various members. Questions to ask that cover these topics include:

- What are the formal methods of influence here? This would include meetings, memos, job appraisals, organisation charts, job descriptions, etc.
- What are the informal methods of influence here? This would include style of talking, where decisions are really taken rather than where they are rubber stamped, who is 'in' and who 'out' – which is not necessarily the same as the formal hierarchy.
- Who is the most influential person? What is the basis of this influence? Is it based on position, power, expertise, charm, length of service, ownership or just being there?

Authority

If we are going to be influential, having authority will help. Authority is an important concept for managers and is widely used in management literature – see for example, Fayol (in Pugh 1971, p103):

> **Authority is the right to give orders and the power to exact obedience.**

Many discussions of authority and influence show some confusion between authority, legitimate power and gaining compliance. This is hardly surprising as the concept is widely discussed in political theory, suggesting there is difficulty in finding a definition. Carter (1979, p1) says:

> **Authority is a concept central to social and political thought, yet its precise nature remains remarkably elusive.**

DEBATE – AUTHORITY AS A POLITICAL CONCEPT

Interpretations of authority inevitably vary with the political persuasion of the writer. Conservative writers will tend to uphold existing forms of authority whereas Liberal, Socialist and anarchist writers will view authority with varying degrees of distrust, which at its extremes leads to the abandoning of authority altogether and the adoption of an anarchist framework. Here are two anarchic views on authority.

Guerin (1970) sees authority as tyranny and as incompatible with the natural order and social harmony.

Wolff (1970) concludes that the legitimising of authority undermines the autonomy of the people.

What do you think?

Power made legitimate by position or expertise is called authority. Without the legitimising of the power in one of these ways the relationship is seen as coercive and unacceptable in societies based on democracy and ideas of personal freedom – see Carter (1979) for a full discussion of this political analysis. Carter suggests that we tend to distinguish two sorts of authority: 'in authority' and 'an authority'. It is an important distinction. The first relies on the position of authority as expressed through organisation charts and job titles – 'in authority' relies on control over resources to influence people. The second sort of authority, 'an authority', is based on personal attributes, credibility or ability to influence people.

Being *in* authority confers the right to control and judge the actions of others. Leadership is the exercise of the power conferred by that right in such a way as to win a willing and positive, rather than a grudging and negative response, and is discussed in Chapter 10. Being *an* authority is often the basis of credibility. In many ways the language of politics, citizenship and judicial studies can help in thinking about this legitimising of the position of leaders and led. Or maybe we shall move beyond the ideas of empowerment to the ideas of self-governance and organisations of citizens, but we are still a long way from that in most organisations.

Credibility

Managers and team leaders are people who are expected to influence people both within and without the organisation. Managers and team leaders are people with authority, stemming from the position they hold: they are *in* authority, with all the formal power that the position confers. Successful managers and team leaders have something more: they are *an* authority, possessing skill, knowledge and expertise that others consult willingly. Credibility is the word used in organisations, particularly among professionals, to describe this prerequisite ability that you need in order to get things done. In the increasingly informal working of organisations this credibility is something you have to earn and maintain for yourself. The job title and organisational position will help but will not be sufficient. Those with high credibility are worthy of belief, trustworthy, convincing and respected. They are listened to and can achieve things willingly and quickly, whereas colleagues who lack credibility meet resistance and have to rely more heavily on the glacial speed of formal mechanisms.

The basis of credibility is usually an appropriate expertise and some contribution of personal qualities such as hard work and enthusiasm. It is a very rare individual who can rely on personal attributes alone to be credible. Leadership is more often made up of hard work, understanding of the organisation's objectives, and position power. The components of a leader's credibility might be:

- Keeping in touch with the main task – it is only by keeping in touch with the main task of the organisation as a whole, and the section in which the leader is located, that new ideas can be based in reality. If they lose touch with their operational expertise they risk losing credibility with their colleagues. Staff can become sceptical about how much they understand current operational problems and the manager or team leader will retreat further into management and administration. This in turn creates unnecessary and superfluous systems of control that infuriate the staff.

- Legitimacy – staff on the receiving end of managers or team leaders exercising authority respond readily only when they perceive the authority to be legitimate. The formal organisation charts, job titles and pay structures provide *in* authority legitimacy. Western society and its organisations have developed a taste for informal means to supplement these. Keeping in touch with the main task and maintaining technical competence is the main feature, but *an* authority is also legitimised by behaviour such as showing willingness to do things, working hard, supporting team members, and demonstrating enthusiasm. Belonging to the organisation and being seen to be committed to it can be crucial in enabling one to influence things. Experience enables some people to develop a 'nose' for appropriate times and actions. They have invaluable legitimacy. The fact that these cannot be learned does not reduce their importance.

- A clear role – we have found that many managerial jobs do not have any clear role. People with these jobs are not in charge of anything and consequently the individuals, who are often hard-working, experienced and keen, will find work to do. Not all of this is helpful as it often interferes with other people's work, particularly where the work created is predominantly administrative and increases the amount of administration done by those required to respond.

For further details of these components of credibility see a series of studies we made (Weightman (1986), Torrington and Weightman (1982), (1987) and (1989b)).

There are several little phrases that suggest someone has credibility at work. Put the person in these phrases:

'You must talk to "our ..."'

'Can I just get your opinion on this?'

'You'll have to wait till ... comes back – they really understand...'

'I wonder what . . . thinks of this'

'We'll ask . . . to join us'

'We'd better put this past . . . first'

'I think . . . may have come across this before'

'I'm sure . . . will know about that'

'Check it with . . . first'

'Copy . . . in with it'

Behaviours that undermine credibility include: appearing to do useless things, adding to the burden of others unnecessarily, and bandwagoning for personal gain. But different cultures and organisations will reflect different things, so any particular organisation may well have other behaviours that add to or subtract from credibility. The important thing is to know what is the basis of your credibility and to work on maintaining it. The consequences of not having credibility are that those working with you will be frustrated and less compliant, peers will take you less seriously, bosses may include you only as a backup to themselves, and customers, clients, and others outside the organisation may come to devalue the whole organisation.

Just as important as acquiring credibility is the process of maintaining credibility. It is no use relying on expertise and practical experience that is five or ten years old. No young member of staff will be impressed with 'Well, we used to do it like this and it was fine' or '15 years ago we had the same problem and I managed to fix it.' Far better to offer the advice as current and try to encourage a mutual problem-solving approach.

CRITICAL INCIDENTS OF INFLUENCE

There are several typical meeting places for team leaders and managers where influence and persuasion are needed. These can be called the critical incidents of the working life of a manager or leader. Critical incident analysis is a technique used to understand someone's work. They are asked to describe critical incidents they have experienced at work. Then an analysis is done to see what competencies are needed to manage these incidents successfully. Examples of critical influencing incidents are given here. One is persuading people to take on different work by delegating to them. Second, there is the building and maintaining of a network of useful contacts. Another area is negotiating with people both in and outside the organisation. Meetings, of various kinds, are another typical persuading encounter. Team leaders and managers spend a lot of their working day influencing and persuading others to do things differently from how they might have been done otherwise. Let us look at some of these critical incidents of influence and persuasion.

Delegation

An issue closely related to authority and credibility is that of delegation. When, where and how do individuals delegate? Most books on management will have a chapter on delegation, as in order to manage the work of another some sort of delegation is involved. Usually this means entrusting some degree of authority and responsibility to others. Normally this is perceived to apply more in the relationship of delegating to those lower in the hierarchy, but this does not have to be the case. For example, we sometimes delegate a colleague to look after a particular part of the project. Most cases of delegation in organisations, however, are from the top down.

Mullins (1996, p570) suggests that delegation is founded on the concepts of:

- authority – the right to make decisions and take actions
- responsibility – the obligation to perform certain duties
- accountability (ultimate responsibility) – which cannot be delegated as the senior is ultimately responsible for the acts of the subordinates. The senior is responsible for ensuring that the job gets done even when they delegate to someone else the actual business of doing the job. This accountability is at the heart of a team leader's or manager's responsibility.

Most textbooks suggest that authority should be equivalent to responsibility. Responsibility without the authority to get things done is utterly frustrating for the people involved. This can end up with many people feeling stressed as they feel they have been landed with jobs to do for which they do not have appropriate authority.

Delegation is not giving people jobs to do – it is giving people scope, responsibility and authority. The test questions to ask are: can the person try their own ideas? Can they develop understanding and confidence? If the answer is yes then true delegation has taken place. This will give them the opportunity to perform, but it also gives them the opportunity to develop new competencies. Delegation may also help to encourage commitment. This comes about as people are motivated by having something more responsible and complex to do. If, however, this is taken too far, stimulation becomes fear and is not conducive to excellent performance. The more specific the instructions and terms of reference, the less stimulation and learning will be possible as a result of the activity. A related concept is empowerment; this is covered in Chapters 7 and 9 which both have a section on empowerment. Empowerment is a form of delegation.

The advantages claimed for delegation are:

- It contributes to the training and development of people. By doing a wider range of tasks, and those that incur more responsibility, we learn how to be more competent.
- It makes use of time more efficient. If work can be shared around there is less likely to be a constraint on getting things done while everyone waits for the overloaded to get round to the task.
- It makes it easier to perform tasks in diverse geographical locations. If all the branches of the organisation have at least one member of staff who can carry out the needed behaviour, again they do not have to wait on some other part of the organisation.
- Expertise and specialisms can be developed and used. By delegating particular kinds of work, individuals can develop expertise because they are dealing with it more frequently and so come to know what to do.
- It is cheaper. In most organisations those in senior positions tend to be paid more than those more junior. Consequently, if we can delegate to those on lower pay it can be said to be cheaper. If, however, they are overloaded and we appoint an additional member of the team whilst the senior is doing nothing, that would clearly not be cheaper.

Some disadvantages of delegation are:

- The delegator is dependent on others to perform appropriately.

- The standard of performance is less easy to control if you do not do it yourself. They may do it better or worse than you.

- It may not fit organisational culture. It may, for example, be an essential part of the credibility of team leaders to do certain activities themselves.

> We are constantly delegating in our personal lives. Think of how you approach asking someone to wash up, look after your plants, buy you a book or let the cat out. Do you let them decide whether to do it or not? What to do? How to do it? How does this compare with the way your mother goes about the same delegations?

Delegation is about trusting each other and having confidence that the job will be done. The delegator is relying on the other to do the work appropriately. In many ways the amount of and type of delegation that is demonstrated within an organisation says something about the nature of the organisational culture. Certainly within a team it says a great deal about the relationship between the team leader and the others. Delegation is an essential part of the way we influence and persuade others at work.

Networking

An important aspect of influence and persuasion is knowing a variety of people, and their knowing us in return. Creating a network of contacts is crucial to getting things done easily. This network is not just the official hierarchy and organisational contacts; it is a much more idiosyncratic combination of contacts that cuts across the more formal relationships. In a useful study of general managers, Kotter (1982) concluded that the work of senior managers could be analysed into the agendas of work that they set themselves and the network of contacts they maintained to implement these agendas. The agendas were made up of large and small aims and objectives, both formal and informal, that the managers were trying to get done. The networks of people were there to help the manager get things done. Having a network of contacts both inside and outside the organisation enabled people to consult about new projects effectively. A network also meant that they heard and understood when things began going wrong rather than having to wait until they had gone wrong. People who rely on formal relationships will be told only what they expect to hear and only at arranged times – when they have to be told.

Agenda-setting is one way in which people impose their will on the situation around them. The other is by setting up and maintaining a network of contacts through which the agendas are implemented. Agendas and networks are interdependent, as it is often through contact with people in the network that the agenda is kept up to date and appropriate. Networks are quite different from the formal structures, although there is no substitute for them in large organisations. Networks are made up of a whole range of people, both inside and outside the organisation, who can help implement the agenda. They are also a source of information about what should be on the agenda. A network is the people who can help things along by speeding things up, providing information, jumping a queue, endorsing a proposal in a meeting, checking data, arranging for you to meet someone with relevant expertise and, of course, doing jobs. Networks are made up of people who work for you, people you have worked with in the past, useful experts, people who understand the system, and a wide range of personal contacts. Expertise and personal charm are as important as position in the organisation for setting up and maintaining networks. There is usually some reciprocity implied in networks – 'You owe me one' is often heard.

Some will claim that this networking can become too political. How can we judge whether we are becoming too political in our behaviour? A useful test is to distinguish between setting agendas for action and using networks to implement the agendas. Political behaviour is potentially useful when it is deployed to put agendas into action. It is counterproductive when it is deployed only to build and maintain networks. Then it is seen as self-serving and can lead to a loss of credibility and accusations such as 'bandwagoning' or 'looking after their own career' are made.

Too much network and not enough agenda is associated with the type of people who are more concerned with their own promotion and position than with getting on with the job. The person who underemphasises networks and concentrates on agendas can be inward-looking and fail to take power seriously – and consequently fail to influence events sufficiently. Both these characters can be found in any organisation, but the former is more likely to be in a managerial position.

> June was the manager of the beauty and haberdashery department of a large department store. She was a friendly, outgoing woman. She willingly went to meetings and conferences and everyone knew her. Her colleagues in the department felt that she never really had any strong view of what should happen and so always followed the latest fashions and management requests. Perhaps June would have been better advised to use her obvious social skills for networking to inform her views and develop an agenda about the department.

> Another example concerns Paul, who was the ward manager of a hospital orthopaedic ward. He was passionate about the needs of people in traction and in hospital for relatively long periods of time. However, his style was rather brusque and intense, so others tended to avoid him where possible. He might have been advised to learn some of the influencing skills of networking and become more influential.

Negotiating

So far we have looked at the informal use of influence and persuasion within organisations. There are also occasions when this needs to be more formal. One such is the process of negotiation. This may correspond to negotiating a contract for supplying a service or products. It may be negotiating one's own terms and conditions of employment. It may be negotiating with a neighbouring firm to develop some waste land as a car park for both organisations. The important thing is that in most negotiations both sides expect to gain.

There are different sorts of negotiation problems. When there are just two players of equal standing it is a situation of mutual dependence. Fifty/fifty sharing is a natural solution to the problem in these sorts of negotiations because it has an appearance of fairness. Getting there may take some time because of the element of ritual and the need for face-saving in some negotiations, but the fairness principle does seem typical of British organisational behaviour.

Another more complex sort of negotiation is where the number of potential parties on either side increases. Then the numbers and bargaining power of each member matter less. Here it becomes more useful in negotiation if the joint group can create a bigger pool to negotiate about – that is, they try to find more customers, clients or users of the product/service so everyone can have a bit more. For example, when purchaser and supplier are negotiating on a one-to-one basis it is reasonable to bargain about the 50/50 split – whereas if there are several providers and suppliers negotiating together there may be more to be said for trying to generate more business than about exactly how it is split. This is certainly a lesson being taken up by conglomerates of leisure and tourist facilities in some towns, who have found themselves a stronger negotiating position by grouping, and marketing the place generally to attract visitors.

Meetings

Meetings are another formal setting for influence and persuasion. All forms of power, authority and influence at work in organisations can be seen at work in the meeting. Many people in large organisations spend a good deal of time attending, and complaining about, meetings. The usual question is 'What is the point of this meeting?' Meetings have both overt and covert reasons for taking place. Some of these reasons are given below.

Overt reasons for meetings:

- Making decisions – the meeting may be the focus of decision-making, with all the appropriate people present to enable a consensus decision to take place or, as often happens, prior discussions have arrived at the decisions and the meeting merely ratifies them.

- Making recommendations – the assembled meeting has to agree what and to whom it wants to recommend. It might be only a subsidiary meeting passing recommendations to a more senior meeting where the real decision will take place.

- Training newcomers to the group – it is often through attending meetings that managers and team leaders learn about the wider implications of the work of their unit and the issues facing the organisation as a whole. Meetings are also a source of learning about the politics and power play within the organisation.

- Analysis and report – organising material for another group. This is particularly the function of working parties.

- Information – exchanging information and asking for information; this usually takes place under the 'any other business' or 'matters arising' sections in formal meetings. This can be a major function of informal gatherings.

Covert reasons for meetings, which in general are good reasons although hidden, include:

- Cohesion – people can feel part of the whole by, for example, chatting beforehand, catching someone's eye or joking. Some regular meetings try to engender this clubbiness by having regular breakfast meetings of the management team or an occasional 'away day' in a hotel.

- Catharsis – sometimes it is useful to give vent to anger even when nothing can be done. At least people feel they 'have had their say'.

- Manipulation – where a particular decision or action is desired and the meeting is manoeuvred into agreeing to this as if it was its own decision. Manipulating the meeting is usually done by more senior staff or a particular cabal who want a particular decision and the meeting legitimises the proposed plans and policies.

As so much time and energy can be spent in meetings, it is worth thinking about how they are run. It is certainly the case that those who prepare for the meeting are likely to be more influential. We (Torrington and Weightman, 1989a) developed a checklist to consider the arrangements for regular meetings. It was designed to assist in running them effectively so that the necessary communication and decision-making could take place. The list of questions might also help when a regular meeting feels wrong, as usually this means something on this list is not clear or agreed on. There are no right answers; it is just a list for you to consider if you are part of a meeting – see Table 11.1.

Making a case

In meetings people in organisations are often required to make a presentation or a case for something. This may be reporting the results of a project, making a bid for funding for a project, trying to sell something to a customer or client, or trying to influence or persuade a group of people towards a particular outcome. The authority, power and credibility of the individual making the presentation will influence how effective and persuasive the presentation is. But there are also technical aspects of presentations that can make the presentation more influential. Some of these are given here. Whatever the purpose, there are some basic ground rules for presentations, which are summarised in Table 11.2. It is perhaps worth noting that the same model can be quite helpful for essay writing as well!

This chapter has looked at influencing: at the specific personal attributes of authority and credibility and the specific techniques of such things as meetings and presentations. Being persuasive and influential is a combination of these personal attributes and the technical skills to develop good networks, negotiations, meetings and presentations. How influential a manager or team leader you are will depend to a great extent on the nature of the relationship you have with the person(s) you are trying to influence.

ACTIVITIES

1 Ask yourself the following questions:

  ■ Who has real credibility round here? What is the basis of this credibility?

  ■ What is the basis of my credibility? Is this based on old expertise? What am I doing to maintain my credibility? Is this mostly based on technical expertise or on personal qualities?

  ■ What do I do to maintain my credibility with my team?

  ■ What do I do to maintain my credibility with my colleagues elsewhere in the organisation and in other places?

  ■ What are we doing to ensure that others can build and develop their own credibility? Are we doing anything to undermine their credibility? Can we do something to prevent that?

2 Make a list of all the individuals who can influence how effective you are in your work, but with whom you do not have a formal working relationship. Then answer the following:

  ■ Is there someone not on your list who would be useful?

  ■ Are there people on the list where communication could be improved?

  ■ What are you going to do about it?

Table 11.1 *A meetings checklist*

Who should attend the meeting?
- A large group to represent wide interests
- A small group to make discussion easier and more productive
- Representatives of each layer of the hierarchy
- A variety of personalities to ensure a lively discussion
- Only those with expertise in this area
- Who should be chair?

What is the brief or terms of reference of the meeting?
- Does this meeting have the power to take a decision?
- Can this meeting make a recommendation?
- How wide can the discussion usefully range?
- Has a decision relating to the topic already been made that cannot be changed?
- Are there some conclusions that would be unacceptable? To whom?

What should the agenda be?
- What do we need to consider and in what order?
- Is there too much to cope with?
- Who can include items on the agenda?
- Will matters arising and any other business take up a lot of time?

What about the physical location and arrangements?
- Does everyone know which room is to be used and is it the right size?
- Is the furniture arranged so that everyone can see everyone else and give them eye contact?
- Is it appropriate to have coffee served? Has it been arranged?
- Is it noisy, cold, likely to have interruptions?

How can contributors be stimulated and controlled?
- Who has something to say?
- How can I get them to say it?
- How can I make the long-winded brief?
- When should I nudge the meeting towards a decision/the next item?

Minutes or report of the meeting
- Who writes them?
- Is it important to describe the discussion and issues or just the actions and who is responsible?
- Who gets a copy?
- What will be the effect of the minutes on those who did/did not attend?
- Who are we trying to influence with these minutes and in what way?

Implementation of proposals
- Who has agreed to do what?
- How can we help each other to get on with it?
- Who else can we involve?
- How can we monitor the implementation?
- Do we need a review date?
- What can I do to get things moving?

Source: Torrington and Weightman (1989)

Table 11.2 *Making your case*

Preparation

Why are you making this presentation?
What are you going to say?
Who are you saying it to?
Where will you be saying it?
How will you say it?
How long have you got to say it?

The structure

Preface
Position
Problem
Possibilities
Proposal
Postscript

The technique

Delivery – beware mumbling, hesitancy, gabbling, catch phrases, poor eye contact, mannerisms and dropping your voice
Language – use short words and sentences
Visuals – they aid explanation and persuasion
Detail – better too little than too much
Timing – better too short than too long
Feedback – ask them

Summary and questions

Look at original objective
Summarise, recommend, propose next step, thank, and ask for questions

Source *Making your case*, Video Arts

---

3 Imagine you are working in the tourist office for your home town. Which facilities in the town would you be most keen to promote? Why might any facility resist inclusion?

4 Answer the questions below about an organisation you know – for example, where you work, your department/school within the university, or some sports organisation.

   ■ What are the formal methods of influence here? This would include meetings, memos, job appraisals, organisation charts, job descriptions, etc.

   ■ What are the informal methods of influence here? This would include style of talking, where decisions are really taken, who is 'in' and who is 'out', etc.

   ■ Who is most influential? What is the basis of this influence? Position, power, expertise, charm, length of service, ownership, or just being there?

   Now list three ways you think you could get some change in this organisation.

5 If you are in seminar group, get everyone to make a 3-minute presentation using Table 11.2 'Making your case'. This can be done with ten minute's notice. If you want some ideas for topics, try:

Why you should visit . . .

Why you should take up . . .

Why it is wrong to . . .

Afterwards discuss which parts of the structure were well done.

HAVE I MET THE OBJECTIVES?

1 What is the difference between 'in' authority and 'an' authority?

2 How can those lacking significant degrees of hierarchical authority influence and persuade others?

3 What does delegation involve?

4 What factors must be considered when organising a meeting?

5 Discuss the importance of credibility.

6 Describe the importance of networking for individuals within organisations.

And finally . . .

What would you advise Hans to do? What from this chapter might be useful? I would probably start by looking at the basis of his authority and credibility, encourage him to build a suitable network. He needs to decide whether a meeting would be useful and, if so, what sort of meeting he wants. He then needs to consult with people to find out whether there is likely to be any sort of compromise possible before the meeting. If these people are used to meeting, the work may get done quickly; if not, it could be a difficult time.

FURTHER READING

This is a chapter where the material comes from such a wide range of disciplines that no specific text exists which covers everything comprehensively.

On the academic side you could look at the relevant sections in a book on organisational behaviour such as Mullins (2002). This is the standard text in the area of organisation behaviour.

More political is the book by Carter (1979), I recommend this to those of you with a taste for the analytical.

Pfeffer (1981) is an excellent academic text that is worth having a look at if you want to go into greater depth.

More fun would be to read some descriptions of how people actually went about influencing others. For this you could look at some of the autobiographies mentioned in Chapter 1, or the Lowndes book mentioned in the previous chapter.

Case studies and profiles in magazines such as *Management Today* or the business sections of the press also have good stories in this area which may include useful insights.

Motivation

*This is an important theoretical chapter for the management of people at work. It appears at this late position in the book to follow the CIPD Standards. It could equally appear at the beginning of the book as it is such a central idea for looking at people and what makes them get up and make a suitable contribution at work. It deals with **theories of motivation** and **alienation**. It also examines the practical application of motivation and the **psychological contract**. Other relevant practical applications of motivation are covered in job design, Chapter 5; rewards and performance management, Chapters 13 and 14; job satisfaction, Chapters 5 and 13; commitment and valuing in Chapter 7; and leadership in Chapter 10.*

OBJECTIVES

When you have finished reading this chapter you should be able to:

- **understand and explain the major theories of motivation**

- **list a hierarchy of needs that affect people's motivation**

- **give examples of things at work that will demotivate people and others that will be a positive motivation at work**

- **distinguish different individual attitudes to work**

- **understand some of the reasons why individuals differ in their attitudes to work.**

Ikbahl's fatigued charity

Ikbahl is the office manager at the headquarters of a charity. He is responsible for 40 people. There is a lot of clerical work to do, acknowledging donations from the public and sending out leaflets. Many of the employees are idealistic young people who feel passionately about the cause of the charity and want to make a difference. Despite this passion there is a constant turnover of staff. Ikbahl feels that too many errors occur in the administration because of the large proportion of inexperienced staff. In addition he feels that good people are leaving because they find the reality of the work dull compared with their initial expectations. There are always plenty of candidates for the jobs, but can Ikbahl improve the continuity of staff? What should Ikbahl do?

Should he accept the rate of turnover as inevitable? Hope that a recession will make people stay in their jobs longer? Try to vary the work by including some tasks outside the office? Look for ways of getting groups to work together and innovate? Have a suggestion box for a weekly campaign? Have a small fund of time/cash for individual projects to increase fundraising? What would motivate these keen young idealists to stay longer?

In common parlance we often say things like 'Jo is motivated by money' or 'Jan really enjoys competition'. The assumption is that we can see motivation. The reality is that we can only hypothesise that people are motivated by some particular factor. We do this by looking at their behaviour and seeing if there is anything different when the particular 'factor' is involved. Motivation is a drive within a person to try to achieve a goal, to meet a want or need.

There seems little doubt that beyond the very basic needs of food, shelter and safety, our wants are culturally determined. For example, in the developed Western cultures we tend to emphasise individuality and achievement, whereas in many Eastern cultures there is an emphasis on the family and group achievements. Fitting in and being accepted is valued highly. These values affect what people are motivated to work for. How stable these culturally determined motivations are, how varied they are and whether they can be influenced, is the subject of much academic debate that is really too theoretical for our needs here; if you are interested, look up the references at the end of this chapter.

MOTIVATION AT WORK

Our prime task here is to examine the motivation of people in the workplace. For managers and team leaders this understanding is important as they are responsible for ensuring that the work output of their team members is satisfactory. For individuals, the understanding is important if they are to understand their own and other people's behaviour at work. Motivating people at work is not just a case of pressing the right button to switch them on, no matter that some managers feel this is how it should be. Indeed, technically, no one can motivate another person. Motivation is an internal state that directs people towards certain goals or objectives.

At the basic contract level, the team leader's or manager's task is to ensure that each individual's motivation is sufficiently engaged. This is done by checking whether individuals are willing to work, to a standard, for the rewards offered. Most team leaders would hope to be able to motivate members of the team to even greater contributions; indeed, some argue it is this capacity that differentiates the leader from the manager. It is important to understand this distinction, as many team leaders and managers treat everyone in the same way and try to manipulate people by trying to 'motivate' them. A better way is to try to understand the needs and objectives of those who work for or with you, and to arrive at some sort of equitable arrangement that their needs as well as the organisation's needs will be met. Put simply, motivation at work is trying to answer 'what is in it for them'.

The balance between the individual and the organisation is sometimes enshrined in the phrase the 'employment, or psychological, contract', see Chapter 4. This 'contract' involves a series of expectations between the individual member and the organisation. These expectations are not defined formally and the individual and the organisation may not be conscious of the contract, but the relationship is affected by the expectations. This means taking into account individual differences in how people interpret the rewards offered. For example, we all differ in our interests, attitudes and needs and that will affect how we react to different aspects of the job, such as its degree of autonomy, variety and amount of work to be done. We also react differently to the people aspect of our work environment. Aspects such as our peers, the nature of the supervision and the general organisational climate can affect our motivation at work. We all have different reasons for going to work and we want different things from work. Some of us are looking for totally involving jobs that offer opportunities for responsibility and recognition, for example becoming general managers. Others are working for little more than the money and the freedom to get on with their life away from work. We have different attitudes to work.

Understanding the motivation of people at work means admitting that certain aspects of the job will have different values to different people. This suggests that we need to understand that those who work with us may not have the same orientation to work as ourselves. To paraphrase Mills (1956):

'Work may be a mere source of livelihood, or the most significant part of one's inner life; it may be experienced as hard graft, or as an exuberant expression of self, as a bounden duty, or as a development of man's universal nature. Neither love nor hatred of work is inherent in man, or inherent in any given line of work.'

An example of the different approaches people take to their work can be seen where some opt for part-time, temporary or contract work, so-called peripheral work, whilst others opt for permanent, full-time work, so-called core work. This can be an expression of a different set of priorities as well as a response to the available opportunities. Why are people so different?

THEORIES OF MOTIVATION

Trying to account for the different motivation of people has intrigued psychologists for a long time. Research models and theories have been proposed from the earliest times. Some of these have been the most enduring theories of psychology, not necessarily because of any real evidence to support them but more because of a felt 'rightness'. Maslow's and Herzberg's are prime examples of powerful, felt right, enduring models that people still find useful for explaining individual motivation.

Psychologists have studied the behaviour of animals and humans to try to find out what it is people will work for – what gives pleasure and what inhibits behaviour. There have been very precise and detailed studies of how animals learn new skills and the difference a suitable reward can make. The word 'motivation' is used technically in these studies to describe the hidden, inner drive or need to seek that reward. Different models of motivation have been developed to try to account for the variation in motivation a person has across time, and between different people.

Maslow's model of motivation

The most famous model of the variation in motivation across time, for the same person and between people, is that of Maslow (1954) – see Figure 12.1. He grouped needs into a hierarchy of five stages. The first two he called primary needs, concerned with our basic physical requirements to sustain life. The last three stages he calls secondary needs, which are learned. These are psychological needs that come into play only when the primary needs are satisfied. They are more culturally determined. For example, if we are hungry or physically exhausted we are less concerned about being sociable. He also pointed out that once a primary need is satisfied it loses its potency and is no longer a motivator. In our example, once the hunger or exhaustion is satisfied the person will be less motivated by food and rest and will be more motivated to be sociable. By contrast, Maslow argued, secondary needs continue to motivate and we seek more of them even when we have experienced some satisfaction of this need.

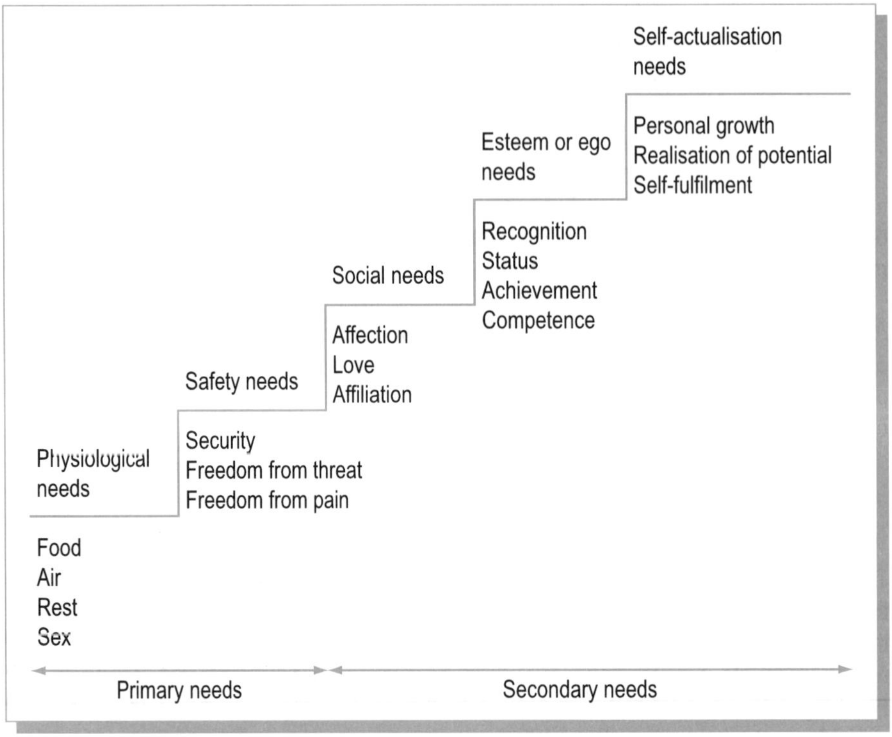

Figure 12.1 *Maslow's hierarchy of human needs*

In one head office I visited, notices had to go out to 20,000 company pensioners. The manager in charge decided that the whole department, including himself, should spend the last half hour of the day, for a week, putting the papers in the envelopes as they sat round a big table. He could, of course, have hired temporary staff or given it to the most junior staff. He saw the opportunity to get the task done efficiently by bringing everyone together. They certainly all seemed motivated by the social gathering and chatted as they did the task.

At work, at least in the developed world, most of us have our primary needs satisfied by regular periods of rest and food, with sufficient shelter to protect us from the climate. Just think of the fuss we make when the heating or air-conditioning is not working. In analysing the behaviour in Western organisations we are mostly concerned with the motivation based on secondary needs. When we look at the range of conditions that organisations are providing for their employees we can see that different needs can be satisfied at work. For example, many organisations recognise that social contact and belonging to a group can be helpful in getting the work done – especially as relief from a tedious task.

Maslow's next level, esteem needs, are met at work through all sorts of status distinctions, for example size of office, company car, having a secretary, use of telephone for overseas calls or not. Many organisations are now trying to reduce these distinctions by having, for example, only one dining room or style of uniform. The aim is usually to reduce the number of spurious symbols of esteem rather than to remove symbols of esteem altogether. Not many organisations give everyone the same pay and conditions of employment! For example, how much freedom to organise one's work varies between jobs. Often those in senior positions have more autonomy as to how they organise their time. Not many senior staff are happy to give over complete control of their diaries to the online diary.

The top of Maslow's hierarchy is self-actualisation or self-fulfilment. That is, trying to become everything you have the potential to become. This idea of 'self-actualisation' has been particularly taken up and developed by humanistic psychologists. The concept has also been very influential in organisations due to the use of management consultants, organisation developers and advisers on change who have pursued these ideals. It is not always such a motivator as there are some constraints. First, it is a learnt, culturally determined, need. Second, the other needs must be satisfied first. Third, not everyone shares the same attitude to work.

Maslow's model is a general model of human motivation. How well suited is Maslow's hierarchy to the work situation? Although he did not devise the model specifically to look at motivation at work, it has become very popular for doing so. Its main strength is in listing what factors might motivate people. Steers and Porter (1991, p35) have taken the analysis forward and suggest various organisational factors that could be used to satisfy the different stages of need as applied to the workplace:

- physiological
  pay
  pleasant work conditions
  dining facilities
- safety
  health and safety well monitored
  company benefits
  job security
- social
  cohesive work group
  friendly supervision
  professional associations
- esteem
  social recognition
  job title
  high-status job
  feedback from job itself
- self-actualisation
  challenging job
  opportunities for creativity
  achievement in work
  advancement in the organisation.

The difficulty in applying a Maslow approach to motivation at work is that many people will not wish to satisfy all their motivations at work. This implies that the motivating factors at work will not be the same for each individual, even where they apparently have the same desires, as some people will be meeting their needs outside of work and other individuals will be trying to meet a lot of their desires at work.

Alderfer (1972) developed Maslow's motivation theory as it applied to work by suggesting that there were three groups of needs:

- **e**xistence needs, to do with survival
- **r**elatedness needs, to do with social belonging
- **g**rowth needs, to do with individual development.

He called this the ERG theory, and he argued that organisations and their team leaders and managers need to address all three of these. Alderfer suggested that where growth is not possible at work the other two needs must be addressed more powerfully.

An indication of how well this Maslow model still fits with the experience of people in work in the UK is revealed in a survey of 1,500 employees within the UK (The UK@work report, 2003). It found that to keep staff happy the following aspects of work, in this order of importance, should be in place:

Safety and security – continuity of employment

Reward – suitably paid

Affiliation – with pleasant colleagues

Growth – personal development and developing organisatons

Work/life balance – with time to lead a personal life.

Herzberg's theory of motivation at work

Herzberg (1968) developed Maslow's model with particular reference to people at work. He described the lower-order needs as having the potential to dissatisfy if they are not met, but once they are met more of them will not increase motivation. These he called the hygiene factors – if managers do not get them right there will be complaints and people will be demotivated; if they are right no one will comment or notice, just like the effect of hygiene in the kitchen. In contrast to the hygiene factors are the satisfiers. People will work for these and want more of them. These satisfiers tend to be intrinsic to the person. The list of satisfiers are more culturally determined than the hygiene factors, so your group may have slightly different ones from those listed in Table 12.1. Herzberg's model has been particularly useful in drawing attention to the way jobs are designed so that jobs are enriched and the quality of life at work can be improved.

Support for Herzberg's model of motivation at work can be seen in the results of surveys carried out in the workplace. For example, one survey by Leigh and Brown (1996), using the phrases 'psychological safety' and 'meaningfulness' – similar but not identical to Herzberg's hygiene factors and satisfiers – found that people worked harder if the following job features were in place:

- psychological safety:
    - support – to have authority and be backed by one's boss
    - role clarity – what is expected, and to what standard, is clear
    - recognition – praise is given

Table 12.1 *Herzberg's theory of motivation*

Hygiene factors	Satisfiers
Company policy and administration	
Supervision	Achievement
Working conditions	Recognition
Salary	Work itself
Relationship with peers	Responsibility
Personal life	Advancement
Relationship with subordinates	Growth
Status	
Security	

Source: F. Hertzberg, 'One more time: how do you motivate employees?' *Harvard Business Review*, January–February 1968.

- meaningfulness:
  - self-expression – express self through the work
  - contribution – make a difference to the main task
  - challenge – feel stretched.

If these are representative of many people's feelings about their work, these points are useful starting places for designing the allocation of work and jobs. They also say something about how people want to be led or managed.

How is behaviour driven by our needs?

The Maslow and Herzberg theories given above are both concerned with what motivates an individual – that is, the content of motivation. If we start looking at the process of motivation, we find the ways in which behaviour is initiated, directed and maintained are also important in establishing and maintaining motivation. Other theories and models have been developed to help understand the process of motivation.

An important model in this area is the *force field* theory of Lewin. Lewin (1952) emphasises that individuals operate in a field of forces that represent subjective perceptions about the environment, the importance of a goal, and the psychological distance of the goal. Lewin uses his theory to try to account for the difference of motivation in people at different times. For example, you and I might both want to meet the prime minister. I see the circumstances as far too difficult; the goal of seeing him or her is not compelling enough to overcome the psychological distance to make any effort to see him or her worthwhile. You, however, may be in more favourable circumstances, or you may want to see the prime minister enough to overcome the psychological distance between him or her and you. As a result, you will be more motivated to try to meet the prime minister than I am.

A model closely related to force field theory is that of *expectancy theory* developed by Vroom and Deci (1974). This concept looks at the influence on our motivation of our expectancy of the success of our actions. The more likely we think it is that we shall be successful the more effort we put in. For example, if I feel that when I go to the library I shall find the books and gain access to the computers that I want, I am more likely to put the effort into going than if I expect to find all the resources 'out' or 'booked'. My expectation of success influences my motivation to go to the library. Another concept that Vroom and Deci use is 'valence', which is the degree of preference an individual attaches to a particular outcome. This can be positive, negative or indifferent. The theory then makes the motivation (M) of the individual a combination of expectancy (Ex) times the valency (V) attached to the outcome, expressed as the equation $M = ExV$.

Another influence on expectancy is the perceived fairness of the results. This derives from how fairly treated an individual feels they have been treated in comparison with others – see Adams (1979) for further discussion. This idea is based on exchange theory, where people expect certain outcomes in exchange for certain contributions. For example, if in seminars/tutorials two of us are always contributing to the discussion and have always done the reading when the others have not, we may begin to feel very demotivated and begin to make less effort. On the other hand, we may delight in the personal attention of the tutor.

MOTIVATION AND WORK BEHAVIOUR

Some people feel that with the increasing use of robotics, automation and the advent of computers, the most tedious jobs have disappeared. The argument continues that consequently motivation at work is no longer an issue for individuals or the team leaders and managers responsible for organisations. However, even if we accept the premiss – which is arguable – our expectations as consumers about standards of service from organisations in both the public and private sectors make it important that people are well motivated at work. This is to say nothing of the humanitarian argument that people should be doing something they want to do! Motivation remains an important part of understanding and analysing the behaviour of people at work, and so improving the working life of those employed in organisations.

Understanding what motivates people at work will also suggest appropriate rewards for them in response to their contribution. Although reward management is a study in itself – see Armstrong (1996) – and is the business of HR/personnel departments, some understanding of different rewards can suggest different ways a team leader or line manager might approach individuals. They include:

- pay – for time; by results; for merit; performance-related; share ownership; profit-related
- other benefits – pensions; sick pay; insurance schemes and other financial benefits
- work/task – variety of work and skills used; autonomy; involvement
- social/people – interactions with others; recognition; feedback.

In many ways, the emphasis of this book on managing people is suggesting a variety of ways of tailoring rewards to individuals so they are motivated to contribute their effort to achieve the organisation's goals.

Steers and Porter (1987, p21) indicate some of the more important variables that influence people's motivation and work – see Table 12.2. These variables also give us a helpful checklist for looking at some of the reasons for poor performance in organisations. There can be a problem with any one of the variables.

Table 12.2 *Steers and Porter's checklist of influences on motivation at work.*

Individual characteristics
Interests
Attitudes towards self/job/aspects of the work situation
Needs such as security/social/achievement

Job characteristics
Types of intrinsic rewards
Degree of autonomy
Amount of direct performance feedback
Degree of variety of tasks
Work environment characteristics such as peers and supervision

Organisational actions such as
Reward practices
System-wide rewards
Individual rewards
Organisational climate

Source: Steers and Porter (1987)

Another checklist that may be useful is Hollyforde and Whiddett's (2002) summary of some of the motivation material and the ways they suggest we might nurture motivation at work.

- Give individuals and teams responsibility for the results of their work.
- Give people clear, challenging, but achievable goals.
- Ensure there are sufficient resources to do the job.
- Give feedback to support, not control.
- Stimulate through variety.
- Have fair systems and procedures.
- Give people complete processes to do, not parts of tasks.

Leading, or managing, people with all the variety of analysis and application is in the end about motivating people to do the work required in the most efficient and effective way. Although this chapter comes late in the book, the concept of motivation is really at the heart of managing people.

Attitudes to work

There are several other important questions about work and people's motivation which need to be asked, such as: what is the meaning of work for individuals? Does work have the same importance for us all? Is there some inevitable connection between certain work conditions and experiences and particular attitudes and feelings? What do we mean by job satisfaction? Is it the same for us all? Most studies in this field have been done with manual labourers in manufacturing workplaces. This is partly because this group of people is easy to study, as they have less to hide. It is partly because they have been seen as a problem by management. By studying the effect of work and the differing attitudes to this work it is hoped that better working practices can be developed for the benefit of the organisation and the workers.

One important influence on work is the nature of that work. The technology used by workers will affect and constrain the way in which their work can be organised. For example, whether a work process is done sequentially with everyone adding their little bit, or whether each individual can perform the whole task, will also have an effect. The sheer physical scale of an operation and the noise generated whilst doing it will influence how the things are organised. Whether the technology must be in the same place for several years or is constantly on the move will determine how things are organised. All of these in turn will influence the attitude and behaviour of the workers. For example, some technologies like printing allow social groupings at work. Others, such as car assembly, are much more difficult to organise in social groups at a reasonable cost. Some tasks, such as shutting down oil wells, are by definition always somewhere different from the previous occasion but tend to be done by an established group. Workers engaged in these different tasks will have different group attitudes and behaviours, on average, compared to others.

The classic study which introduced the concept of 'orientation to work' is that of Goldthorpe, Lockwood, Bechhofer and Platt (1969), who examined the attitude and behaviour of assembly line workers at the Vauxhall car manufacturing plant in Luton. They found that different workers doing similar jobs had different wants and expectations of work. That is, work had a different meaning for them. The study distinguished three main orientations or attitudes to work:

- An instrumental orientation to work means that work is a means to an end outside the work situation. Work is a means of acquiring the income to support a valued way of life.

- A bureaucratic orientation describes people who seek to give services to a company over a long time in return for a career that promises some promotion and increases in salary and security of employment.

- A solidaristic orientation characterises those people who in addition to an economic orientation also value group loyalty to their mates.

This research work suggests that not everyone is seeking self-actualisation through work – perhaps they are resigned to being unable to do so. It is a useful counterpoint to the assumptions made by Maslow and Herzberg.

DEBATE THE MEANING OF WORK

Discussing the meaning of, and attitude to, work involves our basic assumptions about morals, power, equality, the rights of individuals and so on, all of which have a political aspect to them. A unitarist approach to job satisfaction would be to assume that belonging to the team will meet most people's needs. The pluralist, on the other hand, would want a wider selection of rewards and jobs for people to do. This difference in points of view makes research in this area very difficult as different interpretations can be put on the same findings. In addition there is the thorny problem of exactly what do we mean by 'job satisfaction' and the meaning of work. Certainly we need to understand that not everyone is the same. What you mean by 'job satisfaction' may not be what I want from work – nor what I think others want from work. Much of current thinking on performance management is trying to find a reward system that caters for individuals rather than groups. Can you think of two organisations with contrasting attitudes in their approach to rewarding individuals? Does this lead to a difference in attitude to work from the people working in these organisations?

Alienation

Another important concept that can help explain people's motivation at work is alienation. This concept, used in sociology and elsewhere, was originally formulated by Karl Marx to analyse the effect of capitalism on people. Marx used it to refer to people's detachment, estrangement and loss of control over their lives in a capitalist society. Alienation is about the separation of people. It is applied to the way we feel cut off from important decisions, people or outcomes.

The concept can be applied to work organisations. The work we do can feel alien and oppressive. It is thought that it is the way work is organised that leads to this alienation, rather than particular work processes. Individuals can also be alienated from other people because the relationships have become calculating, self-interested and untrusting. This is demonstrated when individuals have become so alienated from others that they are able to behave callously towards them without a sense of embarrassment.

Examples of alienated people can be found in some city dealing rooms where the drive to make a profitable deal means ignoring a colleague who is clearly in distress. This hard approach is often part of the culture and may explain why many people working in these environments 'burn out' and leave the employment early.

People can also be alienated from the product of their labours when the end product is not seen or is remote from their control. Alienation can happen when people are not involved in the original decision about what the work should be. The classic example of alienation is seen in large-scale manufacturing, such as car plants (see Beynon, 1973), compared with traditional crafts such as pottery where the workers can see the results of their labour and are less likely to be alienated. People are alienated from their own labour when they are unable to get the satisfactions at work because they are controlled by others, and so are meeting someone else's requirements and standards as opposed to their own. One example is where two building societies merge and the workers from one society have to adopt the procedures, standards and requirements of the other. The individual operators can feel alienated.

Marx argued that alienation is an objective state. We may feel dissatisfied with our job but not necessarily alienated. We may feel satisfied with our job but be alienated at the same time as we may be missing out on something much more rewarding. An example can be seen in those who have been made redundant and have then developed alternative activities which they find more worthwhile than their former employment and wonder why they did not do this earlier. Before redundancy they were in a state of being alienated.

It is an ideal world where everyone is highly motivated and doing exactly what they would choose to do. We may not achieve this ideal, but that does not mean not trying to improve things. There are real dangers if the organisation of work does not give sufficient consideration to the needs of the individuals working in the organisation. If work is organised so that we are cut off from important decisions, people and outcomes, we can feel the work we do is alien and oppressive – that is, we are alienated. Blauner (1967) argued that alienation consists of four conditions or states:

- Powerlessness – comes when people feel controlled by others
- Meaninglessness – is felt when people do not understand the co-ordination or purpose of their work

- Isolation – is where people do not feel they belong
- Self-estrangement — is when people do not feel involved with their own work.

All of these can happen to people at all levels of the organisation, and they are particularly likely to be found in periods of reorganisation. It can be very difficult to find ways of reorienting people once they have become alienated. It is, therefore, worth picking up on the early signs so that something can be done to make people feel more valued. Attempts to pre-empt these elements of alienation found within organisations include trying to empower staff, setting reasonable objectives, valuing staff and engendering commitment. These concepts are all dealt with elsewhere in this book.

This chapter has been about motivation at work. I hope it has persuaded you that this is not just a mechanical process where you press button A and everyone is 'motivated'. However, you can help colleagues to be motivated if you carefully analyse what is in it for them, from their perspective. If you understand what suits and motivates particular people you can design tasks and jobs so that people are more likely to succeed and feel rewarded. This is surely in the interest of workers, team leaders and managers, and of the organisation you all work for. It also helps team leaders and managers to manage performance, which is discussed in the final two chapters.

ACTIVITIES

1   Do we use all the Steers and Porter's list at work? Could we do more?

2   Which of Herzberg's hygiene factors are currently causing a problem in our organisation? What can be done about it?

3   Are people in our organisation showing the signs of being alienated from their work? For example, are they demonstrating feelings of loneliness, exclusion, or rejection? Do their actions seem mechanical or uncommitted? Is their behaviour not bound by rules?

4   List three reasons why you are doing this course. Include a mixture of personal reasons and pressure from outside. Now get three other people in your group to do the same thing. Compare the results to see where you agree and disagreee about the 'motivations' for doing this course.

5   Think back to something you have done recently in which you were really involved. This may be a social activity, sporting event, a project, a family event or something solitary. Describe the event objectively with the 'who, what and where'. Now describe your feelings during the event. Using Maslow's hierarchy of needs, which of your needs do you think were being satisfied? Would you have felt the same if you had been really exhausted, hungry or frightened?

6   Try to list three different attitudes to work that supermarket checkout people might have. Which of these would be associated with full-time permanent core workers and which with those who work on Sundays only? Do you think there would need to be a difference in the way they were supervised?

HAVE I MET THE OBJECTIVES?

1   What are the five levels in Maslow's hierarchy of needs?

2   What are the differences between Herzberg's hygiene factors and the satisfiers?

3 Why might people have different attitudes to work?

4 What are Blauner's four signs of alienation?

5 Why is motivation not something that is 'done' to people?

And finally ...

What would you do in Ikbahl's position? Would you use your understanding about motivation and attitudes to work to help? I should probably try to use some of the theories detailed in this chapter to remind myself that there are different satisfactions to be had. I should try to connect the work in the office with the ideals of the charity. Some daily or weekly activity that reinforces the connection might help.

FURTHER READING

The special issue 'Motivating People' of the *Harvard Business Review*, January 2003 is well worth getting hold of. It has reprints of classic papers such as Herzberg and several interesting contemporary points of view. There are also some good cartoons.

Other books to look at are:

Armstrong M (1999) is a useful look at the whole area.

Maitland I (1995) *Motivating People*. London, IPD. This is a short, practical book.

Steers and Porter (1991) is an academic text with various articles exploring some of the issues associated with understanding motivation and its application to the work environment. There several editions of this book, so look for the latest edition.

Stimulating Improved Performance

CHAPTER 13

*This is largely an applied chapter but has some material on **communication** theory. Chapter 12 on motivation is also very relevant. The applied material included here covers **performance management**, **core competencies**, **planning**, **performance-related pay** and **managing by objectives**. There are specific examples from the NHS, Price Waterhouse and BIC.*

OBJECTIVES

When you have finished reading this chapter you should be able to:

- **understand the issues associated with managing performance**

- **explain the issues associated with managing performance**

- **discuss how performance management fits in with the needs of the business as a whole**

- **define 'performance'**

- **discuss the importance of communication in managing performance**

- **describe what is performance-related pay**

- **describe the ethics of managing performance.**

Helena's junior

Helena was a senior barrister in a small firm of lawyers in a provincial city. The firm specialised in criminal work. Its barristers were always busy with referrals and there were piles of paper everywhere. Most of the work was paid for by Legal Aid. Helena was mentor to three of the junior lawyers. She felt that each of them should be capable of winning more of their cases – particularly Kate, who had lost all of her cases. This was not very good for business, as solicitors and their clients were trying to ensure that Kate was not allocated to them. What should Helena do?

Should she examine what was being asked of juniors? Would it be sensible to reduce their case loads? Might it be useful to give them more assistance? Perhaps they could hold some training seminars? Or take a look at the reward system? Maybe Helena would be better conducting some individual appraisals? Should she talk to the other seniors to see if it is a common problem? Should she go on a management course herself? Or is the first step to discuss it with Kate?

It is generally presumed that the performance of each of us at work is supposed to fit in with what everyone else is doing, so that the contributions of each of us makes up the whole. In the past a lot of this fitting things together was assumed and left implicit. New people were expected to fit into their groups and gradually 'came on board'. Now the process is seen as being in need of more explicit analysis and description. Organisations are trying to integrate strategy, target-setting, appraisal schemes, training and development, and rewarding the staff. It is argued that this should focus employee behaviour so that each person adds value to the organisation. Associated with this view is that performance and rewards should be linked. As Kanter (1989, p223) said:

> **Can anyone be against the idea that people's pay should reflect their performance? Isn't that how the system is supposed to work?**

Compare this view with that held in many British organisations as late as the 1980s, that men should be paid more than women doing the same job because they have families to support. Or a still frequently held view that 'this is the rate for the job no matter who does it or how well done the job is or is not done'. The aim of the more explicit approach of linking rewards to performance is to improve the performance of individuals and organisations so they are more able to compete effectively in a changing world. In many ways performance management is at the heart of a team leader's or line manager's day-to-day work. It is about how the work can be organised to get the required results.

WHAT IS PERFORMANCE MANAGEMENT?

The increased interest in systematic people management in the past 20 years has led to the development of performance management. A variety of influences made this so – increased competition from other countries and the realisation of their better productivity; the findings of Peters and Waterman's book (1982) on the factors associated with excellence, which had a large influence; and pressure from government bodies such as the training section of the Employment and Education Department.

Performance management usually involves (Marchington and Wilkinson, 1996, p134) the following:

- statements of what is required from people
- communication about where we are up to in achieving the goals
- integration with other organisation-wide schemes such as quality initiatives
- specific individual and team targets set and reviewed regularly
- performance appraisal
- performance-related pay
- reviews of training and development needs
- provision of training and development to meet the needs.

A general summary of some of the areas that need considering when reviewing an organisation's performance management, from a management perspective, is that of Hendry, Bradley and Perkins (1997). I have laid them out as a series of questions that you can ask yourself about your own organisation:

- Reasons –   Why do we want to reappraise the way we manage people and their rewards?

- Objectives – What are the goals of the exercise?

   Which are the critical performances that need to be rewarded?

   What is the nature of our contract with employees?

   We want the performance system to do what – attract, motivate, retain, control?

- External – What stage of the business cycle are we in?

   What is the nature of the national culture?

- Internal – What assumptions do we have about our work and relationships?

   What groups do we have and what is their performance and style?

- Systems – The systems are there to support what?

- Design – How do we define rewards?

   What incentives are we going to offer?

- What measures are appropriate – Can we measure performance?

   Can people see this?

   Is it manageable?

   How is this communicated to everyone?

- Outcome – What effect on behaviour are we looking for?

   What are the criteria of success?

- Monitoring – What review process do we have?

- We might also add costs – How much will it cost?

   Is it worth it?

Performance management is usually taken to mean an increased emphasis on specifying what is wanted and rewarding those individuals who are able to deliver it satisfactorily. The normal stages of performance management, as described in the literature, develop as follows:

- There are written and agreed job descriptions, and they are reviewed regularly.
- There are objectives for the work group, which have been cascaded down from the organisation's strategic objectives.
- There are individual objectives derived from the above, which are jointly devised by appraiser and appraisee. These objectives are result- rather than task-orientated, are tightly defined, and include measures to be assessed. The objectives are designed to stretch the individual and offer potential development as well as meeting business needs.
- There is a development plan, devised by the team leader or manager and the individual, detailing development goals and activities designed to enable the individual to meet his or her objectives. These could be competency based. The emphasis here is on managerial support and coaching.
- Assessment of objectives with ongoing formal reviews is practised on a regular basis; it is designed to motivate the appraisee and concentrate on developmental issues.
- There is usually also an annual assessment which affects pay received, depending on the performance in achieving the objectives.

For many organisations this has led to three separate interviews with staff: the appraisal interview which looks at the past performance, the performance interview which looks at what is expected for the next period, and the development interview which deals with training and development needs and future career prospects. For some, these might be carried out one after the other on the same day, but the distinction between the three is felt useful to keep the idea of performance management clear. One of the major advantages of performance management is that team leaders and managers are forced to give emphasis to formal and planned employee development. Another advantage is that it also enforces a clear role description and set of objectives agreed by team leaders or managers and individuals. On the downside, there is potential conflict between the aim of improving performance – which requires openness and a developmental approach – and the link with pay. This conflict is sometimes resolved by separating the three reviews, performance, development and performance pay, and holding them at different times of the year.

SETTING THE TARGETS

Before we get on to the specifics of performance management in the next chapter, let us look briefly at some of the ways in which people in organisations arrive at the strategies and targets that are supposed to start the whole process off. There are shelves of books on strategy and planning from all possible points of view. Since the 1990s there has been an increased emphasis on the behavioural aspects of strategy. This suggests that the skills or competencies of the people in the organisation are an important part of the success of the organisation, see for example the very influential paper by Prahalad and Hamel (1990). This view emphasises that it is what people do, and their flexibility to scan the horizon and adapt, that determines the sustainability of the organisation. This emphasis on the strategic importance of the people contrasts with other models, which emphasise the financial and technical aspects of the organisation.

> A clothes shop selling fashionable clothes to young people needs sales and purchasing staff who are in the clubs and on the street so they know what is up to date.

Core competencies

Core competencies are the central skills and abilities of an organisation that are the basis of its continuing existence. Sometimes these are widely understood and acknowledged, for example Sony's ability to miniaturise electronic goods. Sometimes they are taken for granted and not sufficiently cherished so they can be undermined in periods of reorganisation. For example, the shipbuilders in Barrow-in-Furness had not built commercial ships for several years and had laid off a lot of employees, and when they started to build ships again they ended up with punitive delays.

An interesting and influential British writer on strategy and planning is Kay (1993). He argues that organisations have core competencies that may depend on particular individuals and teams within the organisation. The important core competencies according to Kay are:

Networks of contacts – these are long-term relationships of shared knowledge, established routines and are co-operative. They can include internal and external contacts. An example would be how housing associations need close contacts with local authorities to operate effectively.

Reputation – this is an attribute of quality that organisations can monitor but not establish quickly. It is costly to develop, but is worth doing if there is a premium for high quality or where repeat business is likely. It is also something that can easily be lost.

Innovation – this can be when an organisation establishes the standard or gets in before others. This gives them a head start, which makes it difficult for competitors to catch up.

Monopolies – exclusive positions because of regulations and contracts – this can happen because there really is room for only one operator where establishing the business is so difficult or expensive or where there are limited opportunities.

Processes – Some organisations rely on their competence at doing some particular thing well that gives them the edge over competitors. An example is Easyjet's online ticketing system, which gave them an early cost advantage over other airlines.

Services or products – this is when an organisation has something that the customer wants.

Not all organisations will have all these core competencies, but identifying which of them is important may help to identify which team and individual performances are crucial for the organisation.

Planning

Perhaps the most commonly used technique for arriving at targets and planning is the simple form of a SWOT analysis. This is a useful device for analysing the situation and then making some decisions.

- *Strengths* – what are the positive attributes of the organisation, department, team or group in this situation? This might include people, traditions, technology and know-how, customer loyalty, finance and other resources, location and reputation.
- *Weaknesses* – what are the negative attributes of the organisation, department, team, or group in this situation? It might include any of the above.
- *Opportunities* – these are usually changes in the environment of the organisation, such as changes in the market, legislation, transport, the economy, other competitors' positions or technology. A successful organisation needs to have sensitivity to pick up on these.
- *Threats* – these can be any of the above – particularly if changes are ignored or not noticed.

When the SWOT analysis or other planning has been done there should be some clear objectives or goals. These outcomes of the planning cycle can then be broken down into suitable chunks and used to set team and individual objectives. The SWOT device can be used in all sorts of circumstance for both large and small projects. The breaking down of organisational objectives into smaller achievable tasks and targets is an important role for the team leader as it helps in the process of clearly communicating to people what is expected of them.

Communication

In all human interactions there are two components – content and process. The content refers to the subject matter or task in which the group is involved. The process is concerned with how this takes place. Usually very little attention is given to process as everyone is so concerned with getting on with the task. However, sometimes the reason for failure is because of inadequate processes. Communication difficulties can be at the heart of this failure.

We (Torrington and Weightman, 1989, pp106–7) found the following examples of communication when we asked 'How do you find out what is going on?':

Bill and Ben – 'Oh, I generally ask Bill or Ben.' Relying on the informal method of management.

Noisy plumbing – 'Oh, my head of department tells me if they think I need to know.' When relying on the cascade system, much depends on those controlling the taps not to over-filter, leaving those at the bottom without water, or over-polluting the message.

Whatever the purpose of the communication, it is a two way process – complete only when the message has been received. Figure 13.1 gives a basic model of the chain of active processes that is involved both by the communicator and the receiver for effective communication to take place. Problems of communication can happen anywhere along this chain. When we want to be effective communicators we need to think about our own performance, but also about the people with whom we are communicating. The old adage 'Who is your audience?' is worth asking before communicating, whatever the medium. Difficulties in communication occur when the purpose of the message is unclear, there are problems in sending or receiving the message, where there is a mismatch between the sender and receiver, and if outside physical factors intervene. Each of these needs to be looked at if communication is poor. If we are trying to stimulate improved performance in our team then clear communication is an important first step.

REWARDING PERFORMANCE

Having decided on the task and communicated this clearly, the third main aspect of performance management is managing the reward. The way in which people are rewarded is central to the regulation of the employment relationship. Pay arrangements are also central to any changes, including cultural initiatives, because they are the most tangible expression of the working relationship between employer and employee. Managerial perceptions of appropriate payment systems have been subject to considerable change and fluctuation over time. The basic principles of paying either for time or performance (or both) are at the heart of any system. Payment for time is relatively straightforward, with set hourly or weekly rates. Paying for performance is altogether more complicated. The nature of the achievement and whether this is achieved by an individual, or a group, can both be considered. Over time, many organisations end up with some hybrid system that includes both paying for time and for performance, as well as all sorts of idiosyncrasies that develop through 'custom and practice'.

We (Weightman, Blandamer and Torrington (1991)) found that people in the North Western Regional Health Authority were paid on 2,008 different levels of pay; 78 per cent of these pay points had 10 people or fewer being paid that amount. We also found wide ranges for such things as weekly hours, annual holidays, pay for being 'on call', and so on.

It is outside the scope of this book to discuss the advantages and disadvantages of different pay systems – for further information on them see Armstrong and Brown (2001). However, it is worth noting that the current fashion of 'pay for performance' approaches to managing

Stage	Process	Check-points
ENCODING	Deciding on the message Selecting the right words Understanding the other person	Clarify your objectives What will the other person want from the message? What will be the emotional impact of the message?
TRANSMITTING	Selecting the right medium Sending the message Giving non-verbal signals	Make sure there are no more than approximately seven ideas to transmit Are words and non-verbal signals consistent? Is the language suitable?
ENVIRONMENT	Coping with distractions Dealing with distortions	Avoiding interruptions and noise Is the seating right?
RECEIVING	Perceiving the message Listening actively	What phrases, facts, and inferences am I looking for? How can I test my understanding of the message?
DECODING	Making sense of the message Understanding the other person	What do they mean? What is the 'hidden agenda'? How shall I handle it if it does not fit in with my beliefs?
FEEDBACK	Encoding the response Starting the next message	To keep communication going: nod, smile, agree To stop the communication: look uninterested, avoid eye contact

Figure 13.1 *The basic communications chain*

performance can really work only in an environment in which the staff are given enough discretion in their jobs to be able to affect their actual performance in a significant way. Otherwise they will become cynical about the whole initiative. It is also the case that for performance-related pay (PRP) schemes to make a significant difference to performance they add about 10 per cent to the salary bill. This is because the performance element of the pay needs to be substantial, say 30 per cent, to be motivating – otherwise it feels derisory and not worth working for. This is not always affordable or appropriate. Another difficulty of PRP is that not everyone can receive the top payouts and it can be quite demotivating to receive average payouts.

Despite all this talk of performance management, the reality is that a team leader or line manager's responsibilities for pay are often merely administrative ones. Their job is to ensure the paperwork associated with hours, overtime and rotas worked is up to date and returned in time for the pay records to be updated before the pay date. Pay administration is a classic

Herzberg hygiene factor; if it is OK no one bothers, but if there is an administrative error then people can be very upset. However, things are changing. Team leaders and managers are being encouraged to be more actively involved in deciding some of the pay of those in their team or department through performance-related pay schemes.

In 1996 Price Waterhouse offered its staff a cafeteria of benefits that it called Flex. A cafeteria of benefits is where the employer offers a range of benefits, and individuals choose their own combination up to a certain cost – rather like choosing food in a cafeteria. In this scheme individuals had the following rewards:

- 80 per cent of the reward figure had to be taken in cash
- plus a minimum of 20 days' holiday
- plus a choice from 10 benefits such as additional holidays, pensions, health insurance, accident insurance, childcare vouchers, retail vouchers, company cars and health club membership at a discount.

This had a tax and National Insurance contribution benefit for the company as well as the obvious benefit for the individual. Mercury Telecommunications also have a large scheme like this.

A team leader or line manager is responsible for engendering commitment from the staff. Rewarding them in ways other than through pay are within their powers. People work for a variety of reasons, as we saw in Chapter 12. To gain commitment, rewards can be such things as valuing the contribution, allowing autonomy, supporting people through personal crises and generally treating people as they would like to be treated. The personal credibility and leadership of a manager will probably enhance the value of these rewards in the eyes of the staff.

MANAGING PERFORMANCE

This chapter is about the basic concepts and issues of performance management. We also need to look at the practice of how to manage performance. Who defines what performance is required and whether it has been achieved will be determined by the nature of the organisation, its environment, and the politics and power associated with the players involved. This context of performance management is dealt with in Chapters 7 and 11. Whoever runs the organisation is ultimately responsible for its performance. They may be accountable to shareholders, customers, clients, staff, the country and other stakeholders. The performance can be organisational, group or individual.

The interaction between members of the organisation over performance will be both formal and informal. We often say to colleagues 'That's great' or 'What's that you're doing?' We observe their behaviour, look at their production, listen to them on the telephone or see them with a client. These observations give us informal information about performance. We are constantly on the lookout for clues as to what others are doing, and learning about their performance and picking up on what is acceptable and what is unacceptable performance in this particular context. We are also perhaps learning new ways to do things that improve our own performance. For example, my ability to use word processing was greatly improved by sitting next to an experienced secretary whilst we finished a report – she was a wizard at using all the devices! Performance management involves formal, systematic ways of gaining information about performance.

The main construct of performance management is that work groups and individuals see what they have to do to make their contribution to the organisation's overall effectiveness. There needs to be a clear link with the organisational objectives. This involves good communication of clear objectives that everyone can understand. The level of involvement of individuals is contingent on the particular culture of the organisation. The organisation's strategy will be stated in various ways, from the formal written business plan to informal chats with senior staff.

Performance is managed by the following processes:

- Organisation-wide
    - incentives to perform are offered
    - quality management initiatives
    - quality assurance procedures such as BS 5750 and ISO 9000
    - Investors in People
    - learning organisation approaches
- Team-department-wide
    - team reviews
    - performance indicators
    - team incentives
    - quality circles
    - assessment
- Individual
    - performance appraisal
    - link to job description
    - development plan
    - performance-related pay.

These terms are discussed throughout the book; the next chapter in particular looks at individual performance management.

One traditional approach to directing the performance of people in organisations is management by objectives (MBO). This phrase is used to describe a system of management that tries to relate the organisational goals to the behaviour and performance of individuals in the organisation. It involves:

- setting targets and objectives
- getting individuals to agree these objectives and the criteria for measuring performance
- continually appraising and reviewing the outcomes.

This concept was introduced by Drucker (1954) and was initially related to the behaviour of senior managers. Since then it has been widely adopted and is now applied to all levels in the organisation through performance-appraisal systems. The cycle of management by objectives is a cycle of interrelated activities, see Figure 13.2. This is still at the heart of many organisations' performance management schemes, although for many it seems rather mechanistic.

The advantages claimed for such a system of performance management are that it:

- concentrates on the areas perceived to be important
- identifies problem areas before they become critical
- identifies training needs
- improves communications
- makes managers actually manage their staff.

Some difficulties, identified by Kane and Freeman (1986), are that:

- individuals do just enough to get the reward
- the emphasis is on the short term
- there is a lack of discretion for team leaders and managers
- flexibility is lost as individuals 'work to objectives'
- there is an annual bottle-neck of interviews after the organisation's goals have been set.

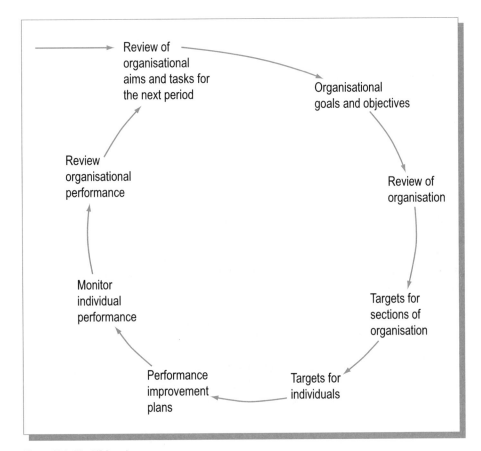

Figure 13.2 *The MBO cycle*

An overriding issue for some is that it can be a top-down procedure if there is no feedback to the original target-setting from those asked to implement them. It can also be seen as very mechanistic, focusing on the stated objectives and not considering individual differences. I mention it here as it is still frequently used in organisations. The next chapter deals with management of individual performance in more detail.

ETHICS OF MANAGING PERFORMANCE

What right does anyone have to manage another person's performance? Can those senior in the hierarchy be blamed for the poor performance of an individual at work? When there is a serious accident, questions such as these become focused. For example, was it the captain of the ship who failed to close the car loading doors who was responsible for the sinking of the ship? Or was it his bosses who were constantly putting pressure on the captain to quicken the turn-around time in order to make more journeys per day? This discussion of the social responsibility and ethics of organisations is increasingly a subject for discussion – see for example Connock and Johns (1995).

The Business In the Community model of corporate social responsibility includes:

Workplace –   treat employees well
respect human rights
employ minorities

Marketplace –   respond to customer needs and concerns

Environment –   renewables
emissions

Community –   communicating
helping
giving something back

We have earlier distinguished between hard and soft approaches to managing people. So it is with performance management. Those with a hard approach will see it as a continuing right and responsibility of those senior in the organisation to set out formal requirements for performance and to monitor the results. Those with a softer approach will prefer to see the developing individual as having the flair to cope with autonomy, and consequently offering his or her best performance to the organisation.

These two approaches are at the extremes, and most organisations use a mixture of both. Increasingly these are brought together in the contract of employment. This has explicit aspects that detail the ways in which the employer can control the work of the employee and what the employee will get in return. It also has implicit aspects, sometimes called the psychological contract, which include such things as the employer maintaining mutual trust and confidence, and the employee obeying lawful and reasonable orders. This explicit and implicit contract of employment is at the core of performance management.

DEBATE – WHAT IS JOB SATISFACTION?

Some of the issues of the ethics of managing performance have been brought together under the concept of 'job satisfaction'. Although originally studied from the point of view of motivation, job satisfaction seems to be something more complex and is now associated with job design and the quality of working life. Whatever is involved, job satisfaction does seem to be an attitude of mind and is undoubtedly an internal state associated with a feeling of achievement. The relationship between job satisfaction and performance is controversial. Earlier researchers felt that satisfaction led to improved performance, but it could be that improved performance leads to satisfaction. However, Luthans (1992, p123) suggests that:

> Although most people assume a positive relationship, the preponderance of research evidence indicates that there is no strong linkage between satisfaction and productivity.

What do you think?

An important concept to help make sense of performance management from an organisation perspective is that of some sort of contract between the employee and employer. The nature of the contract will vary enormously, and individuals vary in what they consider acceptable. Analysing these contracts will tell you a good deal about the particular organisational behaviour. Perhaps using some of the questions given at the beginning of this chapter will give you a start in looking at the implicit contracts that organisations are offering their people.

Improving performance involves the whole range of what goes on in organisations. Suitable targets need to be well communicated to staff who are trained and rewarded. This needs to be co-ordinated with others and appropriate resources made available. No wonder it does not always work perfectly. But trying to stimulate improved performance is the essential leadership and management role.

ACTIVITIES

1 How many of the performance management techniques listed in this chapter have you experienced? Would it have been appropriate to have used more? How would this sit with the desire of some people to be seen as autonomous professionals?

2 Should you do a SWOT analysis of your current project? Would it be useful in helping you sort out where the bottle-necks are in your schedule, and help you to prioritise your work?

3 Think back over yesterday and try to think of different non-verbal communications you experienced – things like people gesturing, sitting in particular ways, the way they are dressed, standing close, touching, etc. If you are in a seminar group you could compare notes.

4 Answer the following questions about your organisation: what does the pay you receive tell you about the organisation you work in? Do the terms and conditions of the people who work in your team vary? What about the non-qualified staff? What about the difference between the conditions of the core and peripheral staff? In what ways are you rewarded other than financially?

HAVE I MET THE OBJECTIVES?

1   What is performance management?

2   What are core competencies?

3   How does performance management fit in with the needs of the business as a whole?

4   What is the communication chain?

5   Can I define performance and performance-related pay?

6   What is the central question of the ethics of managing performance?

And finally ...

What would you recommend to Helena? Would you use any of the approaches in this chapter? What about some sort of performance management? I should certainly recommend that Helena discuss this with the other seniors. I should also recommend that they as a firm set out their objectives and expectations clearly to the juniors. The nature of the 'mentoring' would also be an area to look at. Kate needs immediate attention, with suggestions on how her performance can be improved, and frequent appraisal-type discussions as follow-up. It may be that some more training is required.

FURTHER READING

Current practice is often discussed in the management pages of the *Financial Times* and other broadsheet newspapers. Look at current personnel journals such as *People Management* from the CIPD for specific examples of this practice.

Any human resource management textbook will have material on this.

There are several videos in this area that you might like to try:

■ *The Whole Picture – 360-degree appraisal* – four case studies such as ICL and Thomas Cook, from the Industrial Society (1997).

■ *Coaching for Improved Performance at Work* – case studies such as NatWest and Easyjet, from the Industrial Society (1997). These can be hired by the day.

■ *Feedback for Performance* (1997) Melrose.

Performance Management

This chapter is a continuation of the previous one and both should be read in that order. Theories about motivation, Chapter 12, authority, Chapter 11, and communication, Chapter 13, are very relevant. The applied material in this chapter looks at **performance appraisal, interviewing, assessment, poor performance** and **discipline and dismissal**. Other relevant chapters are 1 on the HR role; 2 on prejudice; 9 on training and development; and 13 on planning. The examples in this chapter are self-generated.

OBJECTIVES

By the time you have finished reading this chapter you should be able to:

■ **understand the basic ingredients for the effective design of a performance review and appraisal system**

■ **describe the basic ingredients for the effective design of a performance review and appraisal system**

■ **describe the basic ingredients for the effective operation of a performance review and appraisal system**

■ **describe a systematic approach for dealing with problems of poor performance.**

Margaret's review

Margaret is the station manager for a medium-sized radio station. Recently it has been taken over by one of the larger media groups. She has been told that she should conduct a series of interviews with the staff who work for her at the station. These interviews should be about their performance and development within the new context. She is deeply suspicious that this may be a precursor to redundancies. She has been assured that this is not so, but rather that the larger company has a policy of managing the performance of the staff systematically through a series of regular interviews. She receives a copy of their policy suggesting they have review interviews to discuss last year's performance, target-setting interviews to discuss next year's performance, and development interviews to discuss individual development needs. Margaret has never heard of anything like it. What is she to do?

Should she show the document to the staff? Discuss it with other members of management? Ask to go through the procedure herself with her boss first? Look for alternatives? See it as an opportunity to get to know her staff better? Just get on with it and not worry about the consequences? Have a joint training session with the staff on performance management and appraisal interviews? Say she does this informally anyway and sees no reason to put it in this grandiose procedure when everyone is very busy and having to work to new procedures after the takeover?

'Managing performance' has become a buzz-phrase of management. What is meant by performance management or managing performance varies enormously. For some, it means manipulating pay and other reward systems so that people will work harder. For others, it means telling staff what they should do. Other people think it means increasing people's understanding of the whole process so that they know what they are doing and why. We shall look at a variety of different models or methods in this chapter, and some of the variety of claims that are made about managing performance.

MANAGING INDIVIDUAL PERFORMANCE

The one certain thing is that nothing quite distinguishes our underlying assumptions about the working relationship as our approach to managing performance and what is seen as acceptable and what is not. Some would argue for the autonomy of individuals to offer their work in whatever way they feel is appropriate. Some would argue that there is a need for outside authorities to ensure standards that individuals apply in their work, while still allowing the individual to offer this work as and when he or she wishes (see, for example, professional groups such as lawyers and doctors). Others, usually managers, want things much more tightly controlled by the employers or managers. Questions about what work should be done, how it should be done, the quality expected, and the rewards for work, are all associated with performance management. Who should take the decisions about these is inevitably wrapped up in the politics of the debate. This chapter looks at some of the issues associated with performance management, as well as describing some of the normal sequence of procedures for managing performance.

Measuring performance

Measuring anything about people inevitably means judging them in some way. Despite efforts to try to reduce the subjectiveness of this judgement, such as the use of a competency approach, there is always a point at which someone is judging another. Where this judgement is to last a long time, and may affect the individual's chances of employment or education, very careful consideration of the assessment process is necessary. This may explain why you can find almost mystical discussion of the assessment process in education journals. Table 14.1 gives a list of basic questions to ask about measuring someone's performance. The answers to these questions will be contingent on the particular setting of the assessment.

Appraising performance

Performance appraisal is a well-established way of providing milestones, feedback, guidance and monitoring for staff. A further development, as described above, is tying this appraisal into a larger and more complete system of performance management. These performance management systems, which are increasingly used (see for example Fletcher, 1997), highlight appraisal as an activity central to the good management of staff. The difference from traditional appraisal 'chats' is that the assessment process in performance management tends to be more rigorous and objective. It is clearly linked to precise job definitions. It is based on organisational objective-setting and individual development plans and it has links with the pay system. For many systems, an element of self-appraisal is also included. This has the advantage that it involves the individuals being assessed – who really know what they have been doing. The individual can suggest ways of improving his or her own work. Self-appraisal is also useful in engendering commitment to any agreed changes.

The essential elements of any performance appraisal are judgement and reporting. The performance is not simply being measured as in the completion of a work rota, it is being judged. This obviously involves discretion, worry about bias and the possibility of being quite wrong. The judgement not only has to be made, but also passed on to other people in such a

Table 14.1 *Questions to ask yourself about measuring performance*

Why are we assessing this person?
- to recruit?
- to develop?
- to promote?
- to redeploy?
- to gain national qualifications?
- because of company policy?

How important is it that the assessment is accurate?

Is the assessment compulsory?

How much time and effort are we prepared to put into the process?

How frequently do we want the assessment done?

Who should do the judging?
- the immediate boss?
- the person themselves?
- their colleagues?
- someone in a position of authority?
- someone with expertise?
- a variety of people?

What sort of evidence is needed to assess the performance?
- Can the individual collect written materials to prove they have done it?
- Must the performance be observed?
- Can it be observed in the normal course of work?

Who has sight of the conclusions of the assessment?
- Is it confidential?
- Just the individual and their line manager?
- Can it be used for other purposes?
- Should it be used outside the team?

What will be the result of the assessment?

Who is responsible for ensuring that the follow-up takes place?

Set a date for assessing the follow-up?

way that the other understands what is intended and takes action upon it. Those devising performance-appraisal schemes devote most of their energies to finding ways of making the judgements as systematic as possible, and the reporting of different appraisers as consistent as possible.

Much of what has been written about the appraisal process concentrates on the personal interaction. In addition, George (1986) suggests that an effective appraisal scheme is dependent on the style and content of appraisal not conflicting with the culture of the organisation. He suggests that the degree of openness that is required in the appraisal process is 'unlikely to materialise without an atmosphere of mutual trust and respect – something which is conspicuously lacking in many employing organisations' (George, 1986, p32). The appraisal therefore needs to reflect the wider values of the organisation in order for it to be properly integrated into the organisation and to survive in an effective form. The appraisal system can in fact be used to display and support the culture and style of the organisation.

The reasons why team leaders and managers might want to appraise their staff include:

- human resource considerations – to ensure that the abilities and energies of individuals are being used effectively. They would hope to find out more about the staff and make better use of each individual's talents and expertise.
- training – it is useful to identify training needs, both for new tasks and to improve poor performance amongst their staff.
- promotion – talking to individuals about their aspirations as well as finding out about their performance can assist decision-making about who is ready for promotion.
- planning – to identify skill shortages and succession needs. If there is a widespread lack of particular skills then some serious planning will need to take place.
- authority – the appraisal system sustains the hierarchy of authority by confirming the dependence of staff on those who lead and manage them. It is one of the rituals that underline who is boss.

The reasons why staff might wish to be appraised by their managers include:

- performance – here is an opportunity to discuss what could be done and how one might go about doing it.
- motivation – talking about the job and the work it involves may remind us why we do the job and why we wanted it in the first place.
- career – bosses can be helpful as they understand the promotion route well, since they have travelled up it themselves.
- feeling – getting worries, frustrations and anxiety off the chest.
- information – learning more about the organisation's future plans.

Many things can impair the judgement, reporting and effectiveness of the performance appraisal. For example:

- prejudice
- insufficient knowledge of the individual
- the 'halo' effect of general likeability or recent events
- the difficulty of distinguishing the performance from the context in which the person works
- different perceptions of what are appropriate standards
- marking everyone 'just above average'
- ignoring the outcome of the appraisal process. For example, everyone will be frustrated if there are no improved resources, training or changes.

Despite these problems of judgement, reporting and follow-up, the potential advantages of performance appraisal are generally felt to be so great that it is worth expending the effort to make it work.

Most people find a problem-solving approach the most effective form of appraisal interview, as long as both appraiser and appraisee have the skill and ability to handle the situation. This approach is similar to the counselling interview where neither party knows the answer before the interview begins. Table 6.1 in Chapter 6 gives a sequence for counselling in this type of interview. It develops as the interaction takes place. Training in this type of interviewing is widely available. This does not mean that no preparation is required before the interview – indeed, quite the contrary. Both parties need to have a good think about the past year's performance, the next year's expectations, and where the changes are expected. It is the comparison of each of their views of these that can be the real stuff of a trusting, problem-solving appraisal interview. Experience suggests that the quality of the interview improves as the confidence and trust of the participants develop. Do not expect too much the first time!

Performance appraisal in various guises is now very common. Different forms are constantly introduced to try to resolve some of the difficulties listed above. Despite the problems, most people feel that a regular, formal encounter between themselves and their boss is an appropriate, if sometimes disappointing, procedure.

Who should judge the performance and how should it be done?

Organisations are constantly trying out different forms of assessment. This is partly because of a felt imbalance with whichever method is being practised, and partly because there is always a desire to make it even better. Different types of assessment that have been tried and which could be included in any particular scheme are:

- self-assessment – where individuals decide whether they are having difficulty or not with some required behaviour, and this can then be the basis of discussion
- peer assessment – not usually done formally unless in examining how effective the team is. But a great deal of informal measurement is done. Clergy in the Church of England are not considered employees because they 'work for God', so when they wanted to introduce appraisal they opted for peer appraisal
- boss assessment – the most common technique in the workplace. This may include observation, exercises and collecting evidence. Usually it does not involve such systematic measures, and is much more informal
- assessment by others who come into contact with the job holder – for a true 360-degree picture of the job holder some assessment by his or her customer/clients or other contacts would be logical, but this rarely happens in works organisations. This includes people working for the job holder. WH Smith use upward and 360-degree appraisal to identify managers' training and development needs
- assessment by outsiders – this is sometimes used to give a certain objectivity, for example in assessment centres. It can be expensive, and there is the question of confidentiality.

Techniques for assessing performance could include:

- observation – this can be both formal and informal. It has the advantage that the assessor actually sees the behaviour to be judged. OFSTED for teachers is an example. It has high credibility, but it is very time-consuming. Also, not everything worth doing is observable.
- assessment or development centres – these are where individuals come together for a day or two and carry out various activities whilst being observed by assessors (see

Woodruffe, 1994). They are useful for focusing on the individual and involving outsiders in the assessment. However, they are expensive to run and are simulations of activities rather than the real thing.

■ portfolios – this is where individuals collect documents and evidence of work they have done and been involved in. The advantages are that individuals are responsible, the process celebrates achievement rather than failure, and it concentrates on continuous development. NVQs use this system. However, portfolios can become very unwieldy to read through, and there is the issue of comparability.

■ record systems – such as work sheets. NVQs use these. They enable comparisons with others but may emphasise quantity at the expense of quality.

Problems associated with performance-management schemes

The problems encountered in running any scheme of assessment are formidable. Here are a few of them, mostly based on the experience of appraisal schemes in organisations:

■ Paperwork – any system of assessment always involves paperwork and documentation, as the essential feature is reporting and schemes invariably include attempts to make the judgements and the reporting consistent between different assessors. This unavoidably involves forms and detailed instructions.

■ Formality – the forms introduce an inhibiting feature into the everyday working relationships between the participants, who usually dislike the idea of formal evaluation. However, the desire for informality has to be balanced against the usefulness of a considered view.

■ Outcomes ignored – often a development or promotion is agreed at the appraisal review and then the manager responsible does not deliver the promised development or promotion. There may be good reasons for this, but if it happens too often it can undermine the whole process. More frequent reviews of targets can help reduce the problem.

■ Performance measured by proxy – this is where the performance cannot be measured easily so some other behaviour, such as time-keeping or a pleasant manner, is measured instead. This is the 'halo' effect.

■ Easily measured bits – people do the easily measured bits to get the bonus, whereas the difficult, soft parts of the job are ignored. This can become a powerful message in the organisation: everyone becomes more and more hard-headed and wonders why they are all feeling so stressed.

■ The just-above-average syndrome – there is a reluctance to say that people are not good enough. Some assessment schemes introduce a forced marking-down below average of at least one area for each individual so that not everything for everyone is marked just above average. A problem of everyone being scored above average is that the high fliers continue to be developed and promoted but nothing is done to develop and deal with poor performance.

■ Incomplete coverage – no system ever covers everyone. For example, those who have just arrived and those just leaving will not be covered. Where there are others being excluded because they are 'past it' or 'on the fast track' this can undermine the system.

■ Ill-informed assessors – sometimes assessors are asked to carry out the assessment because of their job titles or rank rather than because of their knowledge of the job and the job holder's performance. The problem can be even worse if the assessors do not know the context in which the individual is trying to operate.

■ Disagreements – where this happens between the appraisee and appraiser it can sour the whole working relationship. Sometimes this is about the actual assessment of the performance; more frequently it is about the level of financial reward that accrues from this assessment. It needs to be dealt with quickly and fairly; otherwise it ends with the junior person looking for a job elsewhere.

DEBATE – PERFORMANCE MANAGEMENT IS AT THE HEART OF THE EMPLOYMENT CONTRACT

Performance management inevitably has a managerial feel to it. After all, it has 'management' in the title! Questions can be asked of one's right to manage someone else's performance – and when and how one does it. At one end of the managerial continuum are managers who see it as a main responsibility of management to tell people what they should do, how they should do it, and when they should do it. The main management job here is to manipulate the environment and people to get the required performance. For many with this perspective the only problem is getting a precise enough analysis of what is required.

At the other extreme are leaders who feel their responsibility is to elicit the performance from freely operating individuals. Here the task is seen as making sure the goal or performance required is sufficiently articulated so that people will see the need for the performance and offer their best efforts. These in turn are rewarded in individually satisfying ways to motivate people to continue to offer their best.

The contract of employment and how this is interpreted is at the heart of the relationship between people and their bosses. Understanding performance management and some of the associated issues is important for understanding the nature of the contract.

POOR PERFORMANCE

A particular aspect of managing performance is managing the poor performer. We can all perform badly at times. Usually there is some tolerance of this, but where it persists something has to be done about it for the sake of customers/clients, other colleagues, and the individual concerned. Avoiding the issue of managing poor performance does not mean that it goes away. Problems with people at work can be short-term or long-term. For example, most of us are not very good when we have a cold; but there are others who never seem to perform well. It is these individuals who have a long-term performance problem that I want to discuss.

Nigel Nicholson (2003) suggests that there are seven hazards in the way we handle problem people:

■ The mulberry bush chase – we go round and round the same fruitless conversations.

■ Huckster hazard – we continue to tell and sell to try to convince them of our reasonableness.

■ Ignorance is bliss – we do not care what makes them tick.

■ Self-centredness trap – we think of their behaviour from our point of view rather than how they would describe their behaviour.

■ Hanging judge tendency – do we want to solve the problem or sit in judgement?

■ The monochrome vision – discovering one positive characteristic can create a starting point for change.

■ The denial danger – we have to deal with their version of reality as well as our own.

He suggests that when these are operating we need a new approach. Usually this means finding out what their point of view is and seeing where we can go with each other.

Before anything can be done to improve poor performance it is important to establish that there really is a gap between required and actual performance. Required performance can be communicated to individuals in several ways:

■ contracts of employment with an outline of duties

■ formal rule books

■ job descriptions

■ training manuals

■ lists of standards

■ procedures

■ briefings

■ training sessions

■ meetings

■ individual conversations

■ professional training and monitoring.

There may be reasons for an individual having difficulties with any of these. For example, the written requirements may be poorly thought out, inappropriate, or out of date. Any of them may be poorly communicated.

When we need information about actual performance, this can be collected in several ways. For example:

■ personal files

■ time sheets

■ sickness and absence records

■ record cards

■ customer complaints

■ inaccurate work

■ mistakes

■ colleagues

■ comparison with other people's work

■ unfinished work.

After looking at what is expected and what has actually been done, the question is whether there is sufficient gap between the two to require attention.

If a gap is established, the next task is to find the reason for the gap. Only by finding the reason or reasons for the gap can we begin to do something about it. There are three main types of reason for poor performance. First are personal reasons that arise from the person's domestic and individual circumstances. These are outside the organisation's control. The main issue is for how long and to what extent do we allow personal problems to interfere with work. Second are reasons to do with poor management and organisation. Third are individual reasons that arise from the individual not fitting in with the organisation. See Table 14.2.

Having established the gap in performance and found the reasons for it, we are in a better position to do the main work of management, which is to do something about it. Usually having established some of the reasons will give us starting points for dealing with them. There are some other starting points given in Table 14.3. Whatever the starting point, there is a need to discuss the problem performance with the individual concerned; a counselling interview technique based on problem-solving, such as in Table 6.1, Chapter 6, would be appropriate.

Table 14.2 *Reasons for problem performance*

Personal characteristics

- intellectual ability inappropriate due to poor selection or changes
- lack of emotional stability due to poor selection or changes
- poor physical ability which may change with age or job changes
- health problems
- domestic circumstances such as child care, parents or partner
- family breakup.

Organisational characteristics

- assignment or job impossible to do or understand
- lack of suitable planning
- job changes do not make sense to the individual
- pay felt to be too low or poorly administered
- poor investment in equipment
- inadequate training
- inappropriate levels of discipline – may be too excessive or too lenient
- poor management – an individual poor manager or a poor management system
- physical conditions distract from performance if they are irritating
- location and transport problems when relocated.

Individual characteristics

- group dynamics, where someone does not fit in and is excluded or prevented from fitting in
- personality clash – this usually means one of the other reasons, but we all feel this clash occasionally
- sense of fair play abused when different views on the right way to do or say things come into conflict
- conflict of religious or moral values
- inappropriate levels of confidence – may be over- or underconfident.

Table 14.3 *Ways of dealing with the poor performer*

The following are in alphabetical order and are starting points when a problem arises

- *Discipline* The range is from informal to formal, and ultimately dismissal.
- *Dissatisfaction* Fill the gap where appropriate.
- *Goal-setting* Jointly agree specific, reasonable goals and a date to review the performance.
- *Management* Improve the clarity of communicating the task, monitoring systems or expertise of the particular team leader or manager.
- *Outside agencies* These are particularly appropriate where there are personal and family reasons for the poor performance.
- *Peer pressure* Where the performance is very different from the average, those working alongside may put pressure on the person to change.
- *Reorganising* This is appropriate where the problem has arisen through difficulties with work materials, reporting relationships or physical arrangements.
- *Return to work interview* Talk about the absence and future action. Seek professional advice if appropriate.
- *The job* Transfer the individual to a different team or redesign the job.
- *Training* Make sure you give appropriate training, preferably on the job so there is no problem making the connection between the training and the work situation.

DISCIPLINE AND DISMISSAL

All the previous sections have been about disciplining, in the sense of trying to change someone's performance, but at some point a team leader or manager may feel that the process needs to be more formal. It is, however, advisable to keep records of what has happened from the earliest stages just in case things reach the point of formal procedures.

Organisations should have procedures for discipline and dismissal, as the Employment Act 2002 has laid down statutory dismissal and grievance procedures. These include a written statement of the reasons for the dismissal, a meeting between the employer and employee, and an appeal meeting. The HR/personnel department and trade union representatives will know the procedures in detail. It is worth consulting them to ensure that you follow the procedures. Many employers use the ACAS code of practice (1977) as the basis of their procedures. ACAS has also published an advisory booklet, *Discipline at Work* (1987), which is strongly recommended – see Table 14.4 for a summary. There are several areas that may lead to disciplinary procedures besides poor performance – for example, where rules necessary to maintain standards have been broken, such as those covering absence, health and safety, misconduct, the use of company facilities, timekeeping and holiday arrangements.

When all the above ideas, and no doubt others as well, have been tried but have failed to improve performance, there comes a point when a decision to dismiss the problem person has to be faced. Where this is a possible outcome, it is important that procedure is closely adhered to. The legislation is clear. You are advised not to dismiss an employee without involving personnel or some other manager.

Table 14.4 *Checklist for handling a disciplinary matter*

1 Gather all the relevant facts: promptly before memories fade, take statements, collect documents; in serious cases consider suspension with pay while investigation is conducted.

2 Be clear about the complaint: is action needed at this stage?

3 If so, decide whether the action should be advice and counselling or formal disciplinary action.

4 If formal action is required, arrange a disciplinary interview: ensure that the individual is aware of the nature of the complaint and that the interview is a disciplinary one. Tell them when and where the interview is to take place and that they can be accompanied. Try to have someone else from management there as well.

5 Start by introducing everyone present, the nature of the complaint, and the supporting evidence.

6 Allow the individual to state their case. Consider and question any explanations put forward.

7 If any new facts emerge, decide whether further investigation is needed. If so, reconvene.

8 Except in very straightforward cases, adjourn before reaching a conclusion. Come to a clear view of the facts. If it is unclear, what is the balance of probabilities?

9 Before deciding the penalty, consider the gravity of the offence, guidance from procedures, any penalty applied previously, the individual's record, any mitigating circumstances, and whether the proposed penalty is reasonable in the circumstances.

10 Reconvene and clearly inform the individual of the decision and the penalty. Explain the right of appeal and how it operates. In the case of a warning, explain what improvement is expected, by when, and what will happen if the improvement fails to materialise.

11 Record the action taken. Unless it is an oral warning, confirm this in writing. Keep a simple record for future reference.

12 Monitor the individual's performance. Disciplinary action should be followed up with the idea of encouraging improvement. Do this regularly and discuss with the individual your findings.

Source: ACAS *Discipline at Work* (1987)

The 'red hot stove' rule was originally advanced by D McGregor, who likened effective discipline to the touching of a red hot stove:

- The burn is immediate – so there is no question of cause and effect.
- There was a warning – the stove was red hot and you knew what would happen if you touched it.
- It is consistent – everyone touching the stove is burned.
- It is impersonal – you get burned, not because of who you are but because of what you have done.

This chapter about performance management ends this book on managing people. Managing the performance of others is at the heart of managing people. The nature of the relationship will help or hinder this process. The more we can learn about people and how they see the work we are asking them to undertake, the more likely we are to be able to discuss the task in terms that make sense to them. The more we understand about them, the more likely we are to find the rewards that will motivate them to offer exceptional work. Being a team leader or manager is hard work, but I would argue that nothing is more intriguing than trying to understand other people and experiencing the diversity of individuals at work.

ACTIVITIES

1   Why do we appraise in our team? What is in it for the appraisee? What is in it for the appraiser?

2   Who do we involve in the appraisal process? Should there be others?

3   What problems do we have with our appraisal process? Any of the above? What can we do to improve?

4   Practise conducting an appraisal interview using the following format. This can be done in a seminar group or with someone else. You need to work in pairs. I find it works much better if done all in one session, otherwise it gets too involved. The point is to get a feel for the process.

A interviews B about what B did last week – this is information-gathering (15 minutes)

B interviews A about what A did last week (15 minutes)

A and B prepare for feedback and discussion (15 minutes)

B conducts an appraisal interview with A about last week – this is feedback. Look for good practice. Criticise only those things that can be changed (30 minutes)

A conducts an appraisal interview with B about last week (30 minutes)

A and B discuss with each other what they like and dislike about the process. Was it useful to talk about your week? How useful was the feedback? Was the credibility of the appraiser important?

HAVE I MET THE OBJECTIVES?

1   What are the basic ingredients for the effective design of a performance review and appraisal system?

2   Why do leaders and managers want to appraise people?

3   What are the basic ingredients for the effective operation of a performance review and appraisal system?

4   Who might be involved in measuring performance?

5   Can I describe a systematic approach for dealing with problems of poor performance?

6   What are the stages for systematic discipline?

And finally ...

What would you do in Margaret's position? Is there anything of use in this chapter? If I were advising Margaret, I would suggest having a general one-hour meeting with the staff to discuss the document and to discuss what is meant by the performance interviews and also what is not meant by them. Who sees the final assessment documents and what they can be used for is an area of concern to many. This needs clarifying: are they to be used only within the department, or will they be used for promotion and redundancy purposes as well? I would suggest she starts in a small way using a problem-solving approach to one or two easily agreed targets.

FURTHER READING

The current ACAS booklets are always worth looking at in this area.

Try to look at a 'real' organisation's documents about handling poor performance.

Some of the material given in the chapter on motivation, Chapter 12. I would particularly look at the *Harvard Business Review* (2003).

Key words – these are terms that you should understand by the end of the book

Alienation	Ethics
Applications	Evaluation
Appraisal	Experiential learning
Assessment	Goals
Attitudes	Group theory
Authority	HR
Behaviourism	HR planning
Behaviour modification	Humanistic psychology
Career management	Induction
Classical conditioning	Intelligence
Communication	Interviewing
Competencies	Job design
Contingency	Leader's behaviours
Continuous improvement in organisations	Leader's roles
Control/participation dilemma	Leader's styles
Core competencies	Leader's traits
Counselling	Leadership
Credibility	Learning chain
Customers	Learning organisations
Delegation	Learning styles
Development	Legitimising
Discipline	Lifelong learning
Dismissal	Management
Diversity	Management by objectives
Effective teams	Managing change
Employability	Managing time
Employment environment	Meetings
Empowerment	Mentoring
Equal opportunities	Morale

Motivation	Power theories
Networking	Prejudice
Norm	Presentations
Operant conditioning	Psychoanalysis
Organisation	Psychological contract
Organisational culture	Psychology
Organisational structures	Recruitment
Organisation's aims	Role
Perception	Selection
Performance appraisal	Socialisation
Performance management	Sociology
Performance-related pay	Stress
Peripheral staff	Team
Personal constructs	Theories
Planning	Theories of personality
Pluralist	Training
Political theory	Unitarist
Politics	Valuing
Poor performer	Work patterns

Answers to Activities and Objectives

Chapter 1

Answers to activities

1   Psychologists have studied the ways in which people communicate at work and which are effective methods in which circumstances. Other areas of study have been motivation; the design of equipment to aid effectiveness, for example the layout of a cockpit; the characteristics of successful managers; and the causes of stress at work. There are, of course, many other areas. The common factors are the systematic study of people and how it affects their work.

2   This might include study of the various groups and their interaction, the study of the culture of the organisation, or a study of the conflicting roles that are expected at work. The common factors are a study of the socialisation of people at work and the expectations that others have of them.

3   Only you can answer this one.

4   Again, only you know what you prefer.

5   This is one for you. If you are in a seminar group exchange details of your examples to see if you agree about the classification hard/soft.

6   My answers are:

How should we train newly appointed lecturers? What skills do they need? Are these trainable? If so how? Psychology.

What does the Dean do? Who does this job? How do they spend their time? What is their job description? What do other people expect them to do? Psychology and sociology.

What will be the effect of amalgamating two departments? Are there different ways of doing things that need to be similar? Are there conflicting opinions? Have we got the same ambitions and objectives? Sociology.

How can we resolve the complaints from the local residents about the noise coming from the student halls of residence? How representative are the complainants? How frequent are the complaints? What would they want from us? Sociology and psychology.

How can we motivate the porters to allow late evening use of the building? What motivates them to work at all? What are the particular problems associated with evening work? Psychology.

Your answers may well be different; the idea is to start breaking the question into component parts that are more easily answered.

Answers to objectives

1   Social science; psychology; sociology; politics; personnel management; human resource management; all are possible answers.

2   Psychology on the whole looks at the behaviour of individuals and groups. Sociology looks at the institutions of society and the effects of these on people.

3   Unitarists believe we are all one happy team; pluralists believe in equally valid but different groups of people making up the whole.

4   Managers believe in setting appropriate targets and getting people to reach them. Leadership is about eliciting the best from people.

5   Is the leader claiming some superior position or not?

Chapter 2

Answers to activities

The first 6 are up to you. My answer to no 7 is given below, but you could come to other conclusions depending on how you interpret the job title. For example, a nature reserve warden may have a lot of contact with schools or be remote from everyone.

Bar person E	Hotel receptionist E	Long-distance truck driver I
Research chemist I	Nature reserve warden I	Leisure centre manager E
Museum guide E	IT programmer I	Trader on the foreign currency market E

Answers to objectives

1   This would include psychoanalysis, behaviourism and humanistic psychology.

2   Nature/nurture.

4   Physical sensitivity, selective attention; categorisation; limits on our capacity; the environment; individuality.

5   Ensuring that people are employed and developed without discrimination.

6   Celebrating the advantages of having people from a range of different backgrounds.

Chapter 3

Answers to activities

Most of them are up to you. My answer to question 3 is:

3   *What types of learning would be most effective if you wanted to do the following tasks:*

   use the Internet to seek references for an assignment – procedural learning

   become influential in a political party – atttitude development

   understand organisational behaviour – comprehension

   understand a balance sheet in a company's annual report – procedural learning.

Answers to objectives

1   Classical conditioning is stimulus–response whereas operant conditioning is rewarding the response to establish the conditioning.

2   Behaviourism, experimental psychology and experiential learning are the three main ones given here.

3   Kolb suggests accomodator, diverger, converger and assimilator. Could you describe these?

4   Comprehension, reflex, attitude, memory, procedural, were given as CRAMP.

6   An organisation that can change and evolve to meet differing economic environments.

Chapter 4
Answers to activities
These are up to you.

Answers to objectives
1   Those that look at task, technology, procedures or people.

2   Schein suggests five given in the text.

3   Summarised as PEST in the text.

4   By taking their custom elsewhere; by wanting more service; by demanding social responsibility from suppliers.

5   The individual gives effort in return for rewards. See figure in text.

6   Giving people the opportunity to keep up to date and develop so that they can get a job on the open market.

Chapter 5
Answers to activities
These are up to you.

Answers to objectives
1   The seven given in the text are: job rotation; job enlargement; job enrichment; autonomous work teams; leadership models; quality movement; flexibility.

2   Content is *what*; process is *how*.

3   See text.

4   I give nine attributes of effective teams by Guirdham in the text; how many did you get?

5   Something about flexibility would be appropriate here. Also words like 'core' and 'peripheral' would impress.

6   A list of 16 was given in the text.

7   Eight issues were raised in the text.

Chapter 6
Answers to activities
These are largely up to you.

11 My answer would include something about how little time is left for anything else if you include travel time and follow-up time. This might well affect both work and domestic life – the work/life balance. This pressure could lead to stress. I would argue for never having a new meeting or committee in an organisation without removing some other one; having very few regular meetings; increased use of video conferencing. You may have other ideas.

Answers to objectives

1 Culture; demands; control; relationships; change; role; support and development and individual factors.

2 Symptoms of stress in the bad sense include:

- short temper and impatience

- emotional outbursts

- lack of attention to duties

- decreased productivity

- increase in number of accidents

- increased absenteeism, lateness and turnover of staff.

3 I would argue for something about giving clear instructions about what is expected, and rewarding people appropriately. In other words, good people management. But that of course is open to a great deal of debate.

4 Lack of agreement and preciseness.

5 A sequence is given in the text.

6 A four-point sequence is given in Table 6.1.

Chapter 7

Answer to activities

Most are up to you, but my answer for question 3 is:
For Crichton it is his ability and resourcefulness. He is the only one with skills and experience of finding, making and doing practical things. In other words, his expertise.
For the head of the family it is position power.

Answers to objectives

1 The control–participation continuum or the tells-sells-consults-joins continuum.

2 Politics.

3 Six are given in the text.

4 Coercive, remunerative, and normative.

5 There is a table with lots of suggestions in the text.

6 Being allowed to decide at least *how* to do something.

7 Consideration; feedback; delegation; participation.

Chapter 8

Answers to activities

These are up to you.

Answer to objectives

1 What you need; job description; person specification; terms and conditions offered; core or peripheral.

2 A list is given in the text.

3 Important and best left to the HR/personnel department to ensure it is correct.

4 So they are socialised into the appropriate ways of behaving and are clear about what is expected.

5 Check the headings of this chapter against your answer.

Chapter 9

Answers to activities
Question 2 – my answers are:

L = less than 6 months LT = long term E = everyone
S = self confident C = low cost H = high cost

Acting up	L LT S C	Action learning	LT S H
Audio-visual presentations	L E C	Blended learning	LT S C H
Case studies	L LT E S C H	Coaching	L LT E S C H
Delegation	L LT E S C H	Discussion	L LT S H
Distance learning	LT S C H	e-learning	L LT E S C H
Empowerment	LT E S C	Exercises	L E C H
Feedback	L LT E S C	Group dynamics	LT S H
Job rotation	LT E S C	Learning contracts	LT E S C
Learning opportunities	L LT S C	Lectures	L LT E S C
On-the-job training	L LT E S C	Programmed instruction	L LT E S C H
Projects	LT S H	Role play	LT S H
Secondments	LT S H	Simulations	LT S H
Skill instruction	L LT E S C H	Talks	L LT E S C

Question 3

Acting up	K	Action learning	K
Audio-visual presentations	K	Blended learning	K
Case studies	K	Coaching	K
Delegation	K	Discussion	
Distance learning		e-learning	
Empowerment	K	Exercises	K
Feedback	K	Group dynamics	K
Job rotation	K	Learning contracts	K
Learning opportunities		Lectures	
On-the-job training	K	Programmed instruction	
Projects	K	Role play	K
Secondments	K	Simulations	K
Skill instruction		Talks	

Answers to objectives

1   Something about identifying training needs related to the work required now and in the future would be appropriate.

2   Appraisals; changes; individual request; induction; recovery programme.

3   A long list is given in the text.

4   To see if it is of any use and whether it is cost-effective.

5   To increase confidence in dealing with change.

Chapter 10

Answers to activities
These are all up to you!

Answers to objectives

1   See Chapter 1

2   Traits, roles and competencies are all given in the text. Which did you choose?

3   The Adair and the Blake and Mouton models were given in the text.

4   This requires some careful discussion and will inevitably force some personal points of view. For myself I would go for some outcome measurements as well as personal attributes. In other words, did they get the job done?

Chapter 11

Answers to activities
They are up to you.

Answers to objectives

1   *In* is position; *an* is expertise and/or personal attributes.

2   Credibility.

3   Giving people the authority to decide at least *how* things are done.

4   There is a long checklist in the text.

5   This is really a very general question asking you to tie in with some of your other learning about the nature of managing people and organisations. Perhaps something about our increasing taste for informality and treating each other as civilians at work rather than as co-workers.

6   The ability to get things done.

Chapter 12

Answers to activities
Mostly for you. My answer to no 6 is:
You could have the young school leaver trying to get going on a career full time, the student trying to earn money to get by, and the mother of a small child doing part-time work to get out of the house on a Sunday. The first would want a great deal of developing and training, the second would probably need a great deal of flexibility for home and term time and exams, and the third probably wants some social time. But these are all generalisations. In terms of

the Goldthorpe orientations, we could say the first was bureaucratic, the second instrumental, and the third solidaristic, but they would probably all have some instrumental aspects.

Answers to objectives

1   Look at the figure.

2   The first can be demotivating if absent; the second continue to motivate.

3   They have different expectations and experiences of work.

4   Powerlessness; meaninglessness; isolation; self-estrangement.

5   It is intrinsic and hidden; we only see the outcomes of being motivated.

Chapter 13

Answers to activities
They are up to you.

Answers to objectives

1   Integration of strategy, targets, appraisals, training and development, and rewards schemes.

2   The important skills and abilities that deliver the success of an organisation.

3   By linking the behaviour of individuals with the aims of the organisation.

4   See Figure 13.2 in the text.

5   This is up to you.

6   Who has the right to manage?

Chapter 14

Answers to activities
These are up to you.

Answers to objectives

1   You need something here about the nature of judgement and reporting. You could use Table 14.1 to give you some ideas, but try to use some of the material from other chapters too. For example, material from Chapter 13 about strategy and planning.

2   HR considerations; training; promotion; planning; authority.

3   A problem-solving approach.

4   Self; peer; boss; 360-degree; outsiders.

5   Establish whether there is a gap between expected and actual performance; find the reasons for the gap; deal with this.

6   A checklist is given in the text.

References

ACAS (1977) *Code of Practice: Disciplinary practice and procedures in employment.* Available from ACAS, London.

ACAS (1987) *Discipline at Work.* London, ACAS.

ACAS (1994) *Recruitment and Induction.* London, ACAS.

ADAIR J (1982) *Action-Centred Leadership.* Aldershot, Gower.

ADAMS JS (1979) 'Injustice in social exchange' in STEERS RM *and* PORTER LM (eds), *Motivation and Work Behaviour.* 2nd edn. Maidenhead, McGraw-Hill.

ALDERFER CP (1972) *Existence, Relatedness and Growth.* New York, Free Press.

ALLPORT FH (1954) 'The structuring of events: outline of a general theory with applications to psychology'. *Psychological Review.* 61. pp281–303.

ARGYRIS C *and* SCHON D (1978) *Organizational Learning: A theory in action perspective.* New York, Addison-Wesley.

ARMSTRONG M (1996) *Employee Reward.* London, Institute of Personnel and Development.

ARMSTRONG M *and* BROWN D (2001) *New Dimensions in Pay Management.* London, CIPD.

BANDURA A (1977) *Social Learning Theory.* Hemel Hempstead, Prentice Hall.

BEE F *and* BEE R (1994) *Training Needs Analysis and Evaluation.* London, Institute of Personnel and Development.

BEYNON H (1973) *Working for Ford.* Harmondsworth, Penguin Books.

BLAKE RR *and* MOUTON JS (1969) *Building a Dynamic Organization through Grid Organization Development.* Houston, Texas, Gull.

BLAUNER R (1967). *Alienation and Freedom: The factory worker and his industry.* Chicago, University of Chicago Press.

BOWDEN V (1997) 'The career states system model: a new approach to analysing careers'. *British Journal of Guidance and Counselling.* Vol 25. No 4. pp473–90.

BRAMHAM J (1989) *Human Resource Planning.* London, Institute of Personnel Management.

BRYANS PP *and* CRONIN TP (1983) *Organization Theory.* London, Mitchell Beazley.

BUCHANAN D *and* HUCZYNSKI J (1997) *Organisational Behaviour.* 3rd edn. Hemel Hempstead, Prentice Hall.

BURNS JM (1978) *Leadership.* New York, Harper & Row.

BURRELL G *and* MORGAN G (1979) *Sociological Paradigms and Organisational Analysis.* London, Heinemann.

CARTER A (1979) *Authority and Democracy.* London, Routledge & Kegan Paul.

CIPD see IPD.

CLARKE C *and* PRATT S (1985) 'Leadership's four-part progress'. *Management Today.* March. pp84–6.

CONNOCK S and JOHNS T (1995) *Ethical Leadership*. London, Institute of Personnel and Development.

COOPER C and EARNSHAW J (1996) *Stress and Employer Liability*. London, Institute of Personnel and Development.

DAHL R (1970) *Modern Political Analysis*. 2nd edn. Englewood Cliffs, New Jersey, Prentice Hall.

DAVIES K (1972) *Human Behaviour at Work*. 4th edn. New York, McGraw-Hill.

DICKSON NS (1976) *The Psychology of Military Incompetence*. London, Jonathan Cape.

DRUCKER PF (1954) in (1977) *Management*. London, Pan Books.

DRUCKER PF (1989) *The Practice of Management*. London, Heinemann Professional. (This includes reference to his earlier 1954 work.)

DULEWICZ V, HIGGS M and CRANWELL-WARD J (2002) 'Oceans twelve' in *People Management*. 30 May. pp32–5.

ETZIONI A (1975) *A Comparative Analysis of Complex Organizations: On power, involvement and their correlates*. Revised edn. New York, Free Press.

EYSENCK HJ (1962) *Know Your Own IQ*. Harmondsworth, Penguin.

EYSENCK HJ (1976) *The Measurement of Personality*. Lancaster, MTP Press.

FARNHAM D (1999) *Managing in a Business Context*. London, Institute of Personnel and Development.

FAYOL H (1949) *General and Industrial Management*. London, Pitman.

FIEDLER FE (1967) *A Theory of Leadership Effectiveness*. New York, McGraw-Hill.

FLETCHER C (1997) *Appraisal: Routes to improved performance*. 2nd edn. London, Institute of Personnel and Development.

FOOT M and HOOK C (1996) *Introducing Human Resource Management*. Harlow, Addison Wesley Longman.

FOOT M and HOOK C (2002) *Introducing Human Resource Management*. 3rd edn. Harlow, Addison Wesley Longman.

FOY N (1994) *Empowering People at Work*. Aldershot, Gower.

FRASER MUNRO J (1950) *Employment Interviewing*. London, Macdonald & Evans.

FRENCH J and RAVEN B (1958) 'The bases of social power' in CARTWRIGHT D (ed.), *Studies in Social Power*. Ann Arbor, Michigan, Institute of Social Research.

FREUD S (1962) *Two Short Accounts of Psychoanalysis*. Harmondsworth, Penguin Books.

GAGNE RM (1975) *Essentials of Learning for Instruction*. New York, Holt Reinehart & Winston.

GALFORD R and DRAPEAU A (2003) 'The enemies of trust'. *Harvard Business Review*. February. p88–95.

GATES B (1996) *The Road Ahead*. Harmondsworth, Penguin.

GEORGE J (1986) 'Appraisal in the public sector: dispensing with the big stick'. *Personnel Management*. May. pp32–5.

GOLDTHORPE JH, LOCKWOOD D, BECHHOFER F and PLATT J (1969) *The Affluent Worker in the Class Struggle*. Cambridge, Cambridge University Press.

GOLEMAN D (1995) *Emotional Intelligence: Why it can matter more than IQ*. Bloomsbury.

GREENFIELD A (1997) *The Human Brain*. London, Weidenfeld & Nicolson.

GUERIN D (1970) 'Anarchism: from theory to practice'. *Monthly Review Press*.

GUIRDHAM M (1990) *Interpersonal Skills at Work*. Hemel Hempstead, Prentice Hall.

HACKMAN JR (1987) 'Work design', in STEERS RM and PORTER LM (eds) *Motivation and Work Behaviour*. 4th edn. London, McGraw-Hill.

HALL P (2002) 'Grow your own leaders' in *People Management*. 13 June. pp56–7.

HAMBLIN A (1974) *Evaluation and Control of Training*. London, McGraw-Hill.

HANDY C (1985, 1997) *Understanding Organisations*. Harmondsworth, Penguin.

HANDY C (1989) *The Age of Unreason*. London, Business Books.

HARVEY-JONES J (1994) *All Together Now*. London, Heinemann.

HEALTH AND SAFETY EXECUTIVE (2002) *Tackling Work-related Stress: A manager's guide to improving and maintaining employee health and well-being*. London, HSE.

HENDRY C, BRADLEY P and PERKINS S (1997) 'Missed a motivator?' *People Management*. 15 May. pp20–5.

HERRIOT P (1989) *Assessment and Selection in Organisations*. Chichester, Wiley.

HERRIOT P and PEMBERTON C (1995) *New Deals*. Chichester, Wiley.

HERZBERG F (1968) 'One more time: how do you motivate employees?' *Harvard Business Review*. Jan/Feb.

HOLLYFORDE S and S WHIDDETT (2002) 'How to Nurture Motivation'. *People Management*. 11 July. pp52–3.

HONEY P and MUMFORD A (1992) *A Manual of Learning Styles*. 3rd edn. 10 Linden Avenue, Maidenhead, Honey.

HYMAN J and CUNNINGHAM I (1996) 'Empowerment in organisations: changes in the manager's role' in MEGGINSON D and GIBB S (eds) *Managers as Developers*. Hemel Hempstead, Prentice Hall.

ILES PA and SALAMAN G (1995) 'Recruitment, selection and assessment' in STOREY J (ed.) *Human Resource Management: A critical text*. London, Routledge.

INDUSTRIAL TRAINING RESEARCH UNIT (1976) *Choose an Effective Style: A self-instructional approach to the teaching of skills*. Cambridge ITRU based on E and RM BELBIN (1972) *Problems in Adult Retraining*. London, Heinemann.

IPD (1998) *Managing Diversity: An IPD position paper*. London, Institute of Personnel and Development.

JENKINS R (1986) *Racism and Recruitment: Managers, organizations and equal opportunities in the labour market*. Cambridge, Cambridge University Press.

KANDOLA R and FULLERTON J (1998) *Diversity in Action*. 2nd edn. London, Institute of Personnel and Development.

KANE JS and FREEMAN KA (1986) 'MBO and performance appraisal: a mixture that's not a solution'. *Personnel*. Vol. 63, No 12. Dec. pp26–36.

KANTER RM (1989) *When Giants Learn to Dance*. London, Simon & Schuster.

KATZ D and KAHN R L (1978) *The Social Psychology of Organizations*. 2nd edn. New York, Wiley.

KAY J (1993) *Foundations of Corporate Success: How business strategies add value*. Oxford, Oxford University Press.

KELLY G (1955) *The Psychology of Personal Constructs*. New York, Norton.

KLINE P (1989) *Psychology Exposed*. London, Routledge.

KOLB DA, RUBIN IM and MCINTYRE J (1974) *Organizational Psychology: An experiential approach*. London, Prentice Hall.

KOLB DA, RUBIN IM and OSLAND J (1991) *Organizational Behaviour: An experiential approach*. 5th edn. London, Prentice Hall.

KOTTER J (1982) *The General Managers*. New York, Free Press.

KRECH D and CRUTCHFIELD R (1948) *Theory and Problems of Social Psychology*. New York, McGraw-Hill.

KRECH D, CRUTCHFIELD RS and BALLACHEY EL (1962) *Individual in Society*. New York, McGraw-Hill.

KUHNERT KW and LEWIS P (1987) 'Transactional and transformational leadership: a constructive/ developmental analysis'. *Academy of Management Review*. Oct. 1987. pp648–57.

LEIGH T and BROWN S (1996) 'A new look at psychological climate and its relationship to job involvement, effort and performance'. *Journal of Applied Psychology*. Aug. pp355–68.

LEWIN K (1952) *Field Theory in Social Science*. London, Tavistock Publications.

LOWNDS S (1998) *Fast Track to Change on the Heathrow Express*. London, Institute of Personnel and Development.

LUCAS B (2001) *Power Up Your Mind: Work smarter, learn faster*. London, Brealey.

LUTHANS F (1992) *Organizational Behaviour*. 6th edn. Maidenhead, McGraw-Hill.

LUTHANS F and KREITNER R (1975) *Organizational Behaviour Modification*. Glenville, Ill., Scott Foreman.

MARCHINGTON M and WILKINSON A (1996) *Core Personnel and Development*. London, Institute of Personnel and Development.

MARCHINGTON M and WILKINSON A (2002) *Core Personnel and Development*. 2nd edn. London, Chartered Institute of Personnel and Development.

MARQUAND M and REYNOLDS A (1994) *The Global Learning Organisation*. London, Irwin.

MASLOW AH (1954) *Motivation and Personality*. New York, Harper & Row.

MAYO – the Hawthorne research is classically described in ROETHLISBERGER FJ and DICKSON WJ (1939) *Management and the Worker*. Cambridge, Mass., Harvard University Press.

MCCALMAN J and PATON RA (1992) *Change Management: A guide to effective implementation*. London, Paul Chapman.

MESTEL R (1994) 'Let the mind talk'. *New Scientist*. 23 July. pp26–31.

MILLS CW (1956) *White Collar: The American middle classes*. New York, OUP.

MINTZBERG H (1973) *The Nature of Managerial Work*. London, Harper & Row.

MORGAN G (1986) *Images of Organization*. Newbury Park, Sage.

MORGAN G (1997) *Images of Organization*. 2nd edn. Beverly Hills, Calif, Sage.

MORGAN KO (ed.) (1993) *The Oxford History of Britain*. Oxford, OUP.

MULLINS LJ (2002) *Management and Organisational Behaviour*. 6th edn. London, Pearson Education.

MUMFORD E. (1972) 'Job satisfaction: a method of analysis' *Personnel Review*. Summer.

NICHOLSON N (2003) 'Motivating problem people'. *Harvard Business Review*. January. pp57–65.

PAVLOV I (1927) *Conditioned Reflexes*. Oxford, Oxford University Press.

PEDLAR M, BURGOYNE J and BOYDELL T (1991) *The Learning Company: A strategy for sustained development*. London, McGraw-Hill.

PETERS TJ and WATERMAN RH (1982) *In Search of Excellence*. New York, Harper & Row.

PFEFFER J (1981) *Power in Organizations*. Marshfield, Mass., Pitman.

PRAHALAD CK and HAMEL G (1990) 'The core competence of the corporation'. *Harvard Business Review*. May/June. pp79–91.

PUGH DS (1971) *Organisational Theory*. London, Penguin.

REID MA and BARRINGTON H (1999) *Training Interventions*. 6th edn. London, Institute of Personnel and Development.

RICK S (1996) 'Managers as developers or developers as managers?', in MEGGINSON D and GIBB S (eds). *Managers as Developers*. Hemel Hempstead, Prentice Hall.

RODGER A (1952) *The Seven-Point Plan*. London, National Institute of Industrial Psychology.

ROGERS C (1967) *On Becoming a Person*. London, Constable.

ROTHWELL S (1995) 'Human resource planning', in STOREY J (ed.) *Human Resource Management: A critical text*. London, Routledge.

ROWE D (1997) *The Real Meaning of Money*. London, HarperCollins.

SCASE R and GOFFEE R (1989) *Reluctant Managers*. London, Unwin Hyman.

SCHEIN E (1978) *Career Dynamics: Matching individual and organisational needs*. Reading, Mass., Addison Wesley.

SCHEIN E (1985) *Organizational Culture and Leadership*. San Fransico, Calif., Jossey Bass.

SCITOVSKY T (1976) *The Joyless Economy*. Oxford, OUP.

SKINNER BF (1953) *Science and Human Behaviour*. New York, Macmillan Free Press.

SKINNER BF (1965) *Science and Human Behaviour*. New York, Free Press.

SMIRCHICH L (1983) 'Concepts of culture and organization analysis'. *Administrative Science Quarterly*. Vol. 28. pp334–58.

STEERS RM and PORTER LW (eds) (1987) *Motivation and Work Behaviour*. 4th edn. London, McGraw-Hill.

STEERS RM and PORTER LW (eds) (1991) *Motivation and Work Behaviour*. 5th edn. London, McGraw-Hill.

STERN S (2003) 'Are you tough enough to succeed?' in *Management Today*. March. pp46–51.

STEWART R (1967) *Managers and Their Jobs*. London, Macmillan.

TANNENBAUM R and SCHMIDT WH (1973) 'How to choose a leadership pattern'. *Harvard Business Review*. May–June. pp162–75, 178–180.

TAYLOR FW (1947) *Scientific Management*. London, Harper & Row.

THORNDIKE EL (1932) *The Fundamentals of Learning.* New York, Teachers College.

TOFFLER A (1970) *Future Shock.* London, Pan Books.

TORRINGTON D *and* WEIGHTMAN J (1991) *Action Management.* London, IPM.

TORRINGTON D *and* WEIGHTMAN J (1982) 'Technical atrophy in middle management'. *Journal of General Management.* Vol 7, No 4. pp5–17.

TORRINGTON D *and* WEIGHTMAN J (1987) 'The analysis of management work'. *Training and Management Development Methods.* Vol 1. pp27–33.

TORRINGTON DP *and* WEIGHTMAN JB (1989a) *Effective Management.* 2nd edn. Hemel Hempstead, Prentice Hall.

TORRINGTON DP *and* WEIGHTMAN JB (1989b) *The Reality of School Management.* Oxford, Blackwell.

TUCKMAN BW (1965) 'Development sequences in small groups'. *Psychological Bulletin.* 63. pp384–99.

TYSON S (1987) 'The management of the personnel function'. *Journal of Management Studies.* Vol 24, No 5, September 1987. pp523–32.

UK@WORK report (2003) Terms of Engagement in People Management. 6 February. pp14–15.

URWICK L (1952) *Notes on the Theory of Organization.* American Management Association.

VROOM V *and* DECI E (1974) *Management and Motivation.* London, Penguin Books.

WARR P (2003) Letter to *People Management.* 6 March. p24.

WATSON CM (1983) 'Leadership, management and the seven keys'. *Business Horizons.* March–April. pp8–13.

WEBER M (1964) *Theory of Social and Economic Organization.* London, Collier Macmillan.

WEIGHTMAN J (1986) 'Middle management: dinosaur or dynamo?' PhD thesis. Manchester, UMIST.

WEIGHTMAN J (1993) *Managing Human Resources.* London, Institute of Personnel Management.

WEIGHTMAN J *and* FLUDE R (1996) Report for Kelloggs. Unpublished.

WEIGHTMAN J, BLANDAMER W *and* TORRINGTON D (1991) *Pay Structures and Negotiating Arrangements: Report for the North Western Regional Health Authority.*

WEST M (2002) A Matter of Life and Death. *People Management.* 21 Feb. pp30–6.

WOLFF RP (1970) *In Defence of Anarchism.* London, Harper & Row.

WOODRUFFE C (1994) *Assessment Centres.* 2nd edn. London, Institute of Personnel and Development.

WOOLDRIDGE A (2002) 'Back to basics'. *The Economist 2002 The World in 2003.* pp107–8.

Professional standards index

This index cross-references to chapters in the text the main subject areas as set out in the Professional Standards of the Chartered Institute of Personnel and Development for Managing People:

INDICATIVE CONTENT

Index